PRACTICAL BUSINESS WISDOM AND MAGIC

ALSO BY PAT O'BRYAN

- *The Absolute Beginner's Guide to Internet Wealth: Everything You Need to Know to Create Your Portable Empire*
- *Your Portable Empire: How to Make Money Anywhere While Doing What You Love*
- *The Absolute Beginner's Guide to Internet Wealth, Volume 2: New for 2010*
- *Money from Anywhere*
- *Everyday Tao te Ching, A Renegade's Practical Guide to Happiness Today*

PRACTICAL BUSINESS WISDOM AND MAGIC

Pat O'Bryan, CEO
Practical Metaphysics, Inc.
www.patobryan.com

with

Deberah Bringelson
Dr. Steve G. Jones
Nick Ortner
Joe Sugarman
Dr. Joe Vitale

also with

Martha Giffen
Connie Ragen Green
Geoff Hoff
Chuck Pennington
Kate Loving Shenk

ISBN: 978-0-9836900-9-2

Published by Portable Empire Publishing
Terlingua, Texas

For more information, or to learn
how you can publish your book, visit
www.PortableEmpirePublishing.com

CONTENTS

WISDOM

MAGIC

INTRODUCTION

This is a book about how you can realistically design and live the life of your dreams while making money from anywhere.

I wake up to the sun rising over Nine Points Mesa. It pans across the valley, illuminating the mountains all around my cabin.

As the sun hits my solar panels, it charges the battery bank and provides power for my off-the-grid adventure.

I turn on the stereo, put on some Mozart or Gov't Mule, and fill the French Press coffee maker with organic Italian Roast coffee. After the water boils, I bring the coffee to the table by my leather "zero-gravity" chair, sit down, grab the MacBook, and see what's going on in the world.

After checking the news and a few blogs I follow, I open Gmail and my work-day begins. My tech staff may have some questions or information. One of my business partners may have an idea for a promotion.

Before I went to bed last night, I loaded today's sales email in the autoresponder. While I was sleeping early this morning, it automatically broadcast today's promotional email to tens of thousands of potential customers.

If I'm doing a promotion that involves affiliates selling my products, over a million emails may have gone out overnight. Every person who gets an email has asked to receive them.

I check my merchant account, ClickBank, PayPal, and any affiliate programs I'm promoting for. Some mornings, thousands of dollars have poured into my accounts while I was sleeping. Some mornings, it's only a few hundred.

After coffee, the rest of the day is my own.

Welcome to my world of Wisdom and Magic.

Let me explain.

I run an online business which allows me to live wherever I want. My dream was to have a self-sufficient off-the-grid cabin near Big Bend National Park. I'm living that dream.

Now would be a good time for you to start thinking about what your dream is. This book will show you how to achieve it.

My office is upstairs. It's a twenty-foot vertical commute. After coffee, I go upstairs and sit in my comfy red high-backed chair. In front of me, my 27" iMac is ready.

I produce a lot of music. Most of what I sell online is music based. I also produce music for various songwriters as well as my own music projects.

Looking around, I see my drum set, twenty-two guitar cases leaning against the wall, and various new and vintage synthesizers.

I also produce videos and photographs, so the iMac is loaded with professional audio, video and photography editing software.

My main occupation is writing. I have several blogs to keep up with and this is my sixth book. I also write sales copy for my websites, educational material for my clients and students, and provide a lot of content for Social Media sites.

My computer is my factory.

Looking out of the window to the East, I see Nine Points Mesa. To the West, Agua Fria mountain. It's a warm day, but there's a cool breeze blowing.

Today's a video day, so I pull up the files in Final Cut Pro X and start putting the pieces together.

Occasionally, I check my various online accounts. Sales are heaviest in the morning and evening—before and after work for most people—but they come in all day.

After the video's done and on YouTube (if that's where it's going), I may go for a ride in the 4-wheel drive 4Runner. Maybe I'll sit with my friends on the porch at the American Legion Hall and watch the sun go down or hang out on the porch in Terlingua with my guitar. Betsy and I might take the RV to Marfa for a little culture. Big Bend National Park and Mexico are just a half hour drive away.

Later, on the porch here at the cabin, I watch the fading sun turn the mountains red, then purple, and then—depending on the moon—shades of gray. If it's a full moon, I can see the mountains of Mexico to the south. If there's no moon, the stars will seem close enough to touch and the Milky Way will shine like a road across the sky.

Sitting back on the porch, I'm filled with gratitude and reflect on how a broke blues guitar player ended up with such a life.

Wisdom

Just a few years ago I was living with my son in a single-wide trailer, dodging bill collectors and trying to live on a bar musician's pay. In Texas, that was $50 to $100, possibly three nights a week. After gas, guitar strings, and my beer tab, that didn't leave much profit.

The sofa was my ATM, and I'd rummage behind the cushions to find spare change to buy groceries. Sometimes the ATM was empty.

It was expensive to be poor. It was a time of overdraft fees at the bank, late fees on the bills, and lots of bean tacos. I avoided the phone—this was before I had a cell phone—because bill collectors were the most prevalent and persistent callers.

Definition of a musician: Someone who will put $5,000 worth of gear in a $500 truck and drive a hundred miles to make $50.

Then the trailer got repossessed because I couldn't make the payments.

My girlfriend let Patrick and I move in with her.

What do you call a musician who loses his girlfriend? Homeless.

Shortly after, I got the opportunity to tour in Europe, which led to a distribution deal that got my CDs in music stores (remember those?) across the EU. That paid a lot better than playing bars in Texas. Still, that brought its own set of problems.

When I was in Europe, my girlfriend was home alone working full time with three kids in school. The modest piles of Euros I would bring home from the tours didn't seem to go far, and touring put a real strain on our lives.

And, to be honest, the romance of being a touring musician in historic Europe fades quickly: Long, uncomfortable trips in a truck. Uncomfortable beds in hostels. Smoky bars full of people speaking languages I didn't understand. No time to sight-see.

I saw a lot of gorgeous scenery out the window of that truck, but my experience was limited to the venues we were playing and the hostels we stayed in after the show.

Three sweaty guys in an equipment truck. I came to loathe that truck.

I turned 50 and realized that my days of playing 30 shows in 30 towns every month were coming to an end. Touring was fun in my 20s. At 50, it's just a grind.

I was trapped. It looked hopeless.

Close your eyes. Take a deep breath. Open your eyes.

Today, I'm a best-selling author, successful Internet Marketer, one the most highly paid composers on the planet, and living my dream life in an off-the-grid cabin near Mexico.

So, how did I get here?

It was a combination of wisdom and magic.

Around the time my trailer was being repossessed, I met a wise magician named Joe Vitale.

A friend who was dabbling in Internet Marketing noticed that Joe lived in the same small Texas town we lived in and invited him to lunch. He brought me along because he knew Joe was interested in music and I played guitar.

Joe and I hit it off and quickly made a deal. I would teach him to play guitar and he would teach me to make money online.

Joe's a much better teacher than I. Luckily, he found a great guitar teacher named Mathew Dixon later and has become a noted singer/songwriter/guitarist with several CDs out. I'm proud of him, but credit must go to Joe and Mathew for that.

Credit for my early success goes to Joe for being a patient, inspired teacher and I guess some of the credit accrues to me for working my ass off to achieve success.

With Joe's help I quickly developed my own online marketing business.

I already had some rudimentary music recording equipment and a computer. Brainstorming with Joe, we came up with the original ideas for the music-based products we still sell today.

I branched out into other markets. As soon as I learned a new skill, I would write an eBook to teach that skill and sell those eBooks.

I discovered Public Domain intellectual property and repackaged and promoted some Public Domain books. I made some audio books and programs. In the same way that a true artist will make art with whatever materials are at hand, I made products I could sell online with the tools I had.

The learning curves were steep, but I had lots of time and the immediate income—and the obvious potential income—motivated me. I learned how to operate online shopping carts, autoresponders, and merchant accounts. I learned how to build simple web pages so I could sell and deliver the products I was making.

And I built my list.

In the online world, your list is everything. I quickly grasped that I needed to find a large group of people who wanted to buy the products I was making and build a relationship with them through my blogs, emails, and later, through my Social Media accounts.

I started learning from Joe in 2004. By 2006 I was no longer a broke guitar player. I was a successful Internet Marketer.

The world's largest non-fiction publisher, J. Wiley, somehow noticed me and asked me if I would like to write a book about how I made that transition?

And, by the way, would a five-figure advance be ok?

That book was my first best-seller, *Your Portable Empire. How To Make Money From Anywhere Doing What You Love*. Writing that book and watching it travel to bookstores all over the world changed my life.

Since then I've published four more books. Two of them have been best-sellers. Today, I publish through my own publishing company, Portable Empire Publishing.

I discovered that unless you are Christopher Moore or J.K. Rowling, book publishers don't promote your books—they print your books and take most of the money.

I opened Portable Empire Publishing to publish my own books. I can charge the customer less for the book and make a lot more profit. After I explained this to some of my friends and clients, they chose to publish through Portable Empire Publishing, too. You can learn more at http://PortableEmpirePublishing.com.

Video, audio, publishing, writing, web hosting, affiliate marketing...

You've probably noticed that my Portable Empire creates multiple sources of passive income.

That's the first lesson I hope you learn from this book. The whole key to a Portable Empire lifestyle is having multiple sources of passive income.

You're probably not going to get wealthy from the first product you produce and market.

But once that product is online it lives forever. And it can make you money forever.

I was delighted when my first product brought in a few hundred dollars in one weekend. I was accustomed making $50 a night playing guitar in bars. Making a month's income in a weekend was exciting.

That first product is still selling, and I have an online inventory of hundreds of audios, videos, eBooks, books, audio books, and courses.

You make them once and they pay you forever.

The cumulative effect can be astounding.

Because we use the Internet to run our businesses, technological changes can not only be fun and exciting, they can also be scary and frustrating. They can cause you to have to change your business model immediately. Web sites that operated fine yesterday may be non-functional today. Customers who gathered in MySpace yesterday may be on Facebook today, and somewhere else tomorrow. The reader who followed your blog from their desktop computer yesterday may be reading it on their iPhone today.

Technology changes fast, and you have to adapt. When I started out in 2004, the idea of streaming a video was preposterous. It took quite a while just to download a picture. We were using dial-up modems to connect to the Internet. Today, video is a big part of my marketing strategy and we're all watching TV and movies on our computers.

When you write your first blog post, you might feel like you're talking to yourself. And you might be right.

Here's how it works: you keep writing blog posts, you keep building your list and sending emails to your readers, you keep making products and marketing them, you write articles and books, you make videos...

In my coaching program, I've seen it happen over and over again. I watched it happen in my own business. It seems like it happens overnight. Once day you look up and notice that people are reading and commenting on your blog, reading your emails, and, most importantly, buying your products.

In the beginning, you'll be overwhelmed by how much there is to learn and how much there is to do. I can remember working from breakfast until bedtime for days on end setting up this business.

Later, once you've built your Portable Empire, it can run itself.

Keep reading. By the time you finish this book you'll have a strong education in making money online. There is a lot of "how to" information in this book. In addition to my chapters, pay special attention to:

Joe Sugarman's chapter on how he almost failed English and went on to make millions of dollars as a copywriter. Joe's one of my marketing heroes and an all-around nice guy. He's the genius behind BluBlocker sunglasses and many other mega-successful products.

Martha Giffen's chapter on Social Media and how to use it to build your business. Martha is a past coaching client and good friend who has become a best-selling author, media personality, public speaker, and Social Media consultant.

Connie Ragen Green is a former realtor and school teacher who is now a best-selling author, in-demand public speaker, marketing consultant, and success coach. She's also been in my coaching program since it started four years ago.

In her chapter she shares her five-point approach to success. Good stuff.

Geoff Hoff, also a member of my coaching program, tells you to "Don't Fear the Tech." Geoff stays on top of the latest developments in online marketing tech, and teaches and consults on tech issues, as well as writing and creativity topics. Another best-selling author, public speaker, and Internet Marketer.

If you want another resource: a detailed step by step road map for building your own Portable Empire—go to http://moneyfromanywhere.com and get your free copy of *Money*

From Anywhere. That book has helped thousands learn how to set up their own Portable Empires.

The tech details change, but the framework on which we build our Portable Empires doesn't go out of date.

Choose a niche: this is your playground and marketplace. For example, my niches are motivational audios and videos and Internet Marketing. You can have more than one, but it's smart to start with just one.

Gather people who are interested in your niche onto your autoresponder. An autoresponder is a combination email/ database program that allows you to *legally* send commercial emails to people who ask to be in that database. I recommend Aweber: http://pat.aweber.com

Use an opt-in page to get people to join your list. Offer them an ethical bribe, like a report, video, or audio in return for their email address. Make sure your ethical bribe is congruent with the products you want to sell, so you can be sure that the people who sign up for your list are interested in your products.

Use blogs, Social Media, videos, Pinterest, advertising, press releases and any other method you can think of to tell people about your opt-in page.

Create or acquire products that your list is interested in and sell those products.

Repeat.

Remember that we're Internet Marketers. Marketing is what we do, and the basics of marketing haven't changed in decades although the style constantly evolves. The Internet is where we do our Marketing. Previously, marketers used classified ads, brochures, direct mail, and TV commercials—and many still do.

The advantages of selling digital products on the Internet are: no manufacturing cost, no delivery cost, very low storage costs, and the ability to communicate with our customers and prospects for next-to-nothing.

Like the rock star who is an overnight sensation after plugging away for twenty years, you'll know that although it may look like it happened overnight, your success is the result of all the work you did.

Once you "break on through to the other side," life gets easier.

Today, I work from my dream location. I have a small staff of geniuses who handle the technical and design work for me. I work when I want to and choose what I want to work on.

My average work-day is less than two hours.

Some days, when I'm writing or creating a product, I might put in six hours. Other days, I check my email and sales and then clock off for the day.

But, you can't get there with just half of the equation. I know people who have worked harder than I have for longer than I have who are still struggling.

That's the Wisdom part. The "how to" stuff.

In no way do I downplay the action part of the equation. The learning curves can be frustrating but the pay-off is worth it. But you need to combine it with Magic to really make your dreams come true.

You need magic, too.

Magic

I call the Wisdom part your outer game and the Magic part your inner game.

To succeed at your outer game, you have to be on top of your inner game.

My mentor, Joe, ends his emails with the phrase, "expect miracles." It took me a long time to understand why he did that. You see and receive what you expect.

Here's an example. Imagine tight-rope walking over a deep canyon without a net. If the narrative in your mind is "I can do this easily," your odds of succeeding are good. If your inner narrative is "Oh my God! I'm going to fall! There's no way I'm going to make it!" you're probably going to fall.

Winners win. Expect to win. Make those expectations real by starting with simple projects that you can complete and that give you immediate positive feedback. Then build on those successes by gradually taking on more ambitious projects.

And remember that there's no such thing as failure. It's all data. If you try and don't immediately succeed, congratulations! You've identified one way to do it that doesn't work. That makes your next step much easier.

I tell my coaching students: "If something's working, do more of that. If something's not working, do something else."

Here's another important lesson—put service first.

Your happiness and prosperity will be a function of how many people you help.

I remember when I finished my first real eBook. It was called *The Think and Grow Rich Workbook*, and was based on a public domain version of *Think and Grow Rich*, by Napoleon Hill.

I knew it was going to be a hit because 1) *Think and Grow Rich* is required reading to be successful and 2) *Think and Grow Rich* is a dull, thick book packed with out of date stories written in a dull, wordy fashion.

By condensing that book and rewriting it to be easier and faster to read, I knew I had created something that a LOT of people were going to want.

I printed a copy and took it over to Joe's house. We sat on his front porch while he looked it over. I could tell he was impressed.

I asked him about his thoughts for marketing.

He said, "give it away."

At the time, I was still broke. I needed money now. I asked him, "what? Are you serious?"

He just smiled and said, "give it away."

So, I did. And tens of thousands of people have downloaded that eBook and their lives are much better for it.

Profit is important. Money is important. I don't believe you can truly become self-actualized if you're spending your time working a job you don't love because you need the money. Money buys you the time to explore the more important things in life that make life richer and deeper.

It's my experience that jobs lead to a mindset of desperation. I want to live with a mindset of creativity and possibility.

It's a mistake to focus on profit and money. Give. Serve. Focus on how you can make other people's lives better.

By making that book a gift, I made many times more money from it than I would have by selling it. Everybody who downloads that book gives me their email address and goes on my list. Some of them have bought dozens of products from me through the years.

Through the years I've gifted my readers videos, audios, eBooks and webinars. It's "good work." It helps others, and it makes me feel good—and every gift I give comes back to me multiplied.

My friend, Cindy Cashman, once told me, "you can't out-give the universe." She's right. Magic.

Another component of your inner game is head maintenance.

Your mind is an amazing tool. It's more powerful than any computer. But, it can only operate with what you feed it.

Since I started paying attention to what I feed my head, I've noticed that I've become more effective, more focused, happier, and I make a lot more money.

I used to recommend getting rid of your TV, but I've modified that.

TVs are good for watching movies, but I recommend that you take charge of the programming. There is a tendency for very wealthy movie makers to make movies glorifying poverty.

Titanic is a great example. *Fiddler on the Roof* is another. "We're poor, but we're honest…"

You don't want that meme in your head. You don't want any subconscious limitations on your income or your life. If you're honest and a good person, you can be rich *and* be an honest and good person.

Even out here in the middle of the desert, 52 miles from the nearest town, cable is available. I'm not interested. I can get the news I need from the Internet faster, and without hysteria and spin.

I don't need hysteria and spin in my head.

In '04—'07, when Joe and I were in the same mastermind

group, Joe would bring us books to read. I read them. Many of them were about how to think, or how other successful people thought.

The way I had been thinking had resulted in failure. I did my best to delete my default thought patterns and replace them with more effective ones. Books are a great way to do that.

I still read the news online and enjoy a whimsical fiction book (Christopher Moore, Douglas Adams, Kinky Friedman, and Tom Holt, for example.) Joe doesn't pay any attention to the news and doesn't read fiction. Joe's a lot more successful than I am. Draw your own conclusions.

Attraction

Joe Vitale has written several books about the Law of Attraction. I recommend that you read them.

What I've learned is that you really do attract what you focus on. That's why it is so important to control what you put in your mind.

If you focus on failure, drama, conspiracies, and the other junk-food information prevalent in broadcast media and some online channels that's what your mind will be attracted to.

If you give your mind enough data that the world is unfair, honest people work too hard and don't make enough money, and the government is out to get you—that's what you'll attract.

You can create a self-fulfilling prophesy.

I like a mix of inspirational and success-oriented data. The Dalai Lama, Byron Katie, Lao Tsu, Stephen Mitchell's *Second Book of the Tao*, are a few of my favorite inspirational sources.

Napoleon Hill, Richard Branson, Felix Dennis, Dan Kennedy, and Robert Kiyosaki are the kind of writers I go to for success-oriented data.

If you give your mind data that reinforces the belief that this is a world of magic and possibility where people like you can be happy and successful, that's what it will believe and that's what it will focus on.

And you'll automatically attract happiness and success.

I know. It sounds like magic. Try it. It works.

I also meditate. Meditation recalibrates and clears my mind.

It stops the repetitive loops that play in my subconscious. I've practiced meditation off and on for forty years and I find that I'm happier and more focused when I practice.

If you really want to take control of your mind and program it for success and happiness, you should make a practice of listening to the Clearing Audios that Joe and I produce.

Those audios are a combination of precision designed and composed original music that I make with either affirmations, hypnotic instructions, or guided meditation vocals.

The effect is very much like meditation, but the results are much faster. Those audios practically force you to breathe in a relaxed manner and put you in a state of optimum reception to the affirmations.

Ten minutes in the morning can make your day much more relaxed, focused and effective.

We use them.

To help you bring magic to your life, I asked several experts in Inner Game strategies to contribute chapters to this book.

Dr. Joe Vitale is one of the five top marketing specialists in the world today and is known to his readers, customers, and seminar attendees as the world's first hypnotic writer. Joe is also a certified hypnotherapist, a certified metaphysical practitioner, a certified Chi Kung healer, a certified Reiki Master, and an ordained minister. He also holds a doctorate degree in Metaphysical Science and another doctorate degree in Marketing. Joe is a proud member of the National Speakers Association. He's also my mentor and friend.

Joe's chapter is titled How to Program Yourself to Attract More Money.

Nick Ortner is the producer of the documentary film, *The Tapping Solution*, and a best-selling author, speaker, and media personality. His chapter will teach you the magic of tapping.

Dr. Steve G. Jones is a board certified Clinical Hypnotherapist. Steve G. Jones, Ed.D. has been practicing hypnotherapy since the 1980s. He is the author of 25 books on hypnosis, the law of attraction and weight loss. He is a member of the National Guild of Hypnotists, American Board of Hypnotherapy, president of the American Alliance of Hypnotists, on the board of directors of the Los Angeles chapter of the American Lung Association, and director of the California state registered Steve G. Jones School of Hypnotherapy.

Steve's chapter teaches you to take control of your life and power your mind through hypnosis to affect change in your life with positive messaging.

Chuck Pennington, who is an author, public speaker, and tech whiz—and is also in my Coaching Program—wrote a chapter that will lead you to the magic of Masterminds. Read it carefully. I attribute a lot of my success to my participation in Mastermind groups.

Deborah Bringelson, business consultant, public speaker and author, contributed a chapter that will help you Live Your Life Like Magic.

Kate Loving Shenk is a writer, healer, musician and published author of the *Prayer Prescription Series*. She has been a nurse for 29 years and she believes all people are healers, but few are willing to own their power. She also believes healing takes place all the time, whether we are conscious of it, or not.

Kate's chapter will teach you about Prayer Prescriptions for prosperity and health.

I'm proud to have such amazing and powerful coauthors.

We will now take you by the hand and show you how you, too, can perfect your inner and outer games—how you can combine Wisdom and Magic—to create the life of freedom and prosperity you've been looking for.

Like Julia Cameron said in *The Artist's Way*, this is a book you DO. In the same way that reading diet books won't help you lose weight unless you actually implement the diet, reading this book won't improve your life unless you actually *use* the information.

When you read an inner game chapter—Nick's chapter on tapping for example, stop and explore the technique.

When you read an outer game chapter—like Martha's chapter on Social Media, stop and implement that strategy.

Then, go on.

There's no limit to what you can have, do or be.

I give *The Think and Grow Workbook* away at http://ThinkAndGrowRichWorkbook.com.

And you can get a free copy of The Clearing Audio (the audios that started it all) at http://FreeClearingAudio.com.

WISDOM

INTERNET MARKETING—WHEN YOU DON'T KNOW HOW TO DO IT

No money. Limited resources. And a complete newbie. That pretty much describes the email I got today from one of my coaching clients.

Think back. Can you remember when you first started out? First there was the vocabulary to learn. Then, the information overload—everybody wants to help you for a price, and how do you tell the schlock from the good information when you're first starting out?

Maybe you remember it like it was yesterday, or earlier today—because it was.

Then, there's the money. Once you get your funnel working, your autoresponders cranking out offers, and gain the trust of your readers, the money comes. But, when you're first starting out, hosting, domain names, autoresponders, shopping carts—not to mention the flood of get rich quick offers…I'll admit, I fell for a few of those, too.

It may seem like it takes a fortune to get started. If it does, you're doing it wrong. Keep reading, and I'll tell you how to set up your online business and run it for about $30/month.

What's the answer?

Well, there's income and expenses, for one thing. You need to keep the first one bigger than the second one, or you're out of the game.

We'll talk some more about that in a minute.

First of all, what, exactly, is Internet Marketing?

The thing to remember is that *Internet* describes the delivery method. There are still millions to be made with direct mail marketing. You can market on TV and radio, and that's cheaper than it's been in years. And easier, too. Social Networks can be used for marketing—very carefully. If you really want to learn how to sell, get a job selling something door-to-door. It may crush your soul and make you crazy, but it's the absolute best way to learn how to sell.

But, for optimum bang for the buck, it's really hard to beat email marketing on the Internet as long as you remember that the most important word in the phrase is *Marketing*.

To break it down to it's simplest formula, you need something to sell and someone to sell to.

You need to pick a niche. That's a fancy way of saying that you need to figure out what you want to sell. Once you're established, you can veer away from your initial decision and, hopefully, take your followers with you. When you're first starting out, you need to focus on one market to play in.

Then, you need to find an interesting problem.

Now, you probably think there's no lack of problems. You may think that problems are, well, a problem. Nope. Problems are money. Every problem is a (at least one) product.

In my books, I talk about the golf niche. I've never played there, but some of my friends have made dinosaur bucks selling stuff to golfers. It's a niche that's rife with problems. And golfers can be pretty fanatical. They'll spend hundreds or thousands of dollars to shave a stroke or two off their score.

Nice.

Now, all you need to do is find out what problems golfers

are having, find the solution to those problems, and sell them to golfers. If you don't know the answer, take your video cam or MP3 recorder and find an expert and ask them. Record the answer. Put it online. Make a sales page and a download page. When you're first starting out you can use PayPal to get the money.

Find a problem. Solve it. Sell the solution.

That's the first part of the equation.

Next, you need somebody to sell to.

That's a little trickier. Forums are good. Put opt-in boxes everywhere you can. Create or acquire stuff you can give away and trade it for email addresses. Get aggressive with your Social Media—you can build a big list fast with Facebook and Twitter—as long as you're not playing Farmville.

To be a successful marketer, you have to think like a marketer. Yes, you can use Facebook to keep up with your friends and family. I do that, too. But, you can also use Facebook to tell the world about your products, blog posts, and giveaways.

The next problem to deal with is information overload. That one is easy. Just unplug.

That may seem counter intuitive, especially when you're first starting out and you want to learn everything all at once. Fact: you can't. A lot of the alleged information you're getting is actually spam and noise, and when you're first starting out you can't tell the noise from the information.

Pick one or two people you can trust (ask around), and read their emails, their blogs, and their Social Networking pages. Unsubscribe from everyone else's list. Now.

You can always resubscribe later. For now, you need to make some space in your mind to focus on the really important stuff. Too much data will just confuse you.

Also, there is a tendency to want to use technological solutions to solve marketing problems. This rarely works. Remember, *Internet* is just our delivery mechanism. It's how we get the information to our readers. But, the *Marketing* part can't be automated. There is no software you can buy that will let you drop $1 in the top and will spit out 1+ dollars.

You have to get your hands dirty and sell your products. The nuts and bolts of this haven't changed since Babylonian times, and probably before...but the tools are a little better. We've learned a lot about how the human mind works, and what motivates people to buy. But, a lot of my coaching clients go through this—they want to be Internet Marketers without actually doing any marketing. It can't be done.

A lot of my coaching clients have trouble with this. They want to make the money, but they're a little above actually doing the selling. Consequently, they don't make any money. You really do have to learn how to sell. That's actually easy. The hard part is psychological. You have to WANT to sell. Our society has given sales people a bad rap, and in some cases, it's well deserved. You don't have to be scammy or spammy. In fact, that will work against you.

You do have to believe that your product solves the problem that your customers have, and you have to tell them so, give them the opportunity to buy the solution from you, and take their money.

The technology you NEED to start making money is:

1. an email address
2. a domain (that's your URL. http://something.com) I buy mine at Godaddy.com
3. hosting (where you put your websites). Portable Empire Hosting is good. (http://PortableEmpireHosting.com)
4. an autoresponder. I recommend Aweber.com for newbies. It's fairly cheap, and will keep you out of trouble. There are some nasty laws (or great laws, depending on your point of view) about who can send commercial email to whom under what circumstances, and what legal mumbo jumbo has to be in those emails. If you get it wrong, you are breaking the law, and can be prosecuted under civil and criminal statutes. You could go to jail. Or, for a few bucks a month, you can pay Aweber to do all that stuff for you. I think it's a no-brainer.

build your list, and market your products to your list. That's really all there is to it.

INTERNET MARKETING FROM THE BEGINNING—PART 1

The sun rose bright in the Chihuahua Desert this morning. Due to the recent rains, the desert is pretty green. The greasewood and sage are higher than I've ever seen them. Here at Portable Empire West, it's a beautiful day.

As you know if you get my emails or read my blog, I live in a cabin in the desert. I'm 52 miles South of Alpine, 30 miles from Terlingua, and 25 miles from Big Bend National Park . The cabin is completely off the grid—water well, solar power, septic, and propane for heating and cooking. The only physical connection to the outside world are a land-line telephone and Internet access.

This is a good place to sit, think, and look at the big picture. It's pretty much distraction-free. I still read the papers, and the columnists in some of the hipper papers are starting to figure out what I've been saying for years—the current economic recession is not at all what it looks like. Yes, the banks, mortgage companies, and real-estate industries screwed up. Yes, access to easy credit created a population over its head in debt. One in five households with mortgages owe more on their house than it's worth. Those are all facts.

But, the meatball in the batter, to quote Douglas Adams, is the parallel fact that what we're watching is the end of the Industrial Revolution. Millions of jobs are gone, and they're not coming back. Just as there will always be blacksmiths, there will always be auto mechanics, factory laborers, and office workers. In a decade, I suspect all three of those categories to be as rare as blacksmiths.

Why? Because they're inefficient. Those jobs can be automated. If you're in one of those industries, or any of dozens more that are in the same boat, listen up.

Those jobs are gone and they're not coming back. And, that's a good thing.

As I said in my best-selling book, *Your Portable Empire, How to Make Money from Anywhere Doing What You Love*, a job is one of the least efficient ways to make money. By definition, you've got to supply more value than you cost. You're an expense to whatever business you work for. The amount of value you create in excess of your salary is profit to the company.

In other words, every day you clock in at your job, you're leaving money on the table. Why not get paid for ALL the value you produce?

How?

You need a Portable Empire. An online business you can run from anywhere. A way to push money into your bank account with your computer from anywhere you want to be. A business that just takes a couple of hours a day to run, so you can actually enjoy your life.

For now I'm going to give you a valuable short course in how to set up your online business.

The core of a Portable Empire is 1) You need somebody to sell to 2) You need something to sell. All the rest is just details.

Of course, you need a way to talk to your potential customers, and a way to get paid for your products.

You need an autoresponder.

What's an autoresponder? It's an online database of email addresses, names, and any other information you get from your customers that allows you to gather that information and then use it to stay in touch with your readers. In the upper right-hand corner of my blog (patobryan.com/blog) you'll see a form with "email" and "name" boxes. That's an opt-in box. When you put your email address and name in the boxes and hit the Submit button, several interesting things happen.

1. Your name and email address go in my database at Aweber
2. Then, automatically, an email that I composed months ago will be sent to you asking you to confirm your subscription to my list.
3. Once you confirm your subscription you automatically receive whatever ethical bribe I offered you in exchange for your email address. That could be an eBook, audio, video, access to a webinar, or anything else that can be delivered over the Internet.

Those are the "auto" functions of an autoresponder. You can use an autoresponder to deliver digital products, build your list, send people to other websites, and several other valuable things. When you're building your Internet Marketing business, you want to automate as much as you can. The plan is for you to have multiple streams of passive income with as little input from you as possible. "Passive" means that you work once and get paid a lot of times. It's the old "make money while you sleep" idea, and it works.

You can program as many emails as you want to be sent to each subscriber when they subscribe. You can tell Aweber to send the first one immediately, the second one in a couple of days, the third in a week, and so on. So, you write your emails once, and they go to work for you over and over again—your invisible sales force.

There's also another trick your autoresponder can do: broadcasting. I use this a lot, because I tend to improvise. You can email any portion of your list, or your entire list, at any time.

If I get an inspiration, or want to tell you about a new blog post or product, that's how I do it. I've done it from castles in Germany, beaches in California, Judge Roy Bean's law office, and all over the world, including this little cabin out in the desert.

That's how you talk to your readers. You use your autoresponder to find out what they want. I recommend this. One of the biggest mistakes Internet Marketers make is trying to sell our customers what we *think* they need instead of what they *actually* want. How do you find out what they want? You ask them. Use polls, blog comments, or return emails to find out what their problems are, and which solutions they'd actually pay you to provide.

Remember, this is a business. Money has to change hands—and end up in yours—for you to be successful. It seems obvious, but many beginning Internet Marketers seem to miss that.

So, how do you get the money?

Let's assume you've asked your list what they want, what they'll pay for, and created the solution. You then use your autoresponder to tell them it's ready.

You need a shopping cart.

When you're first starting out, PayPal works great as a shopping cart. It's cheap to use and much more powerful than it looks to the casual user.

Over time, you'll develop an inventory of products, and it's useful to keep all your products in a database. Also, you'll want to gather and analyze data on your buyers. If someone buys every product you offer, you may want to do something nice for them. Conversely, if someone buys everything you offer and then immediately asks for a refund, you need to know that, too. This is where PayPal's limitations begin to show.

A shopping cart service like 1ShoppingCart can gather a lot of data, aggregate and analyze your customers, identify sales trends, and help you operate your business in a more professional manner. A good shopping cart service will make you a lot more money than it costs, but don't rush in. Get a few products out there first. Then, as soon as you see that you've got something people want, and have a good feeling about your business and it's chances for success, go for it. It costs the same whether you use my link or not: http://budurl.com/6c5j.

1ShoppingCart, like any complex online service, has its eccentricities. Here's the cool part—it also has an autoresponder. You can run your entire Portable Empire from your 1ShoppingCart account. I use my shopping cart and Aweber *together*, but I've been in business for several years and manage multiple niches, scores of products and tens of thousands of subscribers. If you're just starting out, and sure you want to "go for it," then you'll be fine with 1ShoppingCart and a free PayPal account.

There is a learning curve, but it's not too steep and it's fairly short. There's not that much to learn. Aweber, PayPal, and 1ShoppingCart have excellent tutorials.

Get started now building your Portable Empire. In later chapters I'll discuss how to build a great relationship with your list, how to create or acquire products they'll actually pay you for, and all the rest of the strategies online marketers use. For now, grab an autoresponder and start learning how to use it.

INTERNET MARKETING FROM THE BEGINNING—PART 2

This morning I was awakened by a roadrunner.

He was playing around under my swamp cooler making a little racket. I opened the curtain and looked out to see what was causing the noise—and he jumped up on the swamp cooler to get a better look at me. We were eye to eye, nose to beak, separated by a thin pane of glass. Don't see that every day. I got tired of the game before he did, and sloped into the kitchen to start the coffee.

Today's been a relaxing day—a couple of phone meetings, coordinating some stuff with my staff, doing a little writing. There are rainstorms in the East, puffy clouds overhead, and the sun is playing on the mountains to the South. It all depends on which window I look out. For a real treat, I took a walk through the desert—the sky out here is so big you can see several separate weathers going on at once.

I can enjoy relaxing days like this because my Portable Empire chugs away making money while I lock eyes with roadrunners, keep an eye on the weather and even when I go for walks in the desert.

From my point of view, if that ain't magic, I don't know what is. The barrier to entry is so low as to be nonexistent. Technically, you can create a business, open the doors, and start making sales for less than $20. The cost to make the products, store them, and deliver them is almost nothing. With that kind of architecture, your bottom line will greatly resemble your top line. Gross sales approximate net sales. I can't think of another (legal) business that operates like that.

I also can't imagine why you wouldn't want to get your own Portable Empire up and running.

In the previous chapter I talked about autoresponders and shopping carts so let's assume you have the basic infrastructure of your Portable Empire: your autoresponder and shopping cart accounts.

Now, you need a product.

I recommend starting with eBooks. An eBook is just a PDF file (usually) of a document that can be read on computers, tablets and smartphones.

They're free to make and free to deliver. And eBooks are becoming more popular thanks to the Kindle, the Kindle reader for other platforms (I love Kindle reader on my iPad), and all the other e-readers. People are becoming more comfortable reading books on their electronic devices.

A while back I sat down with Joe Vitale and created the eBook Problem Solver: an audio course on how to write eBooks. We went into all aspects—from the mechanics, to the content, to the inner game problems beginning writers have.

You can get your copy at http://eBookProblemSolver.com.

If you want to move fast, go get the eBook Problem Solver. If you're comfy with a more leisurely pace, keep reading and I'll give you the basics.

Interesting and linear problems.

We're in the information marketing business. The Portable Empire system is based on solving problems for others. I like that. It's got a "good work" kinda vibe, in an E.F. Schumacher way. You make money by helping others, and the more value you add to other people's lives, the more money you make.

People will pay you to solve their problems. Your job is to be on the lookout for interesting and linear problems that a group of people have. For example, I know that a certain percentage of my readers are interested in making money with their computers. A good way to do that is by creating and selling eBooks so I made the eBook Problem Solver. I'm an Internet Marketer, and a lot of my readers are, too. If I were to create a product about automobile mechanics, I'd need to find new readers.

I know a lot about the subscribers to my email newsletters: they're interested in Internet Marketing and inner game topics, and those two topics actually have a lot in common.

Also, through my social media work, Portable Empire Coaching program, and webinars, I have a good feel for what beginning Internet Marketers need to know. They're very curious about how to make money online. So, as long as I create and market products that are congruent with that topic, I know I have a good chance of holding their interest.

I mentioned that your job is to look for interesting and linear products. But what does that mean?

By interesting, I mean that it's interesting to my customers. I use Facebook, Twitter, and polls to find out what my customers might be interested in. And, because most people come to me through opt-in pages, I know they're interested in Internet Marketing because my ethical bribe is a free eBook on Internet Marketing.

What do I mean by linear? Linear problems are those that, when solved, lead to *other* problems. For example, after you learn how to make an eBook, you need to learn how to get it online, how to write a sales page, how to create a download page, and several other things. It's like stairs leading to passive income.

As a marketer, you want to be standing in front of your customer as they reach each level on the staircase with the obvious solution to the problem. Because you already know what the next problem is going to be, you can easily have the solution.

The easiest, cheapest way to deliver that solution is by writing an eBook.

Remember, we're selling information. We are *not* selling it by the pound. If you had an eBook that consisted of just one word, but that one word was the cure for cancer, you could sell a *lot* of copies at just about any price you wanted. The value of the information we sell is determined by the pain the problem we're solving is causing for our customers.

So, once you've found your interesting and linear problem, write the solution down. I use Microsoft Word to write my solutions down. If you don't have Word, you can use Open Office, which is a free word processing program and includes a PDF generator. You can download it at OpenOffice.org.

How do you find solutions?

Interviews are good. If you know the answer, you can interview yourself. Be sure to buy yourself a cup of coffee and a nice dinner. If you don't know the answer, act like a reporter and go get it. Radio-TV Interview Report http://www.rtir.com/ is a good place to find experts. I've made a lot of money by playing the dumb student during interviews. Even if I know the answers, I pretend I don't and ask questions that the *least* informed of my subscribers might ask. This tactic has generated some very valuable interviews.

Traditionally, experts are happy to do the interview with you for a copy of the interview. They want exposure and traffic. You can do the interview as a teleseminar and let others join in and ask questions. You can charge for access to the teleseminar. You can do a webinar, and have the expert's computer be part of the presentation—this is great for online "how to" stuff.

There aren't any rules and anything you negotiate with your interviewee is fine—as long as you end up with the right to market the interview.

There are many ways to gather the data, but at some point you'll want to write down your solution, save it as a PDF, put it online, and then sell it.

THE FIRST THING YOU NEED TO KNOW ABOUT INTERNET MARKETING

Last night I realized I was in a privileged position. No, I'm not talking about cars, cigars, guitars or money. I'm talking about my coaching students.

Some of my coaching students are probably more knowledgeable than I am. They're definitely into different aspects of Internet marketing than I am, and know more about those than I do. That's one of the ways I'm privileged. On our weekly coaching webinars I often learn as much as they do.

But I want to focus on the absolute beginners. Last night, there were several on the webinar, and a few of them asked amazing questions. Those questions were gold. And, they were timely reminders that when you first start on your Internet Marketing journey, things look weird.

We were talking about affiliate marketing: selling somebody else's product in return for a commission.

Through the years I've promoted products for friends and coaching students. For the last month, I've been buying affiliate marketing classes and products and have been testing different niches and sales page styles. I've learned some surprising things about my list, and just about doubled my income.

We were talking about EPC, CPC, and different methods of driving traffic when the questions started coming in—and I realized that the new students had no clue what we were talking about.

So, let's explore what you need to know before you get to the basics.

What, exactly, is Internet Marketing?

Well, it's a little bit like the music business, in that you can be in it for years before you realize that it's a business.

> *Flash back: A bar musician wins the lottery. It's millions. A reporter asks, "what are you going to do with the money?" The musician replies, "probably just play gigs till it's gone."*

One of the hardest things to get across to my new students is that if you aren't making money, your Internet Marketing "business" is a hobby. Yes, I want to help others. I want to save the world and I expect you do, too. But, if you're not making a living from your Internet Marketing business, then you're back at your day job. You can't help anybody until you help yourself.

> *Flash back 2: In my twenties, I read E.F. Schumacher's books, Small is Beautiful, and Good Work. Schumacher wrote about "Economics as if People Mattered." I still practice that. But, if you're not part of the solution, you're part of the problem (bonus quote), and if you're not making enough money to take care of your own needs, you're part of the problem.*

As a coach, I get to watch my students learn and grow. And there is a definite epiphany moment when a student gets that Internet Marketing is a business. There is a psychological hurdle to get over. To most people there's something a little bit nasty (and not in a good way) about selling. However, like other things that appear a little bit nasty at first, selling is a fact of life. In a Capitalistic society, like the one we live in, nobody gets paid until somebody sells something. And, (this may sound familiar) after you've done it a few times, you realize that it feels good, and you start enjoying it. Welcome to the adult Internet Marketing world.

So, let's just stipulate here that a primary function of your new Internet Marketing business is to make money. Enough money so that you've got the freedom to love, think, feel, travel, study, play...and that exact number is going to vary depending on you. Oddly, scientific research suggests that once you surpass about $36,000 a year additional income won't make you happier. I disagree. The more you make, the more you can help others. There's happiness in that. But, for most beginning Internet Marketers, three grand a month is a *lot* of money. Make that your first target.

Here's a basic truth. If you're an Internet Marketer, it's ok to market. Keep your eye on that—at some point, you're going to have to ask somebody to spend some money. And if you're doing it right, when they *do* spend money, you'll get some of it.

Let's look at how to do that.

To keep things simple so I can deal with them, let's divide Internet Marketing into two camps: *Relationship Marketing* and *Metrics Marketing.*

What I do is Relationship Marketing: the Portable Empire System is based on serving others.

Relationship Marketing

Find a group of people with a common problem. Confirm that they'll pay for a solution to that problem.

Solve the problem.

Sell them the solution.

Keep the dialog going. Solving problems, if you're clever, leads to the next problem which also calls for a solution. Solve that one and sell the solution.

Rinse and repeat.

You've heard it said that "the money's in the list." This is bullshit. The Los Angeles phone book is a list, and unless you need a phone number and have never heard of Google, it's worthless.

The money is in the *relationship* with the human beings on your targeted list.

One of my coaching students made six figures a year with a list of about 600. You don't necessarily need a big list. (Go read Connie Regan "RayGun" Green's book, *Huge Profits with a Tiny List* for details.)

To build this list of human beings, I recommend you give something away in exchange for their email address. This is called an ethical bribe and you make the offer on a squeeze page (Class Project #1 for my coaching students) You can see an example of a squeeze page at http://moneyfromanywhere.com.

Here's how it works. Some friends and I wrote the book, *Money From Anywhere.* It's a very valuable introduction to Internet Marketing. When you get your copy, you'll be asked to exchange your email address for it. When you do that, you're telling me some very valuable stuff.

- You're interested in making money online.
- You're willing to a give up your email address in exchange for this valuable information.
- You might possibly be interested enough to buy more information.

Congratulations, you're a human being on my list. Let's get to know each other.

At this point, the marketer's job is to build a relationship. I want to know what you think. I want to know what you need. I want to know what questions are keeping you up at night. I want to help you.

People who email me (pat@patobryan.com) are often surprised when I email them back. I LOVE emails from you. I especially love emails with questions. Those are solid gold. Of course I write back. I don't understand why some marketers don't.

I recommend that you cherish every email you get from your subscribers. Find out what their problems are—and then sell them the solutions. You'll make them happy. They'll make you rich.

As a marketer, your list is your most valuable asset. Especially if you've taken the time to get to know the people on that list and developed a relationship that leads your readers to know, like, and trust you.

People buy from people they know, like, and trust.

As an Internet Marketer, it's expected that you'll occasionally do some marketing. Your list is who you market to. And, as long as you bring your list opportunities that help them—solve their problems—your list will be your business. They'll buy things from you. And whether it's your product, or a cool product you're an affiliate for, if you're doing this right you'll get some of the money. If it's your product, you'll probably get all the money, minus PayPal, ClickBank, and merchant account fees. If you're an affiliate, you'll probably get 50% to 75% of the money.

It's a win-win. I sometimes spend ten hours a day and hundreds of dollars buying, consuming and using other people's products. Some of them are dog-poo. You'll never hear about those from me. Some are brilliant. Those are the ones I send to my list. You save your readers a lot of time, money and effort, and the price is the same whether they buy from your affiliate link or not. And everything you offer your list must—*this is not optional*—have a money-back guarantee so that in case you're wrong, and it's not perfect for them, they can get their money back. The game is fun only as long as nobody gets hurt.

You'll hear Internet Marketers talk about traffic. Traffic means people who go to a website. You need traffic. You can't make sales without it. If you're a relationship marketer, your list is your traffic—and it's the best traffic you can get, because they already know, like and trust you. Your job is to earn and keep that trust.

Metrics Marketing

Another way to do IM is what I call Metrics Marketing.

It's pretty much the same, but the emphasis is on numbers instead of a relationship.

Metrics marketers, in my opinion, have the harder job. They're selling to strangers. They don't rely on their list, because, in many cases, they don't have one.

However, don't discount metrics marketing. Huge fortunes have been made playing this game.

To play it well, you have to solve the traffic problem. Metrics marketers use Search Engine Optimization (SEO), Pay Per Click (PPC), Social Media marketing, such as Facebook ads, Banner ads, ad networks (which place ads on other people's sites), and Google AdWords (the big daddy of all ad networks.) If you're a math geek, you'll probably do well at metrics marketing. It involves a lot of testing, tracking, and, well, math.

The theory is the same. They use the above methods to send people to affiliate sales pages, and make a percentage from every sale. The technical stuff: each click costs something. That's your Cost Per Click (CPC). You want this number to be very low. At the end of the day, you add up all the money you made and divide it by the number of clicks you sent. That's your Earnings Per Click (EPC).

As long as EPC is higher than CPC you're making money. The wider that variance, the more money you've made.

That's the basics. Of course, there's more.

But, if you don't understand the basics, the rest is just going to confuse you.

My advice? Start playing the game. You can't win if you don't play.

When people ask me, "what is the first (or next) thing I should do?" I always answer, "what you WILL do." If you're a people-person, or math challenged (like me), you'll probably enjoy relationship marketing. If you've got a rain-man fascination with numbers and their behavior, you'll probably do better at metrics marketing. It's perfectly OK to mix and match.

Now, go do something.

I ALMOST FLUNKED ENGLISH BUT WENT ON TO MAKE MILLIONS OF DOLLARS WRITING SALES COPY

Joe Sugarman

The Guinness Book of World Records listed Joe Girard as the "World's Greatest Retail Salesman" for 12 consecutive years. He holds the singular distinction of having sold an average of six cars a day over his career. Joe Girard told me:

> *"Joe, I can sell in person to individuals in a personal way—in fact, I can sell more cars per day than anyone else. Yet, I can't do what you do—you sell millions of products to masses of people through the sheer power of print."*

Salesmanship in Print

When you look at it from Joe Girard's perspective, it's hard to deny the awesome power of writing good sales copy—which I call "salesmanship in print"—a power that anyone can take advantage of. You don't need good looks, a charming personality or even great intelligence. In fact, you don't even have to pass English.

This is why it baffles me when people desperately rack their brains trying to find ways to make money—when the greatest opportunity is staring them right in the face. What's even more mystifying is that those very same people, when presented with ingenious approaches to writing copy that sells, take the skill for granted and don' use it to make personal fortunes for themselves.

Flunking English

Not many people know this, but I almost flunked English back in high school. In addition, I don' know many big words, unlike the rest of my advertising and marketing colleagues—and my writing style is quite unsophisticated to boot. Yet, by learning to incorporate into my sales copy all the things about how the human mind reacts to certain words and phrases that I've learned over the years, I have made millions of dollars for myself.

The most important lesson you must remember is this: If you learn nothing else but the proper use of psychological principles in writing sales copy, you will always make more money than you'll ever need.

The Million-Dollar Grapefruit Farmer

If you're one of those people who believes that you're not a good enough writer—and that you couldn't possibly learn to write ad copy that sells—I want to tell you the story of a man who attended one of my seminars. This man was a grapefruit farmer who had never written sales copy prior to attending my copywriting seminar. In fact, he expressed his doubts that he would get anything at all from the copywriting lessons he learned. Yet, by the end of the seminar, he was able to write direct mail copy to sell grapefruit by mail, which, over a period of ten years, has earned him millions of dollars.

Success Leaves Clues

For many years I specialized in space-age" products, and my claim to fame was in building and selling " the better mousetrap"—from state-of-the art smoke detectors to chess computers to new-fangled calculators—to BluBlocker sunglasses and more recently—to products based on stem cell research.

But you don't need a space-age product to make a million dollars. In fact, that is the downfall of most people who enter the marketing field. They find a product, fall in love with it, and try to get the market to buy it. With an unproven product, you could lose a lot of money in the process.

Instead what you should do is find a product that's already selling well—and use compelling copy to sell it better.

Harmonize with the Marketplace

One of the psychological principles I describe in my book, *Triggers*, is simply this: Your product needs to harmonize with the marketplace.

Here's a tip that you would definitely find useful: When you're looking for a product to sell, go to the library and flip through the back issues of magazines—particularly the tabloids. Note those mail order ads that are running week after week, month after month. There's only one reason why those ads keep running—they're making money. Those products are already proven to sell well—they've demonstrated that they harmonize with the marketplace.

Even if there are many companies that are already competing in those product categories (example: weight loss, hair restoration, and wrinkle products, etc.), don't worry. If you apply good copywriting guidelines, your marketing efforts will fare better than those who are making money, despite their poor sales copy.

"Splish Splash I Was Takin' A Bath"

Take a clue from Bobby Darin, a popular singer of the '50s. Darin was a young singer in New York who, for a long time, tried unsuccessfully to break into the music business. He would go from record company to record company trying to convince them to make an album of him singing popular jazz oldies. He was rejected.

So one day, Darin sat down and wrote a song that fitted or "harmonized" with what the public was buying at the time. What was popular at the time was good old rock and roll sung by black artists—it was called the Motown sound.

The song he wrote was called "Splish Splash" and the words started out, "Splish splash, I was takin' a bath/ 'Round about a Saturday night." It had a good old Motown rock and roll sound—and it became a smash hit, selling millions of copies.

Darin recognized what the market wanted, and he created something that harmonized perfectly with the prevailing market. From his earnings, he himself produced a record in the music genre that he really loved—popular jazz oldies. His song, "Mack the Knife" went on to become a multimillion-selling single and made Bobby Darin famous.

To summarize, you must first have a product that harmonizes with your market. If you haven't made a substantial amount of money from your marketing efforts yet, sell only products or services that have a ready market—this is the path of least resistance. Afterwards, with the money you make, you can blaze new trails with other products of your own preference.

MONEY FROM ANYWHERE AS AN ONLINE ENTREPRENEUR

Connie Ragen Green

I'm writing this from the front porch of my house in Santa Barbara, California on a clear day in December. I've just returned from a speaking engagement in London, and in a few days I'm headed down to Central America to spend a week with friends and family members to celebrate the holidays. This would not be of major importance or great significance except for the fact that I am now living the lifestyle I had previously only dreamed of, and it all started when I made the decision to change my mindset, work on my 'Inner Game', and come online to build a business as an entrepreneur.

As a young child growing up in Los Angeles, California and, later, in Miami, Florida we were extremely poor. It was just my mother and I, and we never had a car or a telephone or anything else the other families around us all seemed to have. At age twelve I began working, first by mowing lawns and babysitting, and then by working as a waitress in the local coffee shops. I did manage to go to college, but even then I felt out of place with the other students. My mindset was one of poverty, even though I would not have believed or understood that at the time. Where others saw hope and opportunity, I saw challenges and struggle. After graduating from college I wandered through my 20s in a variety of jobs – claims adjuster for an insurance company, bank teller, manager of a coin laundry, and then as a real estate agent.

It was while working in real estate that I finally began to view my life a little bit differently. Perhaps it was the influence of the people I was working with, or the small successes I was beginning to experience in my work, but I found myself wanting more out of life than what I was getting at that time and believing that that was indeed possible. It was also during this time that I began to experience some financial success. I could see the direct correlation between some of the activities I was engaging in and the closed deals that resulted in large commission checks for me. It felt good to finally be earning more money than I had ever made in the past. The only problem was that I was not engaging in anything consistently enough to be able to identify specific activities that were both rewarding and lucrative. The pieces of the puzzle were not coming together completely for me at that time.

In January of 1986 I had just arrived at the real estate office where I was working at the time to find everyone huddled around a small television set to see the launch of the Space Shuttle. As I got close enough to see the screen a hush fell over the room. The Challenger had broken apart and disintegrated before our eyes. This was the first time a teacher had been aboard, and this immediately made me think back to when I was younger and had wanted to become a teacher myself. I made a conscious decision at that moment to pursue my dream of becoming a classroom teacher, and within nine months I was teaching in a classroom while completing my credential.

This marked the very first time I had taken action in such a dramatically focused way. Perhaps it was the emotional tone of what had happened to Christa McAuliffe, the teacher aboard the space craft, and the others that drove me to follow through with something I was so very passionate about. I had wanted to become a teacher for so many years, but had never taken the necessary steps to meet my goal. I had never even discussed this dream with anyone because I thought it would never come true. This time was different, and it felt good to finally be achieving my dreams and having control over my life and my destiny.

Over the next twenty years I worked as a classroom teacher, serving students in Kindergarten through high school. I even taught some adult school night classes for a couple of years. My favorite grade to teach was fifth grade. The kids at that age were so responsive to an adult role model, and it was a joy to watch them grow and learn. During my first few years of teaching I was able to share my own experiences, interests, and knowledge with the kids each year as part of our learning environment; over time this was eliminated and I could only teach the prescribed course of study. I came to understand that the public schools in America were designed to produce a constant stream of obedient and compliant workers for the corporate and manufacturing sectors of our country. My dream was to teach the creative leaders of tomorrow, not to train young people into submission. One day in the spring of 2005, after a disturbing conversation with a group of school administrators, I came to the conclusion that I would leave teaching in the next year or two and pursue a different path for the next phase of my life.

This left me in quite a conundrum as I had to decide what I really wanted out of my life. If you have had this experience in your own life you may already know what I'm talking about here. It's a complicated process to go from where you are in your life at this specific moment in time to an entirely new way of acting, believing, and interacting with others. You must choose to either go on with the life you currently have and be content with whatever might happen, or be willing to move way out of your comfort zone and be responsible for what you really want to experience during the remainder of your life by playing bigger than you've ever thought possible. I was ready for a huge change in my life, so I took a leap of faith and dug in with both heels.

Over the course of the next several months I began to read everything I could get my hands on to find out who I was, what I cared about, and which direction I wanted to take my life. It was as if my eyes were wide open for the first time in ages, and I was intoxicated at the possibilities that appeared and unfolded before me. I knew then that I could determine the outcome of my life and that any decisions I made would either move me closer to or further away from my dreams. My previous life had been dominated by fear, and now I could see why that was so unnecessary. I was afraid of not having enough money, of being judged by others, of making the wrong decisions in my daily life, of losing my job, of not having friends, and of so much more. Now I was starting to turn that around into a positive approach to my life, where fears could easily be overcome and hope was definitely within reach.

That summer I turned fifty years old, and I felt as though I had the rest of my life in front of me in a way I hadn't felt since I was a young child. That's when I began writing down my thoughts in a journal, and also drawing some simple pictures. I've never been much of an artist, but suddenly I wanted to draw meaningful pictures to express my thoughts and ideas for my future. I bought a pad of drawing paper and some colored pencils and began to sketch. I ended up creating a picture of myself sitting at a desk, looking out the window and having my dogs playing on the floor beside me.

Within eight months that picture became my reality. I moved from the house I had lived in for the previous fourteen years into a brand new home in a city twenty-five miles away. When friends came to see the new house and I showed them the picture I had drawn, none of them could believe it had been completed before the new house was even built.

I was now in control of my future and I began to see things very differently. I realized that I had to take full and complete responsibility for everything that happened in my life, whether it was positive or negative. I reflected on situations in my past and saw that my perception of what had occurred was very different, in many cases, from what was actually going on at that time.

At this point I was ready to jump in and start a business on the Internet as an online entrepreneur. My 'Inner Game', which I consider to be more important than business training or experience, was coming together in a way that made me feel excited and confident in my ability to be successful. I was surrounding myself with positive, upbeat people, as well as spending time each day studying what I needed to learn in order to launch my business in a way that would skyrocket my success quickly. Nothing could stop me now because I had a different outlook on life and was determined to see it through.

This was at the end of 2005, and on through 2006 I set about the task of laying a solid foundation for my business. This included starting to blog at least twice a week, writing articles to submit to the article directories, attending and then hosting teleseminars on my topic, learning more about affiliate marketing, and connecting with others who were doing something similar on the Internet. You must remember that this was before social media, so connecting with others took some creative thinking and implementing. These activities became something I named 'The 5 Pronged Approach™' and I'll be discussing it in more detail later on. Also, I did not have my own product to sell until the end of 2006, so recommending other people's products as an affiliate made the most sense for me. These are all tactics, so now it was time to focus on the strategies that would work so that I could replace my previous income and work exclusively online.

'Inner Game' strategies were the first ones I worked on, because I knew by now that if I had my thinking in order making money and achieving my goals would never be an issue for me again during my lifetime. That was a powerful thought and quite a revelation for me at that time, but after spending several months in a positive state of mind I was confident enough to believe in myself in a way I had never been able to in the past.

I used to stand in front of my bathroom mirror and tell myself that I was smart and dedicated and could achieve any goals I wanted to achieve. Then I would sit down at my computer and write for at least thirty minutes.

This writing was therapeutic in that I was writing about many experiences that had not been very pleasant in my life, and then reframing them in a way that served me better than to just complain and feel like a victim. For example, I wrote about the school principal who had been so unkind to me over the years and reframed that into her seeing the special qualities I possessed and wanting to help me to improve upon them. This was a way of forgiving, accepting, and having gratitude for people I had known over the years.

Writing was also a way for me to hone my skills by getting as much practice as possible. If you are familiar with the concept of the 'Ten Thousand Hours Rule', which states that success in any area of life is a matter of practicing a specific task for at least 10,000 hours, you will see how powerful this concept can be. I thought back to my early days of teaching in the classroom and realized that everything came easier once I had been at it for four to five years, which equates to about ten thousand hours of actual teaching. I had always wanted to become a writer, so putting in my time seemed like the wisest step to take to achieve my goal.

And so I continued to write, learn, and create as my business grew, and within about eighteen months I had replaced my previous income and was now surpassing it. It felt wonderful to finally be in a position to help others build their businesses and to become a teacher once again. Along the way I have connected with so many people that I otherwise would never had met, and some of these people I now count as my dearest friends and business associates. I travel the world for both business and pleasure and meet people on the other side of the planet who are pursuing goals in their lives that are very similar to mine. Working online makes all of this possible.

I have run my business from my home offices in southern California, as well as from the beach in Santa Barbara; from Internet cafés in downtown Amsterdam and rural China; the convention center in Bangkok, Thailand; my family's summer cottage in Finland; a pub in London, and from spots all over the United States where I can easily get an Internet signal.

I won't say that the fears and lack of confidence from my previous life are forever behind me; every once in awhile I hear those little voices telling me I'm not smart enough and don't deserve the success I'm now enjoy. When this happens I simply make a list of what I am most grateful for in my life, along with a list of my accomplishments over the past few years, to know that I am on the right path for what I want from my life on a daily basis.

The life of an online entrepreneur suits my new lifestyle quite well, and I would encourage you to explore this way of life if it resonates with you. It allows me to continue to be a teacher, something that I thought was gone forever when I left the classroom. It has also given me the gift of creativity, and I had not thought of myself in this way at any time previously. Teaching and creating are excellent ways to make a living while also helping others and feeling good about what you're doing each day for the ultimate experience in a rewarding business.

The best advice I have for you is to always keep it simple. People come to me all the time with overcomplicated, complex business plans that make my eyes glaze over. Simple, direct goals where you take action and implement what you're learning will always work best in life.

In 2008 I came up with my original 5 Pronged Approach™ for building a profitable online business. Many things changed over time, so in 2013 I have an all new version of this powerful concept. I'll explain it in more detail here for you.

Blogging/Publishing Books—Your blog is your 'Home on the Internet'. This is where you share more about who you are, what you do, and how you serve others in your business. Writing and publishing books in the natural offshoot for the content you are creating within your blog posts, and that has never been easier to do. With the advent of Amazon's Kindle and Create Space programs for self-publishing, you now have a way to get your ideas, information, and expertise out to the world. I have quite a few books available and will continue to use this strategy to build my business.

Short Reports—Previously I taught that article marketing was the second prong in my approach, but that all began to change at the beginning of 2011. Although I will continue to write and submit a few articles to the directories each month, my primary focus has been to repurpose my content over to short reports. These reports can be sold or given away, and will continue to bring you credibility, visibility, and income for years to come.

Teleseminars/Audio/Podcasts—Allowing people to hear your voice is the next best thing to meeting them in person. Use a variety of modalities to make sure you are heard discussing your niche topic on a regular basis. I continue to host teleseminars each month, and also have a weekly podcast series available as a free subscription in iTunes.

Social Media/Forums/Live Events—I started my online business during the 'Dark Ages of Social Media', which means that there was no social media to speak of during 2006 and into 2007. I did spend time on a few forums at that time, and found out quickly which ones were worthwhile. I now recommend that you spend no more than twenty minutes each day on the 'Big Three' social media sites – Facebook, Twitter, and LinkedIn – and that you join one or two paid forums to connect with others. Attend live events whenever possible, starting with those in the city where you currently live.

Affiliate Marketing—This makes the most sense for you if you are a new online entrepreneur and have no products of your own, or only a few, at this time. I am now what is referred to as a 'Super Affiliate', which means that I can win many affiliate contests, drive significant traffic and sales to promotions I believe in, and earn a mid five figures a month, every single month, from my affiliate promotions. This all started in the spring of 2006, when I made my first affiliate sale and earned twenty-one dollars and sixty cents. I saw the possibilities and took off with this business model. People come to me regularly to help them launch their products and programs, and I teach affiliate marketing to those who want to learn how to do this in their own online business.

So, you may be wondering how your 'Inner Game' comes into play with my 5 Pronged Approach™. The answer is that you must continue to believe in yourself and have confidence each day as you go through the different prongs and apply them to your business. No amount of training, or of knowing the specific winning tactics and strategies for business will make a difference unless you know who you are and what you wish to achieve. This is key to being able to attract money and opportunities from anywhere.

Write down your goals and then take action each and every day to move closer to achieving them. Connect with the people who are already living the lifestyle that resonates with you and learn more about how they made significant changes in their lives over time. Ask questions, seek out knowledge, and then move forward. Know that you can be, do, or have anything you want in your life simply by making the conscious decision and positive choice to take massive, inspired actions towards your goals. What you have to share matters to others, and no one can deliver your message in the same way that you will be able to do it. This is the time to simplify, collaborate, and move forward as an online entrepreneur, so incorporate this new way of thinking into your daily thinking and see what's possible in your own life experience.

Connie Ragen Green is an author, speaker, and online marketing strategist living in southern California. Download free training on how you can get started online right away by visiting http://HugeProfitsTinyList.com.

SOCIAL MEDIA: YOUR GATEWAY TO PROFITS

Martha Giffen

Although it's relatively new, social media has come onto the scene and hit the ground running. Fast. The fact is, it's not an option any more. If used as part of your overall marketing strategy, the remarkable power of social media will help you achieve amazing results.

In my case, I've inked book deals, snagged speaking gigs, secured radio and TV interviews, landed in a couple of magazines, and created a Twitter tweet that brought in $1000. Over and over.

But, I'm getting ahead of myself. Let's start at the beginning.

There's nothing new about networking. Many small business owners are members of their local Chamber of Commerce, Rotary, Lions Club, BNI, etc. These are organizations that encourage business owners to meet each other and have the added benefits of cultivating new clients and gaining referrals.

Social media is basically the same thing. Conversations with a purpose. And that can have a pretty powerful outcome!

I happen to be of the opinion that there's a right way and a wrong way to approach social media. By right, I mean using it to build relationships that lead to an increased prospect list, larger client base and a bigger bottom line without constantly shouting to the world your latest promotion. By wrong, I mean just using social media as one big billboard for your products. You can try it that way, but I can assure you, it doesn't work.

If you are interested in connecting with current, past, and future clients and growing a healthy business, then this is for you. I am going to state what you already know: People buy from people they know, like, and trust.

Ask any small business owner and they will agree. The most successful and prosperous businesses are relational.

Think about it. Whether you are the first person your customer sees when they walk into your storefront or you are the door-to-door salesman, people buy from YOU! Period. Soooooo, let's talk about how to get people to warm up to you on the world wide web, come into your store, and buy your goods!

The Big Three

For the sake of not overwhelming you, and also the limited space one book chapter can hold, I'm going to confine our conversation to the Big Three. That would be Twitter, Facebook, and LinkedIn. Master those three and you can branch out to any other social site and be successful.

There is one commonality of all the sites and that's your profile. I can't say enough about how important the profile information is. Think of it as your first impression and you know what they say about that. You only get one.

All profiles have four parts. They are:

> *Your picture*—Keep it current and use the same one on all sites. (Current is the magic word here. Don't let people meet you in person and not be able to recognize you. Or worse, think you are your mother!)
>
> *Your message*—Take the time to condense your message down to a simple sentence or two. This is important because you want to be identified with your message and if it's short, people can remember it. Doing this will also

give you more clarity about your target audience.
A call to action—Always ask for what you want. Tell them what you want them to do. Give a call to action with some kind of offer.
Link—Where do you want them to go? Your site? Your freebie? Your product? Put the link in your profile.

Taking the time to put a clear, concise profile in place is the way you lay a good foundation for everything else you do on social media sites. Be sure to start with that.

Twitter

Everybody's heard of it but many just don't "get it." Think of Twitter this way: A large group of people in a huge room, some talking all at once, some engaged in small groups, a few just standing in the corner quietly observing.

You walk in. Most likely, you will look around, possibly see someone you know, or someone interesting that you don't know but would like to, and you will strike up a conversation. Right? That's the beginning of networking. Friendly conversation that progresses. As it moves forward, you mention your business, give them a card, tell them you'll call, etc. The point is, it's relaxed. You aren't walking into the room carrying a neon sign that says "buy my stuff, buy my stuff." Make sense?

The same rules apply to Twitter. You will begin to engage in short conversations, people will start to know and like you and you eventually mention your business. Even promote your business.

Now, when you walk into the room at a live business networking event, usually people are wearing nametags. The great thing about twitter is that your "nametag," or who you are, is listed for everybody to see, right underneath your picture. See? No neon sign necessary! And, you can even create a twitter background with your company logo and make that as personal as you like!

Think of your twitter background and profile as your "ad" for your biz. The "relational" part comes in the "tweeting."

The Basics

First, if you have not done it yet, go sign up at http://twitter.com. It's free and will only take a couple of minutes.

Two words of advice here: Always use your real name as your user name, especially if you are trying to brand yourself. And, upload your picture. Twitter is social. Many will not communicate with you if you are hiding behind the egghead! The Lingo. . . .

Just like everything else, Twitter has it's own lingo. Here's the main verbiage:

Tweet – The actual words you type on your status. Tweeting is a synonym for talking.

Retweet – Repeating something someone else tweeted.

It also consists of the use of abbreviations.

Here are a few:

@ before each person's name is used when communicating on twitter. It's public.

d before a person's name is used for private conversation. It's a direct message just between two people. Not public. You can only send direct messages to people who follow you.

RT means you are "retweeting," which is simply repeating something someone else has already tweeted or "said." This is done when someone has made a comment you find interesting, is sharing content you like, or is promoting something your audience would be interested in.

How to "tweet"

Basically, twitter is a place where you have 140 characters to say whatever you want. The words you put out there are your "tweets."

Here are some basics to remember:

Be engaging.

Even though you may eventually use some canned promotional tweets, you need to be there "for real" for the most part. "Retweet" something someone else has said that you think is clever, meaningful, is similar to your own message, or relevant to your list. It's always nice to retweet your own clients and customers.

About your followers . . . .

Treat them with respect.

Your followers are numbered. That makes the math easy. It also can play a nice little head game on you. There are two strands of thought on this. One is you want to have "quality" followers. Followers that are only there because they know you, are interested in your message, or are current customers. The other thought is the higher your numbers, the better. Those folks subscribe to the belief that sales is simply a numbers game and the more numbers, the more chances of making an online sale.

I say both are right. It depends on your market. If your market is the whole online world, then go for the numbers and let the chips fall where they may.

If you are after a targeted market, for example, your local market or a specific niche, my suggestion is to go for quality, and build your numbers from there. That's my own approach and it works really well.

NOTE: DO NOT EVER BUY FOLLOWERS. This is silly, they are usually bots, and it hinders what you are trying to accomplish.

All in all, my philosophy is to start your list with a small targeted market and build the numbers from there. You will slowly build up a customer base with others on the peripheral scattered in. It's a nice mix.

For example, I have close alliances with many people who have online businesses whose products I don't actually need or use. However, I might retweet something they are saying about their product because I know, like and trust them. And also, who knows? There may be someone following me who NEEDS that product and I have just done them a service!

What is the best way to pick up followers? Tweet great content! Give little known facts, links to a great blog post, links about your niche, or links to articles about your niche. People are looking for great content. Give it to them! Turn yourself into the twitter expert about that particular niche. Engage in conversations with others who are interested in the same topics. Never forget, on your website or in social networking, ultimately content is king!

How to find your hungry prospects:

Do a simple Twitter search using your keywords. This can be one of the easiest ways, but is so often overlooked. People who are using those keywords will show up in the search. Follow and jump into their conversations!

Follow the key players n your niche. Then, look at their followers. Chances are, those are your prime prospects too. Follow them! (it goes without saying that you begin a conversation)

Hashtags. Using the # sign in front of your keywords will help you find others who are interested in what you have to offer. You will also find people participating in hashtag chats by using this system. For example, looking for small biz owners? Try #smbiz or #smbizchat or #smallbiz

Use the "Perfect Tweet." This is what I call the tweets that bring in the cash! They have three parts: 1) The call out (ex: NEW BLOGGERS); 2) Solve the problem (ex: Want to make money with your blog?); 3) Give the link. So, the tweets looks like this: NEW BLOGGERS! Want to make money with your blog? Here's a free report: http://profitablebloggernow.com

If you follow these tips, you'll build your credibility, visibility, and send people into your sales funnel. By the way, that "Perfect Tweet" has been used by me many times to promote free webinars that offer high quality products at the close of the webinar. That's money in the bank and how I pocketed my first $1000 from one Twitter tweet :)

Promoting Other People

If all of your conversations are about you, your website or your product, you won't be looking at adding many followers.

What about promoting other people? This is a great way to increase your followers and also create goodwill among other business people.

When you recommend their websites or products, you are telling people "These are my favorites. I like what they are doing. I like their products and you will too!"This does two things for you. After that promotional tweet for someone else, you have endorsed what they are doing and they take note of it and probably at some later date, they will reciprocate. Also, it creates the image of being helpful to your clients and not just trying to push your products on them.

Isn't it always great when someone else says your product is fantastic? Not only does it have the possibility of producing a random sale for you but it increases your brand presence because now, all of his followers have seen the recommendation.

See where this is headed? Into the great big twitterverse of people! Possible customers you would have never encountered. Just because someone else promoted your product!

It's a big world out there! Does it feel like it just got bigger?

A word of warning: Never tweet a link that you haven't actually read! Sincerity is key!

140 Characters Not Enough?

Yes, 140 character is not very many. That's the beauty of Twitter. Nobody has a chance to go on and on about ANYTHING! There IS a way to shorten urls or links that you are tweeting out. Here are three places you can go to shorten the link:

http://is.gd

http://bit.ly

http://tinyurl.com

I use all three and they are all great. You can decide which one shortens enough for you!

Automation and tools

Tools are great but automation is tricky. I don't really like it and don't often do it. Here's why: I am an advocate of relational marketing. I can't be relational if I'm using too many canned tweets. However, having said that, I do use them during my sleeping hours for promotional tweets. Never for engagement tweets.

Twitter is a constant stream of people who are "in the moment." Chances are, they are going to see your tweet if they happen to be on twitter at the same time. Well, that's true, but due to Twitter Lists and some other clever applications, you can overcome this obstacle.

As you progress with your Twitter marketing, you will eventually want to add a few tools. There are more tools created for Twitter than I could ever list here but you might want to check out some of these and see if they are for you.

Here are a few and what they do:

Tweetdeck – A great tool for keeping up with your messages. You won't miss any! This tool is focused on who is saying what about you! You can also tweet from there.
Tweetchat – A tool used to watch a #hashtag stream. Just enter the hashtag and the stream comes up. Has the capability of storing tweets to send out later. You can also tweet from there too.
JustUnfollow—Why bother to continue people who aren't interested in what you've got to say. Check this site to see who's not engaging with you.
TwitterGrader – Let's you know your twitter rank. This is interesting information that you can tweet out.
MrTweet – Can help you find followers.
Twello – Called the "Twitter Yellow Pages" for a reason. It's free and will connect you with more people in your niche. A great place to register yourself! Remember, you

want to be found too! You also have the capability of sending tweets from there.

Hootsuite – A place where you can manage all your social networking in one place. Can tweet from there and see multiple streams. It also has the capability of storing tweets to tweet later. (Note: This is my personal favorite. I even use the mobile app)

Twitpic – an application that lets you share photos on twitter.

Twitterholic – A site where you can get stats on yourself and other Twitterers. Fun information!

#Hashtags

You will notice in some tweets, there are words with the # sign in front. That is called the hashtag. Using the hashtag creates a quick way to identify with a list of people who are all tweeting about the same subject. It's also a perfect way to add followers that are tweeting about your niche

For example, If you type the hashtag #LOA, you will find a group of people tweeting about things relative to the Law of Attraction. Using the hashtag #golf would connect you with anyone tweeting something about golf.

You can even start your own hashtag. Just tweet something using a hashtag and see if it will catch on! You can follow me using #BeSocialBeRich

Twitter Lists

One way Twitter has become easier to stay connected with your core groups is by using the Twitter Lists. It's also a fantastic way to keep your groups separate. Think of it as a filing system for your followers!

You will see it on the left hand side of the twitter page. You can create your own lists to make your life a little easier. And, you should be happy when others add you to their list. That way, you have a little more information about why they are following you in the first place!

When you create your lists, give them clever names. Don't title them "future clients" or "prospects". No, no, no! Would you want to be on a list with that label? Give them names like "Social engagers", "just met", or, like one I'm on, "B'ham peeps." That person is identifying my town, Birmingham.

The Power of Twitter

The great thing about twitter? You gain access to people that you would never have otherwise. In my case, I have found people to interview, chatted with famous authors, gotten technology help, studied a mentor before I hired them, and even had a Hollywood producer give me a phone call!

Use Twitter wisely and you'll be watching your business grow.

Facebook

Another social media site that took off like wildfire is Facebook. Everybody and their brother is on there! Facebook is great for your online business. You have a lot of freedom to advertise and many ways for your "friends" to get to know you.

The Basics

To set up your account on Facebook, simply go to http://facebook.com and sign up for an account. Again, there will be plenty of fields for you to fill in the blanks. There are a lot of categories. Just answer the ones you want people to see. It's my opinion that the more you put out there, the more "humanized" you are and that is good for your business. It's your personal preference.

Your profile will be public. This is the place to let people know who you are and what you are doing. Put the link to your website for everyone to see! There is also a field for a short bio. Be sure you make a short statement that says exactly who you are and what you are doing. "I'm a Mom of three boys" is somewhat interesting, but "I help new online entrepreneurs achieve success with Internet marketing" is more specific. By the way, both of those descriptions describe me, but guess which one brings in clients?

And, I can't say this one loud enough – be sure and put your picture on your profile! People want to do business with you. Let them see who you are!

When looking at the facebook page, you will see there is a "home" and "profile" page. On the home page, you will see the real-time stream of other people's status updates. You will also see on the upper right hand side the "requests" heading. You click on these to find out any friend request, fan page request, etc. On the profile page, you will see your profile, your status updates, your FB "friends," basically all things you!

Facebook also has FB message capability. This is e-mail to your account from other FB members.

There is also live chat capability. You will see at the bottom of the right hand side a little "chat" bar. You can optimize this and see which one of your friends is logged on. You can instant message them if you want to talk in "real time."

Warning on this feature: Do not abuse it! If you want to talk to family members and close friends, fine. Do not IM "friends" that are possible clients or mentors that you don't actually know unless you have a really good reason. It's intrusive. It's also a great way to get yourself "unfriended!"

How to use

Facebook is all about "friends." Who can be your friend on Facebook? Any one you approve. When you make a friend request, nothing happens until the other person accepts. Once that happens, you both have access to one another. It's that simple.

Always remember that social networking for your online business is about branding. Facebook is no different. There are many ways to make your presence known on Facebook.

First, your status update. It is that little line where you say something about what's going on in your life. At the very least, you should update it every morning. Yes, every day. You make it part of your daily marketing routine. It will become second nature in no time! Also, during the day, if possible, update. It's a great way for people to start to know you. Now, I'm not saying tell your deep, dark secrets on Facebook, but if you are meeting with a client, say it. (You can omit their name) If you are finishing a chapter in your book, say it. Why? You need to look like the busy entrepreneur that you are. Let the world know what's going on with you.

Busy businesses get more business. Idle ones watch their silent phones.

Let your "friends" know you are busy. It will result in business AND referral business. Again, it's all about branding. Let your friends know you are churning it out and that you are glad to help them too.

If you have a promotion going on, say it. Give the link to it. If you are interviewing someone, put it out there. Did you just write a great blog post? Put that in your status and include the link! If you have a new product, or are just working on a product, put that in your status. Again, you want people to know that you are the expert or the "to-go-to" person in your niche.

Communicating with Others...

As you begin to add friends to facebook, you will be looking at their profiles also. You have the ability to write on their "wall." This is the stream on their profile where their status shows up. If you have a comment that adds to a discussion, fine. Otherwise, you don't want to write on walls too often. Just enough to let people know you are approachable and not become annoying.

Another caution: Do NOT write any type of ad for your business on someone elses wall. I know it's tempting to say, "Go look at my website" and add the link, but don't do it. Use the golden rule here!

Profile Applications

There are a number of applications (Apps) included with your profile. You will see them as tabs at the top of your profile page. These are: Video, Photos, Events, Groups, Notes, Posted Items, Gifts. These are different ways of enhancing your "friends" exposure to you when they visit your profile page.

Here are a few tips regarding these apps:

Video: You have the capability to upload videos. They must be under 300 MB and less than 20 minutes long. You can upload from your phone or web cam. It also have photo tagging capability.

Photos: To upload photos, click on "Create a Photo Album." You can also tag photos by clicking on the picture of the person. A box will come up for you to insert that person's name. If they are one of your friends on FB, it will appear on their wall as well.

Links: Any time you share a link on your status, it will be recorded here.

Fan Page or Business Page

After you have set up your account, you will want to set up a Fan Page. This was a hard one for me at first. Who wants to be my fan? Well, you will be surprised. You send the invitation to everyone who is your friend on FB and watch them line up to be your fan. They are now called business pages and make more sense. For starters here, upload a nice cover. Be sure and read the Facebook Terms of Service so you don't violate any. For example, they don't allow phone numbers, web addresses and such. Just check it out. Don't know where to get a cover? Try Fiverr.com

You can get a nice one for five bucks!

Next, you will want to set up your tabs. I won't spend a lot of time here but some of the possibilities are: Events, Freebies, Your Blog, Amazon link, Online store, Social media links, etc. Use them as another way to send people into your sales funnel.

NOTE: Remember, Facebook pages are not the same as having your own website. You don't own the page and FB can pull it down or make changes on a whim. Always send people to YOUR site. Treat your FB page like somebody else owns it. Because they do.

Facebook is all about content sharing. This comes in many forms.

Blog posts

Pictures and images

Videos

Quotes turned into images

Shared posts from other people

Remember, consistency is the key. You have to train folks to come to your page. Post every day and post great content and pretty soon your traffic will pick up. Sometime I did in the beginning that worked: I posted a social media tip every single day for the first 100 days of my Facebook page. It became so popular that I still do it!

A Little More Advanced...Facebook Apps

You can go to the left hand column and see "Applications." When you click on there, you will find lots and lots of apps for FB. Here are a few you might like for your online business:

Networked Blogs—A great application if you are writing blogs. You enter your blog link, it shows up on your profile page, and you can invite people to follow it. It's a great way to pick up more readers to your blog.

Twitter Badges—Links your twitter account to your FB account so you don't have to update both.

My LinkedIn Profile—Puts a LinkedIn Badge on your FB profile. Clicking the badge will take people to your LinkedIn Profile.

Facebook Connect—This will connect your website to Facebook

WARNING: Do not use the FriendFeed app. because this posts all links and comments to all of your friends' walls. It is annoying to them! Trust me.

Another place to look for great apps is http://www.facebook.com/apps/directory.php

LinkedIn

LinkedIn is THE place for professional networking. And I don't mean professional networkers. I mean the people on LinkedIn ARE professionals!

There are over 161 MILLION members on LinkedIn, including executives from each of the Fortune 500. That's what I'm talking about when I say it's a professional's networking site.

What does that mean to you? Well, basically when you think about it, professionals have more money to spend, know WHERE they want to spend it, and they (usually) now what they are looking for as far as networking on LinkedIn goes. So, you will find a much savvier audience in some ways, definitely a more educated audience, and hopefully an audience with money to spend.

Who DOESN'T like THAT??

Again, the profile is crucial. Don't stop filling it out until it's 100% complete. This is important when people are searching for you. Because of the internal LinkedIn search, people are ranked higher that have their profiles complete.

The beauty of LinkedIn is in the recommendations. Be sure and ask your customers and clients to fill out recommendations for you. People definitely read them when searching.

Recently, LinkedIn has adopted the "endorsement" system. In my opinion, the endorsements don't mean a whole lot, seem more like a popularity contest and I'm not so sure people doing the endorsing have actually worked with their endorsers.

Stick with Recommendations and you can't go wrong. Another great area of LinkedIn are the groups!

They are excellent places for you to find prospects and start building relationships. AND, don't always narrow your participation to groups within your industry. Gravitate to your alma mater group, former places you've worked, or complimentary industries. Chances are, there will be someone in there who either needs your services or knows someone who does.

In my own case, I'm a member of women entrepreneur groups and work-at-home Mom groups. Both are great places for me to learn, connect, and reach out to others. I let my expertise be known through comments and before long, it trickles down to very real paying clients.

Think of groups like this: Offline clubs and organizations are fast being replaced by online groups. Make sense now?

While we're on the subject of groups, be sure and frequent them often. The more people see you in the group adding value , the more likely they are to turn to you to solve their problem.

Even though LinkedIn is considered a social network, it is more of a business network. Remember, it's not a static site. You don't just throw up a profile and wait for others to contact you. No, you have to be proactive, search out others, share content and find your target market.

Conclusion

Social Media is simply conversation. Getting your message out in a warm and inviting way. It can be used to build loyalty and to expand your brand. In the end, it's still networking and building a network that will support your business. Be approachable. Connect. And have a social media marketing plan.

Of course, I wouldn't be much of a Social Media expert if I didn't include my own social links! You can find me at:

http://www.MarthaGiffen.com

http://facebook.com/marthagiffenpage

http://twitter.com/marthagiffen

http://linkedin.com/in/marthagiffen

Also, remember, through social media, you just might meet a marketing guru that wants to include you in their new book! Happy networking!

DON'T FEAR THE TECH!

Geoff Hoff

One of the main reasons people don't start businesses online is that it seems to require a lot of technical know-how. Just the thought of all that stuff you have to learn, as they used to say in the old Southern dramas, can give someone the vapors. What's HTML? What's an AR? How do I change a DNS? What the heck is a DNS and why does it require changing in the first place?

Okay, calm down. Breathe in and out for a moment. Let's take it one step at a time.

First, let me tell you a little about myself so you know why you should even listen to me. I have always been an artistic type. I majored in theatre in college (and, yes, I spelled it with an "re". I'm pretentious and proud of it.) I taught acting for several years, back during the Lincoln administration. I have also always written; I put together my first short story when I was nine. I also paint, draw and sing (sort of). That's awfully "right-brained" activity for someone who is writing about tech.

File that last paragraph under "If I can do it without getting the willies, so can you".

I was once told by a friend I hadn't seen in several years that he would have predicted I would become successful in any field I tried as long as it didn't involve technology. I would have agreed with him until I stumbled backwards into the first technology gig while working at a law office in the prestigious position of mail clerk. This was back when secretaries used IBM Selectric typewriters. Remember them? You changed fonts by changing the typing wheel. Ah, technology.

The firm was kind of cutting-edge and decided to transition into computers. When they sent their word processing dude to computer training, they also sent me as a backup, since it seemed like I had a brain cell or two.

The secretaries started asking me for help when they ran into problems because the other guy spoke tech and I spoke human and, even though he knew more, they understood me better. From there, I got a job in another law office as their computer guy. And then another. And then, I went out on my own as free-lance.

I still pursued the artistic side, of course, saying I did the computer work to support the writing habit.

Several years later, I wrote a book with Steve Mancini, a satirical novel called *Weeping Willow*. We needed a web site for it, so I dove in and learned how to build one. This was way before any of the wonderful tools we have now. I struggled through learning how to do basic web page coding (called HTML. See? You're learning as you read) and made the pages in a text editor. Then I discovered DreamWeaver, which is sort of like Microsoft Word for web pages, and I thought I'd died and gone to heaven. There was still a huge learning curve, though, and I used to shout and swear and pound the desk and throw things a lot. My cat used to simply shake her head in wonder at this strange being who fed her and took most of the bed.

Before you start to hyperventilate (this chapter is called "DON'T fear the tech!"), don't worry. You won't have to know any of this stuff. Ever. In fact you can have a full-on web presence without ever even seeing any code at all! So relax and follow along with me on the winding journey.

As I got more familiar with the Internet, I started to see some real possibilities and started teaching courses. It was actually working with Pat O'Bryan that it all started to fall into place.

I am forever in his debt. The first was a six week, live course on writing a short story. Putting it up involved a ton of tech stuff that I had to learn. (That course is still available with recordings of the live sessions, by the way. I'm still very proud of it, as technologically primitive as it is.)

Many years later, I discovered a marvelous tool called WordPress. I'm sure lots of the people who contributed to this book have already told you about it and I'll talk more about it in a bit, but I want to say here that it finally made life livable for a rightbrained entrepreneur. And as the years went by, it got easier and easier to use this incredibly powerful and versatile tool.

Well, as I continued to slog my way through all this, once again, people started coming to me for advice on their own sites, so I started teaching courses on online tech. I also started offering a monthly tech service to a select few. Again, one of the things people said was that they loved learning that stuff from me, that it all seemed simple, down to earth and infinitely doable. One fellow even called me the Winnie-the-Pooh of online tech. I like that. And, except for the beard, I sort of look like old Winnie.

And how can you fear something that Winnie-the-Pooh can do?

"So What Does This All Mean For ME?"

That's a very good question. This Geoff guy spent years struggling to learn this stuff, how am I supposed to master it without tearing my hair out? I'd rather eat Brussels sprouts.

Well this is where I send your fears outside to play in the yard with the critters and creepy-crawlies they so love, because you don't have to do any of that stuff. We are in a sort of Diamond Age of the Internet, where there are so many tools that make it easy for you (many of them are even free) that any modern-day entrepreneur can breathe easily, knowing that world domination is only a matter of time. (And by entrepreneur I do mean you. Proof? You're reading this book.)

So, rather than get weak in the knees and swoon into your front room chez lounge with the back of your hand pressed against your brow, let's tackle what you will need to know. (And if you were tempted to make that swoon, I'm really not making fun of you. I told you, I'm pretentious and I do love a good dramatic moment. I'll often indulge in one with the smallest provocation. In other words, I'm right there with you, but save it for something really worthy of a good collapse. Something like when they change how Facebook works yet again.)

As I say, there are now some amazing tools that you can use that make almost everything a snap. Let's explore some of these tools we now have that I didn't have back in the day when we had to walk five miles to school uphill in a snowstorm.

What things will you need to get a website up, especially one that can be used for an online business? Here they are. I'll tell you how to do or get each one after the list.

A Product or Service—In order to make money with your online venture, you need something to sell, a product, service, course. Something. Most online products are built to solve a specific problem. If you have had a problem and solved it, you can sell the solution. Other people in this book have talked about this in detail, so I won't delve more here.

A Domain Name—This is the web address; what people type into a web browser like Internet Explorer or Firefox to get to your site. http://Google.com is a domain name. So is http://Amazon. com and http://GeoffHoff.com – Hey, I'm a marketer, you didn't think I'd let an opportunity to give you my web address go by, do you? That's a free non-tech tip for you, by the way. If you're going to market, market.

A Host—This is where your site actually lives. A host is simply a company that rents space on its computers so you can put your website somewhere and people can get to it.

A Website—That's what the previous two are the start of. To get something to actually show up on your website, we'll install WordPress, which will be done in just a few click of your mouse. No more HTML coding in a text editor!

An Email Service—You have to be in connection with both the people who purchased something from you so you can make sure they use it well and so you can sell them other stuff, and with people who have made inquiries of you or downloaded something you gave away. (Again, other people have explained this in detail.) Sending out email from your Outlook will get you in lots of trouble, so you need a service to help you with this bit. There are several, but we'll look at two below.

A Way to Take Payments—If you want to make money, you have to have a way to get the money from your customers to you. Below, I'll tell you about two of those, also.

A Way to Make Your Products—This is assuming that your products are "digital", which means your customers can download them or view them on the Internet, such as eBooks, audios, videos, etc. I'll talk about the easiest – eBooks—below.

Your Domain Name

There are several services where you can purchase your domain name. In case you want to feel like a bit of a geek for a moment, they are called "Registrars". You don't need to know that if you have no geek aspirations, so don't fret. The one I use is GoDaddy, but you can use any of them that your friends and colleagues might recommend. You find this one at http://GoDaddy.com.

Now, you may have seen domain names that end in .com, .net, .org, .info, etc. At the beginning, only concern yourself with the .com or the .net. Once you have a little experience, you can explore getting others. (What? More than one domain name? Doesn't that mean more than one web site?!? Why yes. I own well over 100 domain names. Not all of them are being used. Connie Ragen Green calls this "virtual real estate". Someday, I will develop some of them. I may let some go. I may sell some. Again, don't fret. You only need one to start with.)

There are all sorts of theories about how to choose a domain name and some of them are really valid, but to start with (especially if you are already threatening to panic) just make it simple for yourself. If it's available, you should get your name

(my name is where I have my main web site) and/or the name of your product, service or the area your products or services will be in. If you're selling Poodle Dog Walking classes, go to GoDaddy and see if poodledogwalking.com is available. If not, try poodledogwalkingclasses.com.

To get a little more geeky (most of you can avert your eyes for a moment, there's a tiny bit of geek stuff here), you can see what actual phrases people are searching for in your area of expertise and buy a domain name that includes one of those phrases. (Notice that neither Pat O'Bryan nor I have done this with either of our main sites. We both have, however, with sites specific to some of our products.)

There is a great tool you can use to see what people are searching for called "Google Keyword Tool". To find it, just type Google Keyword Tool into Google. Start by checking on your niche, like poodle dog walking. Then see what they suggest and if any of those sound plausible. Then go to GoDaddy, see if it's available. If it's not, do more looking in the keyword tool, back to GoDaddy, etc. until you find the absolute right combination. That's how I found my http://SimlpleWebsiteTrafficSecrets.com domain name.

Again, in the beginning, just get something that makes sense so you aren't using all the geek talk as an excuse not to get started. Trust me, that's a trick I've used, so I know all about it.

Your Host

Remember, this is where your site lives. There are millions of hosts out there. Some good, some great, some terrible. The one I use is called HostGator at http://HostGator.com, but I can also recommend BlueHost – http://BlueHost.com.

Yes, GoDaddy also offers hosting. My recommendation is not to use them for that. They are experts in domain registration. Not so much in hosting.

Now, here is one of the two things I'll talk about that might make you a little nervous. You have to point the domain name you got at GoDaddy to your host. Breathe in once or twice. Okay, calm? I'll tell you how here, but I've also created a couple of short videos to show you exactly how easy it is and will give you a link at the end of this chapter you can go to so you can watch those videos.

When you got your hosting, they sent you a welcome email. There are two things that you need from that right now. The "name servers". This is the mysterious Domain Name Servers or DNS we mentioned with awe in the first paragraph. See, you learned another new thing! (And now you will learn why you need to change it!)

They will look something like this:

ns1153.hostgator.com or

ns1.BlueHost.com

and there will be two of them.

Now, simply follow these steps. (Or follow along in the video.)

You don't even need to know why you're doing it. Just trust it will work.

Log into your GoDaddy account and…

…click on "My Account" at the top of the page.

Then, click "Launch" on the "Domains" line.

Find the domain you just purchased and click on that.

It will bring you to an edit page. On that page, find the place down a bit where it says "Nameservers".

In that area click on "Set Nameservers"

Choose "I have specific nameservers for my domain".

In the two fields that appear, replace what's there with the two nameservers you got in your welcome email. Click "Okay".

You have now changed your nameservers! Without even breaking a sweat! If you used this domain name when you got your host, it's all done. If you used a different one, you have to warn your host that you now have a new domain name you want them to host.

To do that, log in to your host, find "Addon Domains" and follow the instructions. It might take an hour or so for the DNS change to take hold, so wait a bit before doing any Addons.

All this means is that, when someone types your domain name in, they are taken to that place you're renting over on your host where your site lives.

See how having a one-two-three check list takes the fear away?

Your Website

Okay, now let's install WordPress. With this free tool and the many add-ons you can use with it (many for free) creating a site and getting it to look like what you want it to is now a breeze.

With the WordPress platform, it is now possible to get your basic site set up literally within ten minutes. Yes, you'll need to do some customization and add some content after that, but getting it set up can be a very simple matter. Here is that checklist.

(Loading WordPress is a bit different in HostGator and in BlueHost. Use the instructions for the one you have. They are both really easy and it should only take you a minute or two.)

HostGator:

In the "find" box toward the top left hand side of your control panel, type "Fantastico" and Fantastico DeLuxe will move to the top of the screen. Click on that.

On the left hand side of the screen, find "WordPress" and click on it.

Click on "New Installation".

There is a pull down menu. Choose the domain you are using from that. (If you have more than one, that is. If you only have the one, that should show up already.)

In the box for administrator uername put in your name or a nickname you will remember. (Don't use "admin"! It makes it easy for the bad guys to do bad thing.)

Put in a password. Don't use an easy one like password123 or your name. Hackers love easy passwords.

The rest can be filled in now or when you go to your WordPress control panel

Click on "Install WordPress". Click "Finish Installation".

You have now loaded WordPress! That was easy. Why was I so scared?

BlueHost:

There is a "Find" box toward the top left hand side of your control panel. In that, type "Simple Scripts" and Simple Scripts will move to the top of the screen. Click on that.

If you already have any WordPress installations, they will be listed on top. Under those, look for "WordPress" under "Blogs" and click on it.

At the bottom of the page, click on the "Install" button.

Choose the domain you will put it on from the drop down menu.

Click "Advanced" and change the admin username from Admin to anything else besides Admin. (Using "admin" makes it easier for the bad guys to do bad things to your site.)

Put in a password. Don't use an easy one like password123 or your name. Hackers love easy passwords.

Accept the terms and conditions.

Click on "Complete".

Either host site will give you the link to log in to the admin area of your new WordPress site. Go there, log in and start playing. There are tons of tutorials online, both free and paid, that show you how to customize it. It's easy and now you know you can do it.

Congratulations. You're a tech god! You've accomplished the only two mildly sweat-inducing tasks we'll talk about today: You have changed your DNS and you have loaded WordPress on your site. Go ahead, do the Snoopy dance. You deserve it!

Your Email Service

You do want to have an email service. Mailing out to your list with your Outlook or Gmail account can get you into a lot of trouble. It's considered Spam, and if you start being known as a spammer, your business will never get off the ground.

Not to worry, there are several good email services. I use one, many of my clients use another. I recommend them both, depending on what you need to accomplish. One is 1Shopping-Cart—http://1ShoppingCart.com and the other is Aweber—http://Aweber.com.

The main difference between the two is that Aweber is only to handle your email and contact lists. 1ShoppingCart does that, but also gives you a way to tie everything to your payment links, manage your products, and, even, when you get a bit bigger, manage your affiliates. (They are the people who sell your stuff and get a commission for it.)

Aweber is easier to set up and they have marvelous help files. 1ShoppingCart can be a bit more challenging and I recommend, if you decide to go that route, that you find someone to assist you.

Once you have your service and have people who are signed up to it, you will send out both AutoResponders (also called ARs – another mystery solved!) and broadcasts. An AutoResponder is an automatic series of emails that are pre-written and go out in a specific sequence once someone signs up. (Aweber calls them Followps.) Broadcasts are emails you send out once to your list. You'll want to get in the habit of doing both if you want to keep in communication with your people.

Your Payments

There are, again, several ways to take in payments. I use two of them, and they were both really easy to set up. One is PayPal. If you've been online long, you have, no doubt, used PayPal to buy something at least once. The other one I use is a credit card processing company called PowerPay. (Most people won't need that for a while. I didn't get my account until I'd been online for many, many years.) They understand online businesses, don't have setup fees and are really willing to take you by the hand to get everything going.

For PayPal – http://PayPal.com – you need to have a premier or business account, but if you only have a personal account, it is easy and free to upgrade.

When you get to the point where you want a more robust system, you can also get a PowerPay merchant account at http://powerpay.biz/—but again, don't worry about this now.

Making Your Products

At the beginning, most online businesses sell eBooks. These are usually PDF books. If you've been online for any length of time, you've probably seen a PDF. But how do you make one?

Well, I'm glad you asked. If you use any of the later versions of Microsoft Word, write your eBook in that. Once it's done and you've made it pretty and informative, go to "File", then "Save As". In the field that says, "Save As File Type", scroll down and choose "PDF". It will suggest a name, based on what you called your document to begin with, but you can change this. It will also want to save it in the same place you've been saving your original document. Of course, you can also change that. So, choose the name, and hit save. It will take a few seconds, then POOF! You are now the proud owner of a brand new eBook.

If you don't have MS Word, there is a free Office program you can download that will do everything Microsoft Office does, called OpenOffice.org and you find it at, yes, http://OpenOffice.org. Find it, download it, install it and open the "Writer" program within it.

Write your eBook there, make it pretty and informative, save it, then, under "File", choose "Export as PDF". A scary looking box will come up. Don't worry, just hit "Export" and it will ask you for the name you want to give it. You can also change where it is being saved here. So give it a name, hit "Save" and you have your eBook all bright and shiny.

How about that! In the course of a very short while, you have mastered what you need to know to get started online. Will you need more? Of course. As you grow, as your business builds, there are lots of other tools you can use, but this is "the basics" and you learned them in no time at all. So much for fear.

Of course, if you still decide you'd rather fear the tech but still want an online business, I even have a solution for you!

Get someone else to do it all for you! I've both done that and been that guy for other people. There is no shame in it at all. Eventually, when your business grows to a certain point, you'll want to start getting people to do stuff for you anyway. Any business owner has to. Start by getting someone to do the tech. Fear gone.

To get the videos that take you gently through the two slightly knee-knocking tasks above, go to http://GeoffHoff.com/fearless

---

Geoff Hoff is a best-selling author of both fiction and information books. He is also a popular blogger, a publisher and a public speaker. He teaches online courses in web based tech, online marketing and creativity in business.
You can find out more at http://GeoffHoff.com
And remember: Don't Fear the Tech!

AFFILIATE MARKETING SECRETS #1

If you missed my video, *Introduction to Internet Marketing*, you can see it at http://budurl.com/236w. I'm going to assume you've watched it.

In that video, I talk about how I use affiliate marketing to fill in the holes in my marketing strategy. The problem is that it takes a while to make a product. Then, you launch it and make some money. And then…crickets. What to do to keep making money while you're making your next masterpiece?

I recommend affiliate marketing.

Check out the screenshot below to see one of the reasons I like affiliate marketing.

Weekly Sales Snapshot

Week Ending	Gross Sales
2011-06-01 (current week)	$1,305.25
2011-05-25	$8,816.52
2011-05-18	$3,829.50
2011-05-11	$4,500.17
2011-05-04	$3,434.50

As you can see, it's possible to keep the income stream rocking while you're creating products.

Here's how I do it.

First, I find a product I really like. This is important. I BUY everything I promote. Then, I look it over carefully. Does it really do everything it says it does? Is it a screaming deal? Is it good for my customers?

If the answer is "yes," to all three, then I will probably promote it.

You'll note that I don't USE every product I buy. My customers are, for the most part, beginning Internet Marketers. I'm not. I have access to resources that beginning Internet Marketers don't. I'm looking at these products from the point of view of my customer. Should THEY use them? Yes!

Earnings disclaimer: because we live in a weird world, I'm going to state the obvious. I'm showing you my earnings, but I don't have a clue what you will do. Nobody can predict the outcome of your actions—or lack thereof. I'm only showing you these numbers to show what's possible. I hope you can do better, but I don't promise that you will. Duh. You know that. I only put this in to keep the lawyers quiet.

I'm assuming you've got a way to drive traffic to a website. We've talked about lots of ways to build lists, and I've come across some pretty cool ones that we'll talk about later. You definitely should focus on building your list. For our purposes, we'll assume you've either got a list, or know how to drive traffic using SEO, PPC, JVs, or some other method. (In the free video I mentioned at the beginning of this chapter there's a section on list-building.)

Dr. Joe Vitale, who is also a heavy-hitter affiliate marketer, and I were talking a while back on a road-trip to San Antonio about affiliate marketing. I mentioned that nobody had ever combined "inner game" with "outer game" and taught affiliate marketing from that point of view. We both agreed it was about time somebody did, so we've put together a really cool program called the "ClickBank Secret Code" for you.

In it, I do an in-depth training on how to use ClickBank to make money. Joe created a 7-step formula for you that will guarantee that you maximize your success and make the most money possible with your affiliate marketing. Actually, a lot of Joe's stuff will be useful for many aspects of your life. But, we focused on how to be successful with ClickBank. You can get it at http://onlinewealthsecretcode.com. In the meantime…let's look at the big picture.

I think doing affiliate marketing *exclusively* is dumb. Why?

Because you're not building a business.

When you create your own products, you've got income streams that last pretty much forever. Over the years, I've created a pretty big inventory of products and they're all still selling. Each one generates an income stream. Some of those streams are tiny. Some are pretty impressive. The important thing is that they all flow into an income river which finances my lifestyle, buys my cars, cigars, and guitars *and* supports my family.

Over time, each of those products touches hundreds or thousands of lives. Maybe you've bought some of them?

Through those products—especially the audios and videos—you and my other customers have gotten a feel for who I am, what I do, and what I stand for in the Internet Marketing world. When you add in my hundreds of YouTube videos, my blog posts, my books and articles…well, it all adds up to a business. I can go hiking in Big Bend and it still generates income. The NLP guys call this "building rapport." Let your readers get to know, like and trust you.

That's what I recommend that you do. Build a business. Don't think in terms of products, think in terms of product LINES. YOU are your brand. Once people know like and trust you, you can take them with you wherever you go.

Build your list, and get to know the people on your list. Find out what they want. Then test that. I've discovered that what my readers say they want and what they will actually buy are quite different. Shock!

I think affiliate marketing is a great way to get started before you've built your first product, and as a means to keep your income up while you're making new products.

The important thing is to keep your momentum going.

I've talked to people who have worked *years* on their first eBook, and deferred starting their business while they were writing.

Don't do that.

Objects in motion tend to stay in motion. You can use affiliate marketing to make enough cash to quit your day job so you can focus on building your business.

So—how do you do it? Well, it's all in that video. The basics are:

1. Go to http://ClickBank.com and sign up as an affiliate.
2. Then, at ClickBank, click on "Marketplace" and find something cool to sell.
    a. Buy it. If it fits in with your business, use it. At the very least, confirm that it's as good as it says it is. Make sure it's good for your customers. They're important. Treat them well. Remember, every product sold at ClickBank has a 60 day money-back guarantee. If the product is great, you'll want to keep it and promote it. If it's not, ask for a refund. You can't lose.
    b. You can also use CB Engine (http://cbengine.com) to find products. Go play with that. It does some cool stuff.
3. Once you're absolutely convinced that the product you're promoting is perfect for your list, tell them about it.

Now, there are some ways to get more sales.

First of all, learn and use the 7-step formula that Joe shares in ClicBank Secret Code. It's killer.

You can also give a webinar for your readers and *show* them why the product is so cool. Take them behind the scenes and show them what it does and how it does it. Then, give them your affiliate link.

You can write an article about the product and put it on article directories. Put your affiliate link in the resource box. This can drive sales for years.

Blog posts are good. The people reading your blog probably already know, like and trust you. Tell them about the product in the same way you'd tell them about a movie you think they ought to see.

Can you think of others?

The bottom line is that affiliate marketing is a great way to get started, and a great way to keep your income stream pumping while you're doing other stuff.

THE FAMOUS YOUTUBE/ GOOGLE TRICK

My buddy Ray is a Nashville-based singer/songwriter.

He's doing pretty well. Clear-channel and the BBC are picking up his songs. He's placed songs in movies and TV shows and he stays on the road pretty much constantly playing his songs at festivals, clubs, and concerts.

He's got some good videos on YouTube, but he's not getting useful views and, consequently, the views aren't converting into CD sales. What to do?

Ray has seen what I've done with my buddy George's video. I produced George's CD and his video. It was a blast. We found some great locations near Terlingua and gathered some friends. We had a beer and sandwiches picnic at an old abandoned movie set called Contrabando.

The reason Ray's so interested in George's video is because if you search YouTube for "Americana Music," George's video has over 260,000 views and shows up at #3 and an alternate cut shows up at #5. That means that the suits in Nashville, L.A. and New York sitting in their air-conditioned offices doing research on the 'net have to see George's video. My hope is that some producer hears that song and has it recorded by an established artist.

Ray's videos only show up if you search on his name...and, honestly, how many record producers or music directors know to do that? Ray's more "famous" than George, but he's not a household name, yet.

I know a lot of "Rays." I have a lot of musician and artist friends who NEED to know how to use YouTube to drive traffic and make sales. I also have a lot of Internet Marketing friends and clients who are confused about this.

Here's how it works.

Google owns YouTube. You may think that YouTube is a place to go to watch videos. If you're a songwriter, you may think—or hope—that YouTube is where music directors in L.A. and record producers in Nashville go to find new songs and talent. If you're an Internet Marketer, maybe you've heard that you can drive traffic and sales from YouTube.

And, you're right.

But, from a marketing point of view, YouTube is a search engine and it works just like the Google search engine.

Google uses a complex algorithm that analyzes web pages—and video pages at YouTube. The details are beyond the scope of mortal understanding but the meta-concept is pretty simple. Google is interested in relevance and authority.

Relevance means: "what does this page say it's about?"

Authority means: "what do other web pages say this page is about?"

Google has little purple robots (bots) that feed off data and report the data to Google's main database. Don't ask me how I know they're purple. I'm a professional and that's proprietary knowledge. Just trust me.

Anyway, the bots go to George's page on YouTube and quickly ascertain that the page is about Americana Music, Country music, free music, and some other things related to those things. George's video is also mentioned on a lot of social media and blogs about music (backlinks). This makes the purple bots smile. It confirms their opinion of what the page is about.

They then report that information back to the database and when somebody does a search on YouTube for any of those things

George's video pops right up.

Ray's video, on the other hand, tells the bots stuff they don't really need to know. They think the video is about Ray, the title of the song, and where you can buy his CD. This is interesting to Ray and his small but loyal group of fans. But, unless someone is searching for his name or the name of the song, he's not going to show up in any searches.

So, how do you set up your video page on YouTube so that you get lots of relevant views and show up on the first page of the searches?

1. Decide what keywords you want to rank for. Imagine that you're your own perfect customer. What do you put into the search bar when you're looking for music? In George's case, I imagined that the perfect customer would be searching on Americana music, Country music and free music. You can use Google's Keyword Tool or a service like WordTracker to confirm your guess about what people are actually typing into Google.
2. When you upload your video to YouTube, name it with your keywords. Instead of vid10032.mov, change the name to freeamericanacountrymusic.mov. Yes, Google is that granular. They look.
    a. Put your keywords in the title.
    b. Make the title the first line of your description.
    c. Put your keywords, and related keywords, in the keywords box.
3. After Google processes your video, get the "share" URL and put that in your description. Many video services "scrape" content from Youtube. By doing this, you get a free backlink to your video every time it's "scraped."
4. Get backlinks from high quality, relevant websites.
5. Write a press release and use free press release services to spread the word. There's some good training at PRWeb. http://service.prweb.com/learning/article/free-online-press-release-training/

6. Use Social Media, such as Facebook and Twitter, to tell the world.

That's pretty much it. If you've done all of these things, you've told the purple bots what the video is about and established relevance. If you've got some backlinks from other pages that are also about your keywords, you've established authority. The bots couldn't be happier.

You'll be happier, too, because your video will attract viewers who will actually be interested in your video.

You could, at the end of the video and in the description, mention your web page and invite the viewers to visit you there to receive more free videos and music. While they're there, let them know how they can buy the music.

There are some tech-nerd steps you can add to this, but if you just do this much you'll be way ahead of most of your competition—and you'll show up in YouTube searches on your keywords.

Now, go get rich and famous!

INTERNET MARKETING PRODUCT CREATION

You may have heard me say this: "In Internet Marketing, all you need is something to sell and someone to sell to."

In other words, you need products and traffic.

Today, let's talk about products.

Let's do a quick review, and then I want to talk to you about PLR products. There are basically five ways to acquire a product to sell.

Make It Yourself

This is where most people start. In fact, this is what brings most people into the Internet Marketing world. They have a passion for something and want to share it with the world.

This is cool. However, the most common newbie mistake is to try to turn that passion into a business without researching whether or not anybody is actually interested and, more importantly, whether or not they're willing to exchange money for products about that topic.

Let's assume you've done your research and discovered that topic is in a niche that a LOT of people are interested in and these people will buy products.

The key here is to find a niche where there are problems to be solved. You know that people have a problem and are looking for a solution. You also know how to communicate with these people so you can tell them about YOUR solution to that problem.

From there, it's a short step to big bucks: package the solution and sell it.

You can deliver the solution as an eBook, audio, video, software...

Make It With Someone Else

We call these projects "joint ventures," or JVs. Here's an example: You have identified an interesting problem and your research has shown you that people will pay for the solution. However, you're not an expert on the topic. You do have the ability to package the solution, put up a sales page, write the sales copy, and drive traffic to the sales page.

So, you find an expert and interview them. Ask questions. Get the answers.

Then, all you have to do is package the solution, get it online, sell it, and split the money with your JV partner.

This is an easy way to break into new niches. You could use a conference call service—there are some free ones—call your expert on the phone, record the call, and put the recording online and sell it. I like it—fast and easy.

Sell Somebody Else's Product

This is called "affiliate marketing." The easiest example of this is ClickBank.com—you register as an affiliate. Once you're approved (easy) you have the opportunity to sell any of thousands of products in multiple niches. Affiliates typically make 50%-75% commission on each sale. If you've got a list or a dependable source of traffic, this is easy money.

For Dr. Joe Vitale's 7-step program on making money at ClickBank visit http://onlinewealthsecretcode.com.

Public Domain

This one seems to confuse people at first. It sounds too good to be true, but it is true. Here's the part most people have trouble with: if something is in the public domain, it belongs to you. It also belongs to everybody else, but the important thing to remember is that it belongs to you. You can sell it and keep all the money.

Here's an example: there are tens of thousands of magazine articles in the public domain. You can gather up a couple of dozen that are on a related topic, package them as a book or eBook, sell it—and keep all the money.

Here's another: You can take one of the millions of books that are in the public domain, change the cover, change the title, and—if you want—list yourself as the author. Once you've determined that something is actually in the public domain, there are no rules.

I've made a lot of money with Public Domain products and highly recommend that you use them.

Private Label Rights Products

The product acquisition method I want to focus on in this chapter is the 5th method (in my arbitrary list). Private Label rights (PLR) products.

And, like the Public Domain option, it's confusing to newbies because it sounds too good to be true.

Pay close attention here, because if you're not already using PLR products to make money, you are missing out.

Here's the short-course on PLR. For a price, usually a surprisingly small price, you can purchase a product that you can then resell. In most cases, the products come with a sales page, graphics, web page and download page in addition to the product. If you know where to find them, you can get good ones for $5.

Now, stay with me, because this is going to be hard to believe. You get all of that for just a few bucks. You may want to do some editing, tighten up the sales page, etc. But, you don't have to.

Then, you can put all this online—cut and paste it, basically—sell it, and keep all the money!

PLR is an umbrella term for a variety of groups of products—the difference is in the license that comes with each product. Let's look at some of the licenses.

While licenses differ with each author and seller, the basic premise is that the license permits buyers to re-brand the content under their own name and brand. In general practice this means that the product can be modified, sold, resold or repurposed in many different formats. In some cases authorship on the original product is allowed and with unrestricted private label, buyers are often able to resell the same rights they've acquired.

Normal resell rights mean that after you buy the item you can sell it to your customers.

There may be limitations, such as that you can only sell the product for a specific price. This term is also known as Resale Rights. When a product comes with Resale Rights it means that you can sell the product to just about anyone and keep 100% of the profit. The product *you* sell though should only include the Personal Use Only Right (PUO), in other words, you don't pass along Resale Rights when you sell this type of product. Your customers are the end user.

When you acquire Master Resale Rights (MRR), you sell the product or service to your customers, and you may also grant your customers the right to sell it. You can also pass MRR to your customers, if you are in possession of transferable MRR. This allows your customers to *also* sell the product with MRR.

Before you buy a PLR package, check out the license. I just went to one of my sources and copied a typical license.

Distribution Rights

Resale Rights Yes

Master Resale Rights Yes

Private Label Rights Yes (non-transferable)

Giveaway Rights Yes

Offered as a Bonus Yes

Full Product Copyrights Yes

Full Graphic Copyrights No

May Modify Product Yes

Packaged with Other Products Yes

Added to Paid Membership Websites Yes

Added to Free Membership Websites Yes

May Publish Offline Yes

May Sell on Auction Websites No

As you can see, there's not a lot you *can't* do with this license. Be sure and read the license before you buy—some are more restrictive.

Get it?

There are a LOT of fun ways you can use PLR products to increase your income.

- Just cut and paste 'em online and sell 'em.
- Use them to get people to opt-in to your list.
- Use them as bonuses when you sell another product
- Put them in a membership site and get paid by the month for them
- Give them away as rewards to loyal customers

What other creative ways to use PLR products can you think of?

Bottom Line: PLR products are an amazing opportunity for you. Don't let the fact that it looks to good to be true or too easy slow you down. This is how the "big boys" do it—in fact, some of them would prefer that I didn't teach this. But, it's important information and I want you to have it so you can be successful, too.

Pat created a course on making money with Private Label Rights products. You can learn more at http://instantplrprofits.com.

DOOM. GLOOM. JOBLESSNESS. TURMOIL.

If you *just* look at the surface, it looks like the worst of times. But, just take a peek under the surface and you'll see that—if you're smart—right now is the best time to open a business since the Great Depression.

Why?

Because the cost of opening a profitable business has dropped to almost nothing.

I've written several rants about how the Industrial Revolution is O.V.E.R.

Labor and capital intensive businesses have closed down or moved to where labor is cheap. Computerization, artificial intelligence, and robotics have made most of the jobs our parents had obsolete. You can't legislate the past back into existence. The quicker you adjust to the realities of "now" and take advantage of the possibilities, the farther ahead you're going to be.

Let's look at some of the possibilities:

1. You could open a factory, hire labor, and make something. Fifty years ago, that might have been a good idea. Today… you'll need several million dollars and you'll get your butt handed to you. Anything that can be made in a factory in the United States or Western Europe (where most of my readers are) today can be made cheaper and just as well

with cheap labor or robots in Asia. You'd like to think that customers would pay more for something made in the West, but—next time you're in WalMart read the labels. Politics and philosophy go out the window when the pocketbook is involved. And, most of us don't have millions laying around.

2. Open a franchise. Twenty years ago buying into a franchise was the smart move. Today…
   a. Taco Bell—If you have a passion for operations-excellence and team building and you can commit to building at least 3 restaurants over 3 years Taco bell wants you. A stand-alone restaurant runs between $1,200,000 and $1,700,000, but these figures do not include the land or lease costs.
   b. Subway Sandwich Shop—With location flexibility and an easy-to-run operation built on simplicity and efficiency, our start-up costs are lower than most restaurants. The initial franchise fee is $15,000, and total investment can be as low as $78,600. Individual costs vary.
   c. Snap-on Tools—These stores-on-wheels sell tools to professional mechanics. Each Snap-on truck comes equipped with a computer, wireless Internet access and a DVD player for product demonstrations. Average initial investment: $135,390
   d. 7-11 Convenience Store—The 24-hour home of the Slurpee is the largest franchisor (by outlets) in the world. US military veterans get a 10% discount on the initial franchise fee. Average initial investment: $393,800

- from about.com and Forbes Magazine

You get the idea. And even after the huge investment there's no guarantee your franchise is going to make a profit.

OR

3. You can buy an online business—fully operational and ready to go—for about the cost of a taco at Taco Bell or a sandwich at Subway.

At that price, you can put up a new one every day. You can focus on one niche, or branch out into any niche you like.

Very quickly, you can have multiple streams of passive income surging into your bank account.

It's kinda fun. You can sit and watch the sales receipts as they flow into your email account. I like to check and see where my customers are. There's a sale to a woman in France…there's one to a guy in Poland…somebody in California….

Imagine you—sitting at home in your comfy clothes, a cup of coffee or tea on the desk next to the computer, possibly with your feet up…watching your computer screen and smiling. Or, imagine you at the art gallery or on the beach, knowing that when you get home your online businesses will have made you money while you play.

The benefits are amazing. I have friends who use the money they make online to collect race cars, exotic guitars, and swiss watches. That's cool. For me, it's being able to help my family and friends and live a stress-free life. That's my goal.

What's yours?

With the low investment, you can have a positive cash flow from the very first sale. What other business can you invest in that will give you that?

So—where do you find these businesses that cost less than Tacos? Check out my PLR course at http://instantplrprofits.com.

RUNNING AN INTERNET MARKETING BUSINESS FROM THE DESERT

Last Saturday was my Birthday. I spent it with a dozen or so friends at a very cool bar on the Rio Grande river.

Apparently the birthday and the events and locations surrounding it made me a little philosophical. I'm living my dreams down here on the border. I want you to live your dreams, too. This may help.

This is kind of a long chapter, but I think you'll get some value from it.

Enjoy!

There were rain clouds hovering over the desert. Layers of dark clouds obscured higher layers of puffy white clouds, backlit by the sun giving them a golden edge. In the West, long vertical draperies of rain fall about 30 miles away.

Out here, you can smell the rain long before it gets to you. The greasewood bushes (creosote) emit a clean herb-like odor that smells just like rain ought to smell. We open the windows and/or go outside and just inhale and absorb it. It's wonderful.

I run my Portable Empire from my off-the-grid cabin in the desert. The cabin is 25 miles from Big Bend National Park and maybe 28 miles from the Mexican Border. It's completely off the grid: solar power, well, septic, propane. It does have a landline telephone (cell phones don't work out here) and high speed Internet access, which I've always found to be odd since I'm more than 50 miles from a city.

It's a small two-story cabin and my office is on the second floor. I have an iMac for editing video and audio, a MacBook Pro for writing and such.

Various guitars, keyboards, microphones, video and still cameras, and other tools are within easy reach.

Out my window, I can see 9 Points Mesa a mile or two to the East. Every morning the sun comes up behind that huge mesa, and it takes it about an hour to crest the top. That's the most stunning hour of the day. The light is muted like a Japanese watercolor until the sun bursts around the South side of the Mesa and sweeps like a spotlight over the desert.

The muted colors become vibrant—almost cartoon-like. In the spring and fall, that's a good time to take a walk. In the summer, that sun will take the skin right off your bones.

That's "my" time. I make a pot of locally roasted Italian roast coffee in the French press and sit on my porch. At first, the colors are barely visible. Gradually, they get more intense as the sun gets higher behind the mesa.

Of course, in the evenings the show is in the West. The mountains in the west are farther away. As the sun drops toward the mountains, I move back to the porch, light a cigar, possibly open a bottle of Malbec, and watch the fireworks. Some sunsets are just beautiful sunsets. A few nights ago it was so stunning that Betsy ran around the front and side yards with her camera oohing and aahing and snapping photos as the sun turned the clouds orange, magenta, and red—and then purple, teal and blue—and then set, revealing a Milky Way overhead that you could almost touch. I don't know how many stars there are in the sky, but you can see them all from here.

I find myself spending more time in the desert. I almost wrote "my desert." My cabin is in the middle of ten acres, which is a small yard out here, but I can't see any of my neighbors and they can't see me. That solves a lot of wardrobe issues when the weather is nice. This is harsh country. It's not for everybody. I can see three abandoned homesteads from my front porch, and the desert is littered with them.

Some people come down here and stay a few months and find that it's just too hard. Too hot. Too dry. Too isolated.

A smaller number of people come down here and fall completely head over heels in love with the place. I'm one of those.

My work day.

After the sun is up and I've had my coffee, I head upstairs and start my work day. Technically, I have an 8 foot commute, but the stairs make the trip a little longer. Call it 20 feet. Takes less than 30 seconds.

I settle in my comfy red office chair and get to the work at hand. In the last two weeks I've chipped away at writing a book, scripted and recorded a sales video for a new product, written an extended autoresponder series, edited a lot of video and photos, hosted two webinars, coordinated a complete make-over of our shopping cart system with my tech guys, supervised "the squirrels" (that's our pet name for the junior tech guys) putting together a new program, and promoted various affiliate products.

Bottom line, I've done everything it takes to run and grow my business that I would have done back in the city.

Some days, I work 6 hours. Some days, 1 or 2. Occasionally, I just check email and then go play. It depends on my goals for the day and what needs to be done.

The trick to making money online.

Here's a gift for you: In Internet Marketing, you make your money by having ideas. My most important job is visualizing what should exist and doesn't. Look at the world and see what should be there and isn't.

Once I identify that, it's simply a matter of making it exist. I outsource a lot of that.

Seriously, my most profitable time is spent leaning back in my comfy chair with my eyes half-closed as I explore the needs of my customers, review the existing solutions I have for them, sneak up on a new product idea, trap it, and bring it home.

But sitting back in a chair and staring off into the middle distance doesn't do you any good if you haven't done the necessary preparation.

First, you have to know who your customers are. I talk to mine a lot. Email, blog comments, surveys. I even have my customer service guy forward interesting customer service emails to me so I can see where the gaps are. In a perfect world, we'd never get a customer service email because our products would be so streamlined and self-explanatory that it wouldn't be necessary. We're not there, yet. In fact, we're nowhere near there.

My latest survey was extremely illuminating. I asked my customers what they wanted and how they wanted it delivered. Did they want an ebook or a video or a webinar?

I asked them what problems they were having, what solutions they wished they had, and what their most valuable tool (that they already owned) was.

The trick.

That's the trick. Get your customers to tell you what they want. Then, create it and give it to them. That's my job.

Actually, my job is to identify the problem and visualize the solution. Any part of the actual creation that I can outsource, I do. I don't need to build web pages for example. Neither, I suspect, do you—although that's one of the things my surveys tell me newbies want to learn.

I can get a web page built for $5. It's knowing what should be on the web page that pays the big bucks. That's why the research is so important.

The other side of the equation has to do with having up to date information to use when creating solutions. I'm pretty well known in the industry and have helped thousands of people get started in Internet Marketing. Some of them are rich and famous, now. I'm proud of that.

My dirty little secret.

Here's my dirty little secret—although I run a successful coaching program and people in my field consider me an expert,

I'm also a member of a couple of other people's programs. I spend a small fortune on other people's products. I read a LOT. I'm on a lot of other people's lists.

I know what I know. I don't know everything they know. The more I know, the more useful I am to my clients and customers. The more I help my clients and customers, the more money I make.

I recommend that when you're first starting out you find one teacher and stick with them monogamously until you've figured out the game. It takes a while to learn the vocabulary, flowchart the money, and figure out who you are in the overall universe of Internet Marketing. Once you learn the basics there are a LOT of ways to implement them. One of my buddies runs around giving talks in a glorified jock strap. It works for him—people don't forget. Others are completely anonymous. You'll find your own path.

Then start branching out—be very clear about what you don't know and find the experts who can teach you.

Once you start making money, start spending it—on courses and products in your field. And *use* them.

The rest of the story.

I've also played four or five shows on guitar at various venues, participated in a CD release party for a CD I produced, taken some good photographs, edited video, hung out with friends, eaten some delicious meals, seen some breathtaking scenery, and had a birthday party.

In other words, I pretty much do what I want when I want and keep my business running and growing while I'm at it.

That is what having a Portable Empire is all about.

Let's talk about you.

Now, let's talk about you, your life, and living your dreams. You may have heard me say it's hard to achieve self-actualization if you're broke. Now, broke is a variable. I know some people living in very nice homes and driving new cars who are broke. When your liabilities exceed your assets and/or your expenses exceed your income, you're broke.

So, you need to focus on growing assets and income and keeping liabilities and expenses low—or non-existent.

That's my secret to success and happiness by the way.

I've been broke and it sucks. Bad. I've been scared to answer the phone because I didn't have a good story for the collection agency, or the money to pay them. I've had cars repossessed and homes foreclosed.

Never again.

More importantly, you need to have the money to comfortably live the life of your dreams.

In the meantime, look at the world and imagine what should be there that isn't. Then put it there.

INTERNET MARKETING: THE WAVE OF THE PRESENT

I'd love to know the wave of the future, wouldn't you?

We're in the business of making money from home, the coffee shop, or on the road. At least I am and I highly recommend it to you. Betsy and I are flying to Nashville this weekend to pick up our new RV. That's my new office. Look out road, here we come.

I really find it attractive—bopping around in my gym shorts, t-shirt and birkies—"working" from coffee shops and hot spots. I don't even own a watch any more. I don't have appointments. I owe my lifestyle to the technology that facilitates it and the knowledge and information I've acquired and bought over the last eight years.

It would be useful to be able to anticipate the technological and social changes that will define our industry next year.

Since my time machine is in the shop, let's talk about the wave of the present. What's happening now is pretty futuristic, especially compared to how most people are practicing Internet Marketing.

The most important thing for us to remember is that the Internet is inherently inefficient. That inefficiency is where the profit is. For example, brick and mortar businesses, whose owners are definitely not Internet Marketers, are still paying $500 for WordPress sites and thousands of dollars for the sort of websites we can crank out with Dreamweaver or WordPress in an afternoon. Local businesses are paying hundreds or thousands of dollars a month for SEO services that we know how to purchase and implement for less than twenty bucks.

Knowledge is power my friend.

So, let's look at some recent changes.

Channels—This is probably the biggest change. Although you still need your own website, and should have a specific domain and site for each product, the real action is happening on channels like Amazon, YouTube, and Facebook because that's where the traffic is. Specifically, about 85% of all web traffic is ending up on the main channels.

This is an opportunity.

YouTube, for example, is owned by Google. They're paying for the site and bandwidth and driving massive traffic to their site. You job is to provide content for them and attract all of that traffic you can. Then, of course, take that traffic back to your site.

You can play SEO games with those channels that would get your own site blacklisted and sand-boxed. The trick is to remember that the channel sites are, at their core, search engines. Use keywords cleverly, and you can grab traffic and send it to your opt-in pages. Fun!

Video. I saw this coming years ago. I started producing videos for the web back when you couldn't stream video over the web. When download speeds got fast enough, I was ready. Now, your computer is becoming a TV set. Think about this for a minute…

Over the next year people will continue unsubscribing from cable TV and instead stream video from their computers to their TV sets. Content providers and networks are beginning to bypass the cable companies and stream directly to consumers on paid streams or, in some cases, for free.

Pandora and other music streaming services are making radio stations obsolete. New video services along with YouTube and other channels that generate original programming (Netflix Originals) are making the concept of TV channels obsolete.

This is a HUGE opportunity. Get started now. With what we know about Internet Marketing, we're in a position to compete head on with the big boys in the video world.

On a more immediate level, video sales pages are crushing written sales pages. Video on your blog will increase readership and make your blog sticky as heck.

And, all it takes is a cheap video camera or the video camera in your phone, iMovie or Windows Movie Maker, and a little imagination.

A third major change is quality.

There will always be a market for crap. McDonalds will always sell a lot of burgers. Reality shows and smarmy dramas will still attract audiences. But, in the Internet Marketing space, the bar is a *lot* higher today. The information you can get for free today is much better than the information we paid for a couple of years ago.

Word gets around.

There's going to be a shakeout in our industry, and the only way to thrive and survive is to provide the best quality—and the definition of "best" is changing fast.

A lone gal or guy with a laptop computer can still start a business and get rich in Internet Marketing. But, the level of competition has ratcheted up several notches. We're competing with Internet Marketing companies that are highly organized and fully staffed.

It's gotten easier and cheaper. WordPress is free. SEO is free. Using channels is free. Fiverr and outsourcing provides you access to a huge virtual staff for very little money.

It's a jungle. Luckily, for now, it's a big, friendly jungle and the predators are pretty nice.

THE FUTURE OF INTERNET MARKETING

Predicting the future is a fool's game, but, like Pocket says in Christopher Moore's book, *Fool*, "I'm duty bound to be foolish." So, what's coming up next?

First, let's predict the present.

The industrial revolution is over. In the information economy, you don't need much "labor." For example, Apple opened a huge new data center in Maiden, North Carolina and only hired 50 people to work there. And not locals—because the locals don't have the skills to run a data center.

So, if you're relying on a job or looking for one, now might be a real good time to think about joining the Information age. The jobs are gone, and they're not coming back .

More predicting the present. Remember Frontpage, Dreamweaver and HTML? History. WordPress has taken over. This is a continuation of the trend towards making technology easy. When I first started playing with computers, you had to know how to program a computer to get anything done at all. This was long before the Internet.

The Internet changed everything.

Initially, to get a web page online, you either had to pay big bucks to a programmer or learn HTML. Then, the WYSIWYG (what you see is what you get) programs like Frontpage came along and anybody could put up a website—but most of them looked like moo poo, including mine.

Now, anybody can put up a professional looking site, add amazing functionality to it, and make it dance with WordPress, and WordPress is free.

That's really very, very important. The barrier to entry just disappeared. You now officially don't need ANY tech skills to be a successful Internet Marketer. Or, any money.

Now, what about the future?

Well, just about the time web sites got easy and free to make, they're becoming obsolete.

The iPad changed everything for people who could or wanted to drop $600-$800 on a tablet. Betsy and I each have one and we use them a lot more than we use our computers. Most of what I do on the iPad that's not Internet Marketing related involves apps. I use *Zite*, which is a news aggregator, for example. *The New York Times*, *Wall Street Journal*, *Huffington Post*, the BBC, PBS, and most other news sources have apps.

Hell, Bjork's new album is an iPad app.

If I'm not inside an app, or even if I am, I probably have Pandora streaming music. I might watch a movie on Netflix. The number of actual websites I go to is diminishing rapidly.

The big change is going to happen as tablets get cheaper. A lot of people are getting Kindle Fire tablets this year. They're like an iPad, but cheaper. They are in the $100 range. Still not quite an impulse buy, but well within most people's budget.

What this means is that the traffic we're used to attracting—people surfing the 'net—is getting siphoned off into dedicated apps. They're not surfing the net.

hmmm…

I don't know how to make an app, and even if I did, how would I get people to download it and use it?

Speaking of people surfing the 'net, here's a fascinating factoid for you: in 2012, the top ten websites on the interwebs got 85%

of the traffic. The big kahuna is Facebook. Facebook dominates, accounting for 38% of all referral traffic, followed by email and Twitter, which held 17% and 11% of referrals, respectively.

That leaves you and me competing with over 9 billion other websites for a shrinking long-tail of 15% of the traffic.

We can throw money at Google Adwords and other ad networks to try to direct that traffic to our websites.

For now.

Do you have an iPhone yet? I do. I love Siri. She's a genie that lives in my iPhone, and she can make phone calls, take notes, create reminders, find stuff like restaurants and hotels. She's amazing.

Here's an interesting thing about Siri. When Apple bought her, they stripped out most of her functionality. She had the capability to not only find a hotel, but also to book a room. She could find a restaurant and also make a reservation.

Apple got rid of all that stuff before they released her to the public. For now.

Why?

Because there's a goldmine there.

Google makes billions of dollars with their search engine.

People pay big bucks to be at the top of the page on a Google search. Why would anybody who has Siri use Google?

Apple has to find a way to monetize Siri so that we pay big bucks to be what Siri finds when she's looking for something in our niche. Or, Apple may just walk away from those billions of dollars in potential income. I'd bet against it.

But wait, there's more. Hotels pay commissions for booking rooms. That's one of the ways travel agents used to make money. Remember travel agents? It's how Expedia and Travelocity make money. Who needs a travel agent or Travelocity if Siri can book your hotel room for you? There's another huge income stream that Apple hasn't tapped yet.

I can think of a lot more. Imagine if Siri had a ClickBank affiliate account.

Once Apple figures out how to monetize Siri, you'll find yourself using her a lot.

A lot of people are buying iPhones, but they're still a tiny minority of phone users. That will change—Siri is portable. Apple could, and will, release Siri for iPads and Macs. Apple could also release Siri as a standalone program that would install on anything with a microprocessor.

And Google has a voice recognition app. So does Microsoft.

And they all work on phones.

A couple of months ago, a gaggle of Internet Marketers came to Wimberley to visit. I took them to a local restaurant and we hung out for a few hours talking about Internet Marketing. Every one of the Internet Marketers had their phone in front of them. We weren't making phone calls. We were checking sales at ClickBank, answering emails and text messages, posting pictures and comments on Facebook and tweeting.

Imagine this: you walk into your house with your phone and tell it to broadcast from your TV. You sit down on the couch, pick up your bluetooth keyboard, and log onto Facebook through your phone which you can see on your TV. You check a few emails then walk down the hall to your office where your phone automatically connects to the monitor on your desk. Facebook and your email show up. You pull up some music on Pandora which is broadcast through the speakers on your desk. You write a blog post that is immediately online.

The technology for all of that exists right now—and I think that's where we're heading.

Google Goggles and other wearable computer technology could simplify the process a lot. No more need for monitors, speakers, etc.

I'll still need computers for a while. I edit video, produce music CDs, and stuff like that. Computers are still necessary for the creation of content.

But, most people just consume content. Very soon all they'll need is a phone (and maybe a screen, keyboard and speakers) to watch movies, listen to music, surf the 'net, play with apps, play video games, hold video chats with family and friends… pretty much anything people do online can be done on a phone now. I suspect that future phones will drive the final nail in the computer's coffin.

What does this mean for us? How do you do Internet Marketing in this environment?

Initially, all this scared me. Seriously. All the stuff we've done for the last decade or so is going to stop working. How will we continue growing our businesses if the environment our business grows in changes so dramatically?

Then, I remember that *Internet* is the modifier. Marketing is what we do.

Direct marketing has been around for centuries and most of the techniques we use to make our money were conceived in the 1920s and perfected by the '50s.

We find people with problems. We solve the problems and sell those people the solutions.

We've been using email and websites to do this for so long that we think that's what we do. That's not what we do. That's just the medium in which we do it.

Direct marketing has been done with classified ads and post office boxes. Postcards. Lumpy envelopes. Television. Radio. As each new technology appeared, we've adapted.

Internet Marketing, the way most of us do it, peaked in about 2004. In Internet time, that's centuries ago.

Some marketers will adapt and thrive. Others won't.

I used to be scared, but now I'm excited. This could be huge fun. The trick is to close your eyes and trace the trajectory from where we were to where we're going. Then, get there first.

INTERNET MARKETING TIME MACHINE: DANGER, DANGER

Why you have to "Come From the Heart" if you want to be successful.

Let's climb in the ole time machine and go back to a major Internet Marketing Seminar held in 2005. It was the largest gathering of its kind and was hosted by one of the most successful Internet Marketers on the planet. Tickets were $2,000 each.

The stage looked like something the Rolling Stones might use. Huge PA system, huge video screens on each side, back-lighting, spotlights, and lots of sparkle. The lights went up, the music died down and, to rowdy applause, the host mounted the stage in his Italian suit.

He showed us pictures of his new house—it was as big as a small town. He off-handedly told us how many millions of dollars he'd made that year. We gasped in lust and surprise. He was rich, we weren't. Shut up and listen. We suck. He rocks.

Those of us in the audience sat waiting, pens in hand, while this guru opened the curtains on the secret of success.

> *Sales pages must have blue backgrounds and red headlines. He dictated fonts and sizes to use for headlines and body type. He revealed other timeless truths.*

I can't remember many of them now. It might have been how to manipulate a loophole in Google's search algorithm to trick it into putting your page at the top of the searches. It might have been how to trick adwords into letting you buy traffic to an affiliate page by taking advantage of a loophole in adwords or how to game ClickBank. It could have been how to spin articles and clone web pages to trick the search engines.

A few months later, everything he told us was obsolete.

Some of the other speakers at that event were even more clever. One guy sold premade adsense sites that were guaranteed to bring you consistent income forever!

A LOT of people bought that. How could you not? Guaranteed free money forever?

Less than two weeks later, Google changed their algorithm, the adsense sites stopped working, and…well, I haven't heard anything about that guy since.

Every product sold at that seminar was relegated to doorstop status within two months.

That's the heart breaking problem with learning—and teaching—Internet Marketing. That's also one of the reasons I started putting on UnSeminars.

The stuff you CAN teach—how to build a WordPress site, how to optimize it with SEO, how to use article marketing to drive traffic, and so on—is basically just busy work.

It gives the teacher something to teach and the student something to do, but its long term value is zero.

What?

Don't blame me. I'm just telling it like it is.

So, what should we learn? What should we teach?

Keep reading.

In Mark Joyner's book, *Integration Marketing*, he has an interesting story that I'll paraphrase here because I can't be bothered to cut and paste it:

A tough, highly respected general was facing a classroom of future officers. He asked, "what is the most important skill a general can have?"

The class answered with the usual: "bravery, strategic thinking, politically connected father, an uncle in the arms-running biz, Carlyle group stock, etc."

Eventually the general set them straight. "The most important skill a general can have is the ability to see the battlefield."

That's also the most important skill an Internet Marketer can have.

On last night's Portable Empire Coaching UnWebinar, I started a discussion about this and got distracted. I'd like to try again.

First of all, I don't see the business world as a battlefield. I know it's a popular way to look at it, but it leads to the attitude that it's not enough to win—the other guy has to lose, too. I disagree.

I visualize Internet Marketing as a game.

I think it's possible to play the Internet Marketing game and win without causing anyone else to lose. I don't believe in competition and am working diligently to lose my bad habit of comparing myself to others. It doesn't matter how much money Frank Kern is making this week, for example. As long as my business is hitting or exceeding its targets, Frank and Armand and Mike and John and the gang don't really have anything to do with me. I assume they're doing fine, but I don't know.

I'm playing my game and winning. That's good enough.

So, we could reframe that as "The most important skill an Internet Marketer can have is the ability to see the whole game." Most Internet Marketers play in a small corner of the game board. Interestingly, that's also what they teach. If they've found success with blogging, for example, they teach blogging. If they've found success with PPC or SEO, that's what they teach.

The problem with that is that the details—how to put up a WordPress site, how to optimize for (today's) SEO criteria—although easy to teach, are pretty much a waste of time to learn. Six months from now, those skills will be obsolete.

It's interesting that you could have three or four Internet Marketers in a room, they can all be wildly successful, and yet, when you look closely, they're actually in completely different businesses.

All of those businesses are part of the game.

For example, there are lots of extremely successful marketers who use PPC (pay per click), SEO (search engine optimization), and other forms of what I call Metrics Marketing to drive traffic to affiliate sites.

They were probably math majors in college. This part of the game requires serious math and stats chops.

They may not even make products. If they have a list, they're focusing on maximizing immediate sales and aren't concerned with building a relationship with the readers on that list.

They're real concerned with CPC (cost per click) vs EPC (earnings per click), and clicks are where the action is.

We're in the same business—on the same game board, so to speak—but we don't do the same things.

We have the same goal: we want to make sales.

On another part of the game board, there are marketers who create products and put them on ClickBank, or offer them through their own affiliate program. They focus their energy on attracting affiliates. To them, their first client is the affiliate—that's the first sale they have to make. Then, the affiliates go forth and drive traffic to the product.

The more successful they are at "selling" the affiliates—getting them excited about the new product and enticing them to hit their lists—the more successful their promotion will be.

I'm on some of their lists. Their strategy is "buy or die." They promote vigorously to their list, and the subscriber can either ignore, buy, or unsubscribe. And again, there's no attempt to build a relationship with subscribers.

Recently, I've started playing on this part of the game board myself. It's not the focus of my business, but it's a nice ancillary income stream.

The part of the game board I've been playing on skince I started is called Relationship Marketing. It's what I know, so it's what I teach. That's what I recommend that you learn, because it's not busy work. Once you've built a list and established a relationship with the humans on that list, it doesn't matter what new bright shiny object (BSO) comes along. Earn the trust of your readers, and you've got a business that will support you forever.

I definitely work on building my list, but I work even harder on building a strong relationship with the humans on that list. I give away a lot of free eBooks, videos, audios, etc. In fact, you could learn everything you need to know to build your own business online just by studying the free stuff I give my subscribers.

I answer emails from my subscribers. I don't do much free coaching, but I do try to point them in the right direction and I will tell them to not buy something if I don't think it's right for them.

I write books. I've written five, and three have been bestsellers. I get emails daily from people who have read those books, and they know my story. There's a lot of good Internet Marketing training in those books, but there's also stories of my years as a blues guitarist. I traveled the world, bopped all over Europe, played in Mexico and all over the US I take my readers with me on those trips.

I've had an interesting ride since I started my Internet Marketing business. I was a single dad. I have kids who are grown now, but still find ways to make my life interesting. I'm a real human, and I didn't just appear fully formed on the Internet Marketing stage. I've made a lot of mistakes. Some people really don't like me. Some do. I put all of that into my books.

In Relationship Marketing you are the product. You brand yourself. Even those of us who are not movie star pretty need to put our pictures on our products, web pages, books, etc. We're in front of the camera in our videos. Our social marketing sites like Facebook, Linked In, Google+ are personality driven. Mine has a lot of art, music and politics on it, in addition to Internet Marketing information.

Here's how Mark's book, and the story of the General, has changed my business: I'm making a concentrated effort to see more of the gameboard, and to play outside my usual corner of it.

Which brings us back to the question: what should we learn? What should we teach?

Let's remember that in the phrase Internet Marketing, the word Internet describes the delivery system.

The word Marketing describes what we're doing.

At its core, the Internet Marketing business is just direct marketing using the Internet to deliver the marketing materials. If you read direct marketing training books from decades past, they make pronouncements of eternal truths that are now totally obsolete.

What kind of envelope to use, when to use postcards instead, whether to hand-type, or have your sales material printed professionally, on and on…

I suspect we could find a book on how to market in Morse Code using a telegraph if we looked hard enough.

It's all direct marketing.

And, here's an eternal truth you can count on: "People buy from people they know, like and trust."

Here's an interesting concept: picture infinity.

Right. You can't.

That's why we use filters.

There are between seven and eight billion people on the planet today. Some percentage of them have access to the Internet and read the same language that you write.

That narrows it down to a few billion.

Still too big.

Let's say your niche is mechanical goldfish. That's not a very good niche, by the way, but stay with me here.

You need to filter the people who are interested in mechanical goldfish from that "few billion." You need to get them onto your autoresponder, so you can teach them about mechanical goldfish, become their go-to guy for all things mechanical goldfish, and sell them solutions to their mechanical goldfish problems.

If you're in my coaching program, you recognize that this is where "Class Project #1" comes in.

You'll do the stuff we all do—you'll blog, you'll write articles, you'll optimize your sites—knowing that in a few months most of that will be dust in the wind. But, for now, it gives you something to do—and it helps.

But, if you're smart, you'll see the whole gameboard. You'll realize that we're really not pioneers—we're following a tradition that is at least a century old.

By seeing the big picture you'll be able to bend and change as new stuff comes along. Go ahead and use it. It will work for a while.

The danger is that you'll get so caught up in the busy work that you're doing that you won't see the big picture.

I hear it all the time: "my clicks used to cost a nickel. Now, they're a dollar. I'm going broke."

Or, "I had this great Korean girl write me a few hundred articles, then I used this fancy software to spin those into thousands and thousands and I spammed them all over the Internet and had all these great incoming links and was making all this money and now I'm not making any sales."

Or, "I put up my WordPress site and did all the SEO stuff I was taught to do and it used to work. Now, it's not working. I don't know what to do."

You may have heard me say that Internet Marketing comes down to:

- You need something to sell
- You need someone who wants to buy it

- Everything else is just busy work.

The Portable Empire System is based on helping others and getting paid for it. Both parts of that sentence are important. When you help others, their lives are better—and they'll remember who helped them achieve a better life. When you help others, you feel good about yourself. You're actually making the world a better place.

It's all about coming from the heart. If you try to operate your business strictly on a "maximize shareholder equity and income" basis, you'll possibly make some money in the short run. In the long run, you need to "come from the heart" when you deal with your customers.

If you're just working the numbers, eventually somebody else is going to beat your numbers. There will always be a lower price, better SEO, bigger advertising budget…but, when you come from the heart and actually do good work by helping others the longer you're in business. The longer you're in business the more people you help. And the more people you help the more positive energy you create.

Which is why your business will grow from year to year, even in "interesting" economic times.

So, that's what I think we should learn, and what we should teach.

GAZING INTO MY CRYSTAL BALL...

I'm writing this from my RV on the shores of Canyon Lake. Betsy is curled up on the bed with her iPad. I'm sitting in a comfy Captains Chair writing on my MacBook. Earlier, after dinner, we shared a good maduro cigar and watched the sun go down from a deck near the water. As the sun set, the water turned an amazing copper color...there was one boat moving slowly across the water. Overhead, a sliver of a moon peeked out of the darkness.

In the startup world, they call it "pivoting."

You start in one direction, build your business, attract traffic— and you don't get the results you want. Instead of continuing to do something that doesn't work , or quitting, the smart entrepreneurs pivot.

It's like I tell my coaching clients, "If something isn't working, stop doing it. If something is working, do more of that."

Lately, I've seen some changes in Internet Marketing that have caused me to implement some pivoting strategies. You might want to look at my situation and consider your own business. It may be time to pivot.

Here's an example. I was in Dallas recently, where I spoke at an Internet Marketing seminar. The night before the seminar,

I was in the bar with a group of speakers and attendees. Every person at our table had their phone in front of them. Some were texting, some were updating Facebook or Twitter feeds, some were checking sales, some were doing research.

There was not a computer in sight.

This is a big honking deal.

A couple of years ago, we would have had laptop computers on that table.

Our phones are not only more powerful than laptop computers were a few years ago, they're portable in a way that computers can't be. I don't even know why we still call them phones. I hardly ever talk on mine. I'm more likely to be surfing the 'tubes, reading a book, checking e-mail or checking sales than I am to be talking on the thing.

So…looking into the swirling mist of my crystal ball, I predict that we'll learn how to monetize phone traffic.

Now, this is gonna be a tough one. I occasionally get spam texts from a payday loan service in San Marcos, Texas. They want to loan me $6,000 real bad.

Here's the problem. I don't need a loan, and if I did, I would go to my banker and arrange one at a reasonable interest rate. I don't know how they got my number, but I am not a good candidate for a payday loan.

I feel like spam texts are an intrusion that is much more personal and intimate than a spam e-mail would be.

When I'm surfing the 'net on my phone, I'm sure there are ads on the pages I go to. I don't see them unless I'm consciously looking and I never click them. (Well, I do click the political ads I disagree with.) Have you?

And, on a phone, the ads are so small that it's not just "banner blindness," it's "I can't even see 'em."

So far, the only people I know having any luck with mobile advertising are local marketers. A restaurant with an opt-in text-number list can drive local traffic to a 2-for-1 deal, for example.

I predict we figure it out.

There are some very bright people working on this. So much of the content on the web is advertiser supported that it's impossible a solution won't be found.

Here's how that affects Internet Marketers—have you ever tried to read a long form sales page on your iPhone? It just doesn't work. Video sales pages are *marginally* more effective.

The genius that cracks this one is gonna make jumbo dollars.

John Reese thinks the future is tablets. He's been right a lot of the time, but he's also been wrong. He's got the pockets and the imagination to give it a good shot. I wouldn't bet against him, but I'm hesitant to get real involved in designing apps for tablets.

It seems like every news site I visit has its own app. Lots of businesses have apps. I've had a couple developed, myself.

I don't want to clutter my iPad with apps. I'd rather read *The New York Times* as a website than as an app. The same thing goes for *Huffington Post* and *The Washington Post*.

We're spending a lot of time penned up in channels—YouTube, Facebook, Twitter. Peering deeply into my crystal ball this reminds me of CompuServe and AOL Online. Somebody really smart will find a way to chunk the Social Network experience up a level so it resides as a macro on top of whatever else you're doing online. That will be as big a deal as the day we found our way outside of AOL Online and discovered the World Wide Web.

The next level up from there, I predict, has to do with the Internet of Things. Google is working hard on this. Microsoft is also putting a lot of energy and resources into this. I have no idea how it's going to play out. Google Goggles—the eyeglasses—look like the way to go.

As a marketer, after I get through enjoying the concept, I think about how to monetize it. Imagining the experience, the first image I get is walking into my kitchen wearing Google Glasses to find a big Pepsi logo on my refrigerator with scrolling text moving around the sides...and I don't drink Pepsi. When I take the glasses off, the logo and text disappear.

My crystal ball gets all foggy when I ask it about this…

Here's another place where we can consider pivoting: e-mail marketing.

People still check e-mail on their iPhones, but less and less as time goes by. Facebook, Twitter, texts, IMs…those are taking the place of e-mails. My son and his friends hardly ever use e-mail.

Nobody's talking about this, but e-mail open rates and clickthrough rates are down industry-wide.

If something's not working, do something else, right?

The question is: what?

The answer, for now, is to use channels to connect with people. A good YouTube video can drive a lot of traffic. There's the added benefit of having a lovely backlink if you SEO the description correctly.

Facebook is also useful for gathering your readers in one place so you can talk to them. Direct marketing on Facebook is a dud, but it's good for getting your readers engaged. Pinterest shows promise. Twitter kinda lost my interest for a while, but has recently gotten more interesting. Like I mentioned above, I think the functionality of the Social Networks is going to get absorbed into the overall 'net experience. For now, they're essential.

The ultimate answer is to create a relationship with your email readers that makes them want to open your e-mails.

Here, in my opinion, is the biggest problem that we have to solve.

This is the big pivot.

Internet Marketing consumers—the people who buy our information—have made it very clear: they want a pushbutton solution. They want to make "riches beyond the dreams of avarice" without doing any work or learning anything.

Those of us who are actually making good money online know that such a thing does not exist. There are learning curves. No matter what you know today, or what's working today, six months from now it's out of date.

Successful Internet Marketers join coaching programs, buy training—I spend tens of thousands of dollars and hundreds of hours a year keeping up with the latest strategies and technologies. I have to.

And yet—try putting that on a sales page.

Test it yourself. Send out a promotion for an Internet Marketing product that tells the truth. "You're going to have to do some work and you're going to have to learn some stuff to make money." Then, follow that with a promotion for "this new oneclick wonder will drive massive profits to you with no effort, almost immediately."

The results will drive you, in my case, to a bottle of Malbec and a late night of reflection.

The bigger picture.

Here's the bigger picture. As Internet Marketers, we're doing what E.F. Schumacher called "good work." The job market has undergone a fundamental shift. It's not just a temporary blip. This is the new reality. There are fewer jobs and they're going to require higher levels of training.

When I was growing up the people who didn't finish high school had employment options. They could work at gas stations, for example.

Since then, the world has become automated.

Computers are wonderful, magical things. The prediction was that as computers took over the menial labor, humans would be faced with the problem of how to spend all their leisure time. And, for some, it's worked out swimmingly. If you own a gas station, you need one employee, not ten. Grocery stores and big-box stores are replacing clerks with automated checkout lanes. The guys who used to install lug nut #4 on the left rear tire in the Chevy factory have been replaced by robots.

This trend will continue. Anything that can be automated will be automated. Short term, whether it's good or not depends on where you're standing in the picture. If you own the gas station, your labor costs got slashed and your profits went up. If you used to pump gas, you're on the streets.

Instead of leading to lives of luxury and leisure, where all humans can spend their time improving their minds with literature and art, it's led to poverty, desperation, and massive unemployment.

This ties in with my previous point about Internet Marketing. If you're prepared to do the work and learn some stuff, this represents a tremendous opportunity. It opens up a global market where you can—alone with your computer—run an international marketing company. Drop shipping, Amazon, Alibaba, information products—it's simply a matter of matching the demand with the supply. There's room for everybody.

It seems like we should be teaching this in high school. It seems like the government should open up Internet Marketing academies for the unemployed.

Unfortunately, that's not going to happen.

So, what then shall we do?

I'm going to keep learning, and teaching what I learn. I'm going to analyze what's working and what's not working—and do more of what's working and stop doing the stuff that doesn't work.

MAKE MONEY FROM ANYWHERE—AND HOW TO GET THERE!

Make money from anywhere. That's the goal, right? Click a button and cash floods your bank account.

My previous books have had a lot of the "make money" part of *Money from Anywhere*. This chapter is the "from anywhere" part.

The last time I was in Terlingua, I pulled into Ted's recording studio and saw what was either a big van or a very small RV parked at the loading ramp. It was Ray's Winnebago Rialta, the likes of which I had never seen before.

Ray's a Nashville singer/songwriter who travels around the world singing his songs, and for the last few months he'd been traveling around in the Rialta. He showed me around: kitchen, bathroom, queen size bed, propane, extra batteries, generator… and explained that you could live on the road in this thing without the need of hookups. It was totally self-contained.

I wanted one.

When I got back to Wimberley, I started researching little RVs in general and Rialtas specifically. It turns out that they don't make them anymore, and they're very popular. And, because they get almost 20 miles to the gallon, they're just going to get *more* popular.

Fast forward a month or so, and I get a phone call from Ray. He's going to sell his Rialta and move up to something bigger. Do I want to buy his Rialta?

Well, duh. Yes. Please.

Which explains why I'm sitting in the luxurious Arlington Hotel in Hot Springs, Arkansas writing this chapter. By the way, the Arlington is a time machine. It looks and feels like nothing's changed here since the '30s. Lots of art deco flourishes, polished brass, murals and plants. There's also a Starbucks in the lobby. Add a cigar bar and I'm moving in.

Sunday, I got on a plane to Nashville. Monday I drove around Nashville and surrounding areas with Ray as my copilot. We went to the Flying J truck stop outside of Nashville, and he showed me how to hook up to the water, sewage, and electricity. Well, eventually, you have to dump your waste water: http://budurl.com/mkya.

Monday night, Ray and I met at the Nashville Whole Foods and talked about traveling and I started to feel confident enough to hit the road.

Serious RVers like Ray just pull into a truck stop, WalMart, or sleepy neighborhood and spend the night. It makes hotels irrelevant and also makes it possible to travel pretty much free.

I want to get closer to home and practice in familiar places before I start camping on the road.

Yesterday, I spent a few hours in Memphis, Tennessee. The last time I saw Beale Street was at least 30 years ago. I was on the road with a rock band, and we played a couple of weeks here at a very cool club. Back then, Beale Street looked like Baghdad. Bombed out. Dirty. Deserted.

Today, it's like 6th Street in Austin, but instead of cover bands playing '80s rock, they've got old black guys and gals playing very good blues. Personally, I prefer Beale Street. I had a big ole plate of ribs at B.B. King's, bought some souvenirs, and walked around listening to music. Almost every club had live music and it was uniformly good.

Today, I woke up early in the Arlington and ate breakfast across the street at the Pancake House—which has been in business since 1940 and doesn't take credit cards. Then, I set up shop here in the lobby.

And that's the "Make Money" part.

I'm promoting a friend's new book, which my publishing company published. So, using my autoresponder, I sent an email to my readers to tell them about it.

Then, check the bank account and email. Most of my emails are handled by Customer Service, but some require my attention. Answered those.

The new "UnSeminar People" Facebook group is taking off. So, I logged onto Facebook, posted some pictures, and checked in on my group. Lots of fun conversation going on there.

Then, back to email. We're preparing a new launch. It's got a lot of moving parts, but it's all stuff we can get in place before the launch. That should cut down on the post-launch stress. My tech guy and I are talking about different ways we can achieve our goals.

I have a couple of affiliate marketing promotions going on right now so I zip over to ClickBank and check on sales. Nice. EPC exceeds CPC significantly.

Now, upload pics and write a blog post and I'm through at the office for today. I started work around 7 this morning. It's 8:39 right now. I should be on the road by 9:30.

After this is posted, I'm going to get in my new RV and point it south. I have no idea where I'm going to spend the night tonight. Will I get brave and actually sleep in the RV? Will I find another hotel as cool as the Arlington? Will I decide to drive straight to Wimberley (about 11 hours)?

I don't know. And, I don't want to.

And that, for me, is the beauty of the Portable Empire lifestyle.

I could do this forever. Especially after I figure out the camping in the RV stuff.

I know it's possible to do serious mid-six-figures a year with a laptop computer from just about anywhere because I've been doing it for years.

I know it's possible to teach others how to do it, because several of my coaching clients are doing it, too.

I'm gonna hit the road like Jack Kerouac with a Gold card. That's living.

By the way, they tell me the Arlington Hotel is haunted.

I think I hear a clarinet leading a big band around the corner and the swishing of ball gowns…it's awfully early in the day for ballroom dancing, isn't it?

JOBLESS AND LOVING IT

It's over.

That economy you grew up with?

Yea. That one. It's over.

And they lied to you.

Who?

Your parents, your teachers, your counselors.

I'm assuming they told you what they told me: get a good education so you can get a good job. Then, get that good job and keep it.

I thought that sounded like a waste of a life back when I was young and hearing it the first time. Turns out I was right. For many reasons.

One of the things I love about reading Kinky Friedman's books is that occasionally he'll talk to his cat. And not just kittytalk. He'll get down and dirty and explore the important stuff with his cat. The cat has not been known to respond verbally, but occasionally will respond in other ways.

I figured this was just a literary device until I started doing it, too.

My cat's name is Ming. In her youth, she was a brave hunter of lizards and would proudly bring me her trophies. It was disgusting. But, she was so proud. I never let her know how I really felt. Now, she's matronly and hunts for rays of sunlight to lie in. She's black and white, and (don't tell her) her head is a little small for her body.

This morning, she was lying on our large leather couch, listening to Pat Metheny, while I was waking up in my zero-gravity chair, drinking my morning coffee and reading the news. When I got to one of the articles I must have spoken out loud: "Don't they know the industrial revolution is o.v.e.r.?" I asked.

The cat just looked out the window at a pair of cardinals.

"Those manufacturing jobs are gone. They've been going for the last twenty years. The recession has provided cover for manufacturers to ditch workers they don't need, replace the workers with computers and robots, and ship the very few jobs that require humans to places where humans are cheap."

And, good riddance.

I don't know why YOU think you're on this planet. I've heard all kinds of goofy theories. But, I damn sure ain't gonna spend my precious time on this beautiful spinning globe attaching bolt 12 to the left-hand door on this year's model, be the 50th cost accountant on the 31st floor, or any other kind of grunt work.

I'm here to enjoy gorgeous sunsets and sunrises. I'm here to drink delicious wine, smoke good cigars, and enjoy the love of my woman. I'm here to make and appreciate art and music.

The cat looked at me as if to say, "who says?"

"I say. It's my life. Nobody else gets a vote."

The cat returned to watching birds through the window. She's heard it before.

I continued, "The recovery is working as planned. The stock market is up. Large corporations are holding huge reserves of cash. And they're making capital investments in machinery, automation, and 21st century solutions to 21st century business problems. On a smaller level, I am, too. I'm surrounded by computers and spend a huge chunk of my operating capital on software, servers, video cameras and editing equipment, and product creation tools. I outsource and use contract labor for stuff I need done. I have no employees."

At this point that cat lowered her head and gave me a strange look.

"I NEED 25 guitars!" I said, possibly a little too loud. Can't stand a judgmental cat.

And, in a way, I do. A lot of my income comes from products that have music and I make all the music in my office/studio. 25 guitars, 4 amps, bass, mandolin, 5 keyboards, pippa, pre-amps, compressors, mixers, and some very groovy music production software—those are all investments. I pay them once. I use them for, in the case of some of the guitars, decades.

The cat, possibly pacified, jumped down off the couch and waddled (she's a little overweight. Again, I don't mention it to her.) to her food bowl in the kitchen.

It only makes sense.

To compete in the "new" economy, in whatever we're going to call the post-post-industrial age, it's imperative that companies streamline, automate and outsource. The US is the land of innovation. iPads are made in China, but they were visualized here. Cars are made in Korea, Mexico, Canada, and Japan. But they were visualized here. If there's any truth in the "American Exceptionalism" concept, and I'm not convinced there is, that truth would be that we're exceptional at looking at the world, seeing what's not there but ought to be, and making it appear.

That's a noble job. That's a life.

Ming, apparently temporarily sated, walked across the tiles from the kitchen to the living room and stood directly in front of my chair giving me an accusing look. Looking down, I said, "I don't know what to do about the people who just want a job. I can't wrap my mind around that concept. It's a living death."

You know what I mean, right?

I know people who have worked 30 years at jobs they don't particularly like and are not particularly good at. They drag themselves through each day doing the least they can get by with. On the weekends, they either trance out in front of one tube or the other or drink cheap-swill beer until they've achieved another kind of trance. Or they combine the two, especially during football season. Then Monday comes around and they get up hating it, work all day hating it, and come home hating it. Eventually, they get to retire and do what they really want to do…if they live that long…and if they can remember what it was they wanted to do all those years ago...and if their health will let them do it, whatever it was.

That ain't living.

I'm going to get bumperstickers made. You've seen bumperstickers that say, "I'd rather be fishing," right? Mine are gonna say, "If there was something I'd rather be doing, I'd be doing it." (That's a reference to *Skinny Legs and All* by Tom Robbins, btw. Ming seems to think you might not know that.)

I tried having a "real job" once, when my son was small. I was a single parent and thought I wanted stability and security. I knew they didn't exist, but it seemed like the responsible, grown-up thing to do, so I gave it a shot. I lasted a year. It was terrible. I hated it, and it hated me. I would show up late, shirt wrinkled, tie askew, shoes unpolished. I was good at it, and my boss hated to see me go when I quit, but it damn near killed me. I was drinking every evening and all weekend—and not in a good way. Jobs are a prison, bosses are wardens, and even if you've got a benevolent warden like I did, and a comfortable cubicle, you're still in jail. Doing time.

I used to drive my father to intense teeth-grinding when we'd talk about my future. I'd ask him, "what are people for?"

I felt like I needed an answer to that before I committed myself to any kind of long-term plan. "What, exactly, am I here to do?"

Ming knows what she's here to do: eat and look at me with a sideways, judgmental look. I had no clue. I didn't know what I was capable of or what the options might be. I'd sit on my dad's hand-me-down furniture, drinking his Louisiana coffee in the backwoods pine forest where he lived, and ask him BIG questions—questions I felt like I had a right to have answers to before I committed myself to thirty years of grunt work. He would grit his teeth, chew his cigar, and be irritated.

So, first of all, it's my opinion that jobs are dumb. You can have your own opinion, but you can't have your own facts. The fact is that an employee is an expense. By definition, an employee has to generate more income for a business than that employee costs or the business goes broke. Think about it.

In college, I had an economics instructor who, on the first day of class, announced: "the sole purpose of a corporation is to maximize shareholder value. If you disagree with that, get out of this classroom." He was looking right at me when he said it. I had caused some ripples in the cow-college business school I attended with my hippie sensibilities. He was having none of it.

I aced his class, btw, and he really didn't like that.

But, in a way, he's right. It's not the way it ought to be. It is the way it is. Businesses exist to create profit for the business owners. If you're an employee, the business owner is required to minimize your stake and maximize his. What we're seeing in the economic world today is a massive power grab by "capital" and a total capitulation by "labor." The fact that the political party doing the power grab also has a huge labor component, and has convinced the poor bastards that it's in their best interest to support economic changes that will bankrupt them is heartbreaking. But, it's unlikely that anybody who watches Fox TV also follows what I'm doing, so there's really nothing Ming and I can do for them. They can vote themselves into the poorhouse. And they will.

At this point, Ming, who is a closet Marxist, jumped onto the zero-gravity chair and sat on my lap. She read over the preceding and put her head down, purring.

So "capital" wins. "Labor" loses.

What to do?

Well…years ago, I read *The Marx and Engels Reader*, which was a simplified, comic-book level analysis of Marx and Engels' writings. I got it immediately. I reached different conclusions than they did, probably because I knew lots of "labor," and knew that they weren't going to organize, throw off their chains or do much else except drink a lot of PBR, watch a lot of TV, and bitch about their jobs.

I wanted to be "capital."

I realized that I needed to own my own business so that I would never be at the mercy of a boss.

Then, later, I realized that corporations got all the breaks. Knowing that they existed to maximize shareholder value, I incorporated. I own all the shares.

Now, when I create excess value, it shows up as profit for the corporation—but it's my corporation. I make exactly as much money as I'm worth.

Ming lifted her head and nodded at my computer. I had clicked through to an article and read this about the mysterious lack of recovery for the middle class:

> *But there is no mystery. What other result would you expect from the financial ruin of the once-great American middle class? And make no mistake, the middle class has been ruined: Its wealth has been decimated, its income isn't even keeping pace with inflation, and its faith in the American economy has been shattered. Once, the middle class grew richer each year, grew more comfortable, enjoyed a higher living standard. It was real progress in material terms.*
>
> *But that progress has been halted and even reversed. In some respects, the middle class has made no progress in a generation, or two.*
>
> *This isn't just a sad story about a few losers. The prosperity of the middle class has been the chief engine of growth in the economy for a century or more. But now our mass market is no longer growing. How could it? The middle class doesn't have any money...*

source: MarketWatch

Good catch, cat. That's the other problem.

We're on a trend of the rich getting richer and the poor staying poor, and the middle class is being drug down an alley, raped, and mugged.

This is from that same MarketWatch article—and MarketWatch is associated with *The Wall Street Journal*, which is about a conservative as it gets:

> *The rich recovered; the rest of us didn't.*
>
> *If losing half your meager life savings weren't bad enough, the middle class has also been falling behind in terms of income for decades. Families in the middle make most of their money the old-fashioned way: Working their fingers to the bone for 40 years for wages and a modest pension.*
>
> *Their wages have been flat after adjusting for inflation. In the late 1960s, the 20% of families right in the middle were earning almost their full share of the pie: they had 17.5% of total income. Their share has been falling steadily ever since. Now, that 20% is earning just 14.6% of all income. Meanwhile, the top 5% captured a growing share, going from 17% in the late 1960s to 22% today.*

In a perfect world, the poor and middle class would rise up, demand equality, and wrest back their share of the wealth from the rich, right? It ain't gonna happen.

I can tell Ming disagrees. She finds violence distasteful. She jumped down off my lap and went back to her sunny spot on the couch.

"Can't take the truth, huh?" I asked her.

Rubbing it in, I said, "The middle class and poor are going to be drowning their troubles in cheap beer and watching TV, and you know it."

At this juncture, the cat left the room.

It's not just the cat. I've had old friends un-friend me on Facebook over this one. But, here it is: you are responsible for your own wealth. You are responsible for your own life.

Here's another one that annoys people: If you're not part of the solution, you're part of the problem. The more money you have, the more you can help others. If you're broke, you're just another one who needs help.

It's easy to see the future on this one.

Unemployment will continue to rise. Labor is so 19th century. The guy who checked your oil and pumped your gas at the filling station is gone and so is his job. Cars, appliances, and electronics devices are either made by computers and robots or by people in other countries who can afford to work for less than you can. Things are just going to get worse if you're labor.

As a country, we're happy to slit our own throats and bitch about it. Where do you buy stuff? Where you can get it cheapest, right? And "cheapest" means it was made by robots or Chinese slave labor. Sad, huh?

What's the solution?

1. Own your own business
2. Take responsibility for your own success.
3. Take advantage of reality.

What do I mean by "take advantage of reality?"

1. Jobs are going, going gone.
2. It's better to be rich than it is to be poor.
3. Capital get the breaks. Labor gets screwed.

So, you want to be capital. You want to own the business.

The current reality is that it's never been easier to start and run your own business, and it scales quickly and easily.

You can start an online business—what I've been calling a "Portable Empire," for less than $50 if you have a computer and an Internet connection.

You can be making money with your computer in a week. You can replace a day job in six months to a year—if you've got good information and work smart.

What about "scaling?"

There is a reason I have three computers on my desk. They're factories. While one is rendering video, I'm writing on another. Sometimes the third is processing audio or any of a number of other tasks.

The big scaling happens online.

First, you put up one website. You arrange for people to find it. You build your list and sell the product on that website.

That's a business. You can start one in the next ten minutes if you like.

Then, you let that business continue doing its thing and you make another one.

I have hundreds. I made them one at a time. Each one contributes something to the cash flow of my business.

Ming remembers the bad old days. When I started this business, Ming, my son and I lived in a single-wide mobile home and I tried to pay the bills by playing guitar in bars. It sucked bad.

Then the trailer got repossessed.

There is NO WAY you are broker now than I was when I started.

All you have to do is do it.

How?

First, watch an Introduction to Internet Marketing video at http://budurl.com/236w.

You're reading one of my books on Internet Marketing. I have others that I give away for free. Check the products page on my website at http://patobryan.com/products.

I also have a coaching program. It's good. Learn more at http://PortableEmpireCoaching.com.

That ought'a get you started.

Just now Ming walked into the living room and climbed back into my lap. I let her read what I'd written. She looked a little hurt until I reassured her that she wasn't "people." It's ok for cats to expect to be taken care of.

Outside the window, a pair of cardinals did a mating dance. Ming slept right through it.

UNPUBLISHING FOR 21ST CENTURY AUTHORS.

Yes, the book publishing business is suffering. In some ways, it's dying. The Borders bookstores in Austin closed and they're shutting down stores across the nation. Book sales are down everywhere but Amazon. Traditional publishers are cutting back on the *number* of books they accept for publication, and printing *fewer copies* of the books they do publish.

You'd think now would be the dumbest time in history to start a publishing company, right? The only thing dumber would be to start a record label.

So, you want to take a guess at my next project?

If you guessed, "start a book publishing company," come on down. You win. (If you guessed, "Start a record company," you're a little premature. Let me tilt at this windmill first.)

Before you call the little men in the funny white coats to haul me off to Kinky Friedman's Bandera Home For The Bewildered, let me explain.

You do know why you want to be a published author, right? To establish yourself as "the expert." You can charge more for public speaking, and get better gigs. Your online business will be seen as more professional, so you can sell more products at higher prices. Also, it's fun. There's nothing like holding your freshly printed book in your hand—seeing your name in the "author" place on the cover—and knowing that thousands of people all over the world are "listening" to you by reading your book. You want that.

Recently, I taught a class on self-publishing to 80+ bright new authors. If you're an author, you need this course. Go to http://publishedauthor.me and see why. The course consisted of six intense webinars, and we covered all aspects of being an author in the 21st century as thoroughly as possible. Some of the attendees told me that the course was the best investment they'd ever made.

However, what we—the attendees and I—learned was that not everybody can, or will, do everything it takes to successfully self-publish their book.

There were two areas where the authors got derailed: marketing and tech stuff.

Let's look at marketing first.

I come from a music background, so let's use the music business as an example.

Back in the sixties, record companies would sign bands and support them while they grew. If it took a few albums for them to hit, the record company was willing to wait for the investment to pay off. They made enough profit off their established acts that they could pump some of those profits back into baby bands. They also supported artists who would never become profitable, because the art they were making brought so much prestige to the label that it paid off. Captain Beefheart, Ultimate Spinach, and some Miles Davis projects, for example, had little or no commercial potential—but the labels nurtured them anyway. Other artists, like Joni Mitchell, started slow and ended up redefining the art form and selling piles of records.

The down side was that, with a few exceptions—most of whom are still touring today if they're alive (think McCartney, Stones, David Gilmour, Clapton)—most artists were lucky to scrape by and were grateful to make a living out of their careers.

The record companies, the mafia, and the publishing companies took most of the money.

Today, it's a totally different model. The business, if you're going to play with the record labels, is based on singles. Your first one better sell, or you're not going to get to make a second one. That's why most recording artists are self-publishing.

Recording studios, which used to be silly expensive to build and maintain and were run by funny geeks in white lab coats, are now cheap and easy to use. A good laptop computer and a few hundred dollars worth of software, a decent mic, a keyboard, and you can make a great record. *If* you can make a great record.

What's missing from that model is both a good and bad thing: the gatekeepers: The A&R guys who chose which bands to invest in, and consequently, which music we got to hear. And the producers—producers are the guys (usually) with the golden ears. Think George Martin. The Beatles, without George Martin, would have been nothing at all like The Beatles I grew up with. Those orchestras, odd instrument choices, complex instrumental harmonies, and the over-all sound of those records—that was George Martin. Ahem. SIR George Martin.

When you're making your "record" in your bedroom with a laptop computer and some software, you have the technical ability to make a great record, theoretically. But, there's the part about which songs to record, which instruments to play, how to record those instruments, choosing which performance to keep and which to erase, and how to mix and master the final recording so that it sounds like a real record. Talent, experience, and luck: that's the tricky bit.

Book publishing has a similar history. Back in the day, publishers would pick writers who had talent and potential and nurture them. Some authors never made a profit for their publishers, but brought so much prestige to the imprint that the publisher continued to put out their books. It gave the publishers a cachet of credibility that splashed onto all the books they published.

The gatekeepers were vigilant. If you couldn't get the attention and backing of one of the major publishers, you just didn't get published. Occasionally, a book would "take off" and sell millions of copies, and that funded the books that didn't sell.

I got a real world education in publishing when my second book was picked up by the largest non-fiction publisher on the planet. Now, I thought, I have hit the big time. Fame and fortune are assured.

Wrong. Here are some of the surprises:

1. I don't think my editor ever even looked at the manuscript. He had a pretty good idea that I could use my marketing skills and platform to sell enough copies of the book to make it profitable. That's why they signed me. Dr. Joe Vitale and I were on the same publishing imprint, and our joke was that they weighed the books, they didn't read them.
2. Publishers do NOT market books. Read that again. It's true. Fame and fortune may ensue if you get signed by an established publisher, but it will be because YOU marketed the book.

   The punch line is that the publisher still takes most of the money. You write the thing. You sell it. And the publisher takes most of the money.

   When it did start to sell, and sell a lot, they were able to get it into bookstores all over the world, for which I am grateful. However, today, that's not such a big deal. The bookstores are closing. Also, there are other ways to get into the bookstores.
3. When it came time to discuss my next book, the publisher told me to wait until the first one had sold a certain number of copies. Then we'd talk. They had no opinion of my writing talent, whether or not the book was helping people, or whether I had shown enough potential on my first book with them to justify helping me build my writing career. If it sold XX thousand copies, they'd do another one (and take most of the money). If not, they weren't interested.

How about them apples?

That's the publishing world six years ago. Today, it's even tougher. Fewer books are selling. Bookstores are closing, so a publisher's ability to get books in bookstores is not relevant any more.

You can now describe the book publishing business in one word: Amazon.

That's why I self-published my last three books, and why they're only available at Amazon.com. The last one, *Money From Anywhere*, was also a best-seller. This time, though, there was one huge difference in my experience. As the author *and* the publisher, I made the money. Instead of making about $1 per unit, I made about $14 per unit. That's a huge deal.

I wrote the thing. I (and my friends and coauthors) sold it. Same as before. But, by cutting out the middle-men, I showed a profit almost immediately and will end up making more money on that book than I made on the one published by the big publisher.

Cool, huh?

That's when I decided to share what I had learned about selfpublishing and offered the Published Author.me course. Some of the people who have taken that course will go on and become successful self-published authors.

Some won't.

Here's why, and this is the second thing that caused some of my authors problems.

When you self-publish, *you're* the publisher.

That means you're also the editor. You have to make sure your text is clear, you make your points, and the writing style is interesting.

That's tough.

Like the guitar player in his bedroom trying to make a record, you're faced with infinite possibilities, and some of those possibilities will make for a very dull book. That's why there are so many bad records being made, and so many bad books being published.

It's hard to edit yourself. You're too close to the project.

That also means you're the layout department. People really do judge a book by its cover, and it's rare that the person with the talent for writing a good book also has the talent to design a compelling cover.

You're also in charge of formatting the book so it prints attractively. There is an art to this, too. There are also a lot of fiddly technical issues to deal with. If you're using CreateSpace to publish your book—and I recommend you do—they're very picky about the layout. You can find yourself in publishing hell over an eighth of an inch margin and not understand why.

Even if they accept your manuscript and print it you might end up with an unreadable mess with a dull cover.

We spent two hours during the Published Author course with an expert in these things, and he showed us how to do it. I'll be rewatching that video on one computer with Microsoft Word open on another computer for a while. It's hard.

That's why I'm starting a publishing company.

Stay tuned—we're gonna change the world, one book at a time.

AUTHORS, THE GAME HAS CHANGED

Authors, the game has changed. And, that's a very good thing. Now is possibly the best time in history to be an author. Let's hop in the time machine and zip back to the 1960s for a minute.

No, not those sixties. I was too young to be a hippie, damn it. I would have been. However, for me the sixties were a time of flying my bicycle through the woods and down the streets of our lower middle-class suburban neighborhood. Rows of almost identical little houses, backyard hot-dogs, little-league baseball, black and white TVs with three channels, listening to the kids across the street play Beatles songs in their garage…it's kinda misty, looking back.

We lived in Beaumont, Texas. It's an ugly oil town, but we lived on what was then the outskirts. There were forests. When I was ten, they seemed huge. A mile or so past our subdivision, there were dirt roads with farm houses. Today, it's all ticky-tacky houses and concrete. Back then it was in transition from rural to urban.

For weeks, possibly months, my dad had been tapping late into the night on the old manual typewriter he had won in a short-story contest. It was the music I went to sleep to.

Dad was a writer. He started out working on newspapers. He did some ghost writing, mostly vanity-press biographies of oil barons. And, some of his ghost-written books did real well.

However, when it came to writing his own book, well, that was a different story.

One day, he handed me a large, fat envelope with the manuscript of his latest book and asked me to pedal down to the mailbox at the entrance to our subdivision and mail it for him. I did. After that, the tapping stopped for a while.

Personal note, on nights when he wasn't tapping on his typewriter, my father would sit on the couch in the living room with a martini or scotch and listen to music on our old Magnavox record player. He liked Broadway sound tracks and Gershwin. After a few drinks, he would conduct the record player, like a very relaxed conductor would conduct an orchestra, if a conductor was sitting on a couch with a martini and used a cigar for a baton. I like that image.

Anyway, all my dad got from his tapping was a large pile of rejection slips.

Back in the sixties, there was a huge barrier to entry to becoming a published author.

You couldn't buy books anywhere but a bookstore, and bookstores only sold books that came from established publishing companies. So, if a publishing company didn't publish your book, you were pretty much out of the authoring business.

A few nights ago, I published my fifth book. It took about ten minutes. We'll get to that in a minute.

Six years ago, my second book, *Your Portable Empire, How To Make Money Anywhere Doing What You Love*, was published by the largest non-fiction publishing company on the planet. I think Dad would have been proud.

He would also have been surprised. I sure was. Did you know that publishing companies don't market books? If you're J.K. Rowling they do. But, if you're one of the thousands of unknown authors who are publishing their first book and you're not already famous you're going to have to do your own marketing.

Let's look at the math. That book sells for $24.95. I get about $1.50 for each book sold but because of the creative accounting that publishers use (they're a lot like record companies), it's actually much less than that. That book was an Amazon.com best-seller, and sold many thousands of copies. For each one, I (presumably) got $1.50, and the publisher and seller split the other $23.45.

And for what?

That book became a best-seller because my friends and I marketed the hell out of it. We're marketers. That's what we do. What did the publisher do? They had the book printed, which is cheap. In a minute, I'll tell you exactly how cheap it can be. In fact, I'll show you how to do it for free.

After we had done our promotion, and the book was on the front page of Amazon.com, they printed a lot of them and got them into every bookstore on the planet. That book is still in some bookstores, which is kinda cool—but nowhere near as cool as it was a few years ago.

Now, I must admit that it gave me a thrill to walk into the Barnes and Nobles in Austin with my son and show him my book on the bookshelf along with all the other "real" books. I used the opportunity to remind my son of his grandfather, who never got to have that feeling. I'm glad my son got to see that, because *it will never happen again.*

Have you been to a bookstore lately? I have.

Last time I was there the Barnes and Nobles in Austin was a ghost town. The coffee shop/Internet cafe was busy, but nobody was buying books. Then it closed.

I haven't bought a book in a bookstore in ages. I download most books to the Kindle app on my iPad. If I want a hard copy, I order it from Amazon.com—it's cheaper, easier, and they've got lots of books that a bookstore just can't keep in stock.

If you're an author, this is important. To be a published author, you need to get your book at Amazon.. The marketing is up to you because the marketing was *always* up to you.

So, if having your book in a bookstore *was* a good reason to use a publisher, that reason is gone. You need your book at Amazon.com. That's where people buy books.

Today, you can publish your book for free, and get it automatically on Amazon.com. It takes about ten minutes. You upload a PDF, graphics for the cover, and that's it.

When I got the first six copies of my book, *Money From Anywhere*, I was proud and amazed. They're beautiful. The quality of the printing is first-rate. I gave Joe Vitale the first copy. The book is about 180 pages long and I can order as many as I like for $2.80 each. That, my friends, is a miracle. I have a published book that is available on Amazon.com and it didn't cost me anything to get it published. If I sell one, Amazon takes a cut, but I get most of the money.

Now, it's all down to marketing. The difference this time is that I can actually make some money from my book.

Now, I'm not sure I'm a better writer than my dad was. After all, he was my father. It's impossible to be objective. However, I've learned a lot about writing books, marketing books, and the *business* of writing books that my father never knew. I wrote my latest book in two days. I can write a book in ten minutes. And I can get that puppy published and sell it.

Let's stop for a second and be grateful we live in such times. Never before, in all of history, have authors had this kind of power.

If you've got the gumption and talent to create your book, and the tenacity to tell the world about it, you can be a successful author—with all the psychic benefits that come with that—and make a living from your art. There's no barrier. At all.

If you're an author you know what this feels like: you send your manuscript to a publisher, you check the mail every day hoping for a response…you wake up in the morning, sit in front of a cold cup of coffee and wait because somebody else has your future held hostage. Then, the envelope arrives. It could be your ticket to fame and fortune.

It's not.

It's another rejection slip.

You put it in the filing cabinet or desk drawer with all the others and either send out another manuscript or nuzzle up to your .45. It's a hard life.

You don't ever have to feel that way again. If you want to get started now, go to http://PublishedAuthor.me and get started.

It's an amazing time to be an author.

HOW TO BE RICH?

How to be rich? Specifically, how can *you* be rich?

Let's play with that for a while, shall we?

One of the most important tactics a business owner can implement is "pivoting." When something's not working, stop doing it. Fast. When something is working, do more of that. There are times when "something else" is what you should be doing.

The trick is to define "working" correctly. One definition of "working" is whether or not an expenditure in energy, time or money is returning a profit. Another one, and the one we go by here at Practical Metaphysics, Inc., is whether or not it's fun. In 1996, I claimed "If it ain't fun, I ain't doin' it" as my motto. I recommend it highly.

The few times I've strayed from that, the results have been predictable. I'm looking for life experiences that make me smile now and will make me smile in my dotage. They've got to pass the death-bed test. When I'm lying on my death-bed, looking back at my life, will what I'm doing *right now* make me smile as I remember it? If the answer is yes, I'm on the right track. If the answer is no, it's time for a change.

The experiences that money can buy usually aren't the ones that turn me on. Poverty sucks. I like being rich. But, if money is the *only* reason I'm doing something, it's time to stop doing it.

Now, it's confession time.

Time passes. Things change. People change.

I looked up recently during one of my cleansing trips to the desert, and realized that some of the things that I was doing for money had stopped being fun. The details are personal, but the lesson is universal. Inertia and habit are powerful forces. I kept doing what I'd been doing because that was what I did. I'd changed, other people had changed, and the marketing environment had changed.

Surprisingly, I wasn't having fun. It used to be fun. Oh well…

The solution is obvious: stop doing what I'm doing and do something else.

Because I'm a family guy and business owner, step one is to replace the income that doing the not-fun stuff is bringing in. Lots of people rely on me financially.

That's the easy part. I kinda knew this was coming, so I've been going to seminars, buying training courses, reading and researching and just generally traveling down roads I'd never been down and metaphorically kicking over rocks, peering behind trees, and climbing to the top of hills just to see what was on the other side. A chance conversation with Marlon Sanders, an aside during a webinar with Eric Louvier, a video on Ryan and Perry's site…the heavens parted, the sun broke through the clouds, angels sang (think side 2 of *Abbey Road*) and I heard the voice of god—or maybe it was James Earl Jones—describing my new business model.

The above describes a trick I learned reading a Robert Heinlein book called *Friday* decades ago. When I'm looking for an answer I promiscuously pour data into my head. I keep the question I'm trying to answer in my mind and let my subconscious sort the data for me through the frame of the question I'm trying to answer. Eventually, the answer appears. Very seldom does it appear from the direction I think it will. It never fails.

Yesterday, I had a long meeting with my top tech guru and lined out our new business plan. He immediately got it. And, it turns out that he was getting bored with what we've been doing and was ready for a change, too. He's been spending some time at the cabin in the desert with his family lately. Maybe that's it.

Now, let's talk about you.

I recently read something interesting in The Economist, which is a pretty good 'zine if you're curious about economics. The good news is, comparatively, you're rich. There are billions of people on this planet living on less than $1.25 a day.

In the rich countries—the US and Western Europe mostly—we talk about *relative* poverty. Which is interesting because it's a variable and arbitrary designation. Check out this quote from Wikipedia:

> *A measure of relative poverty defines "poverty" as being below some relative poverty threshold. For example, the statement that "households with an accumulated income less than 60% of the median equivalized household disposable income are living in poverty" uses a relative measure to define poverty. In this system, if everyone's real income in an economy increases, but the income distribution stays the same, then the rate of relative poverty will also stay the same.*

Everything depends on who you compare yourself to. I remember a dinner I went to a couple of years ago where I sat between Joe Vitale and Kevin Trudeau. Comparatively speaking, I was broke. At the American Legion hall on hwy 118, near my cabin in the desert, I drink beer with guys who make about $300 a month and live in trailers in the desert with no utilities. Comparatively speaking, I'm very rich.

Which is it?

Here's another example. I was at a seminar in Houston a few years ago and the speaker told a story: one of his clients said something like, "I'm doing fine. I have the nicest house in my neighborhood." The speaker told him, "you need to move to a better neighborhood."

To me, there's *so much* wrong with that. First of all, basing self-esteem on any possession is a loser's game. Second, the speaker—who is a high-dollar consultant in the "get rich" niche—is basically telling the guy with the house that he shouldn't ever be satisfied. If his house is the nicest in the neighborhood he needs to change neighborhoods so that…what? so he can feel insecure?

That's sad.

Another way to put that would be to say that according to my beliefs and values, that's a pretty pathetic way to live a life.

So, how can you be rich?

First of all, you have to decide what "rich" means. You have your own beliefs and values.

What makes you happy?

Try to differentiate between what *others* have told you will make you happy, what *advertisers* tell you will make you happy, and get down to what *you* know will make you happy. Consider taking a few days off with no T.V. (actually, consider taking the rest of your life off with no T.V.), no Internet, no advertising and see if you can get in touch with what really turns you on.

There's a huge difference between something that's *supposed* to make you happy and something that *actually does*. Once you learn that distinction, you're almost there.

Then, think about who you're comparing yourself to.

Here's a hint. I know some really rich people. They are not the happiest people I know. In fact—and this is a data point that caused me to really examine my beliefs and values—some of the happiest people I know are living on almost no money at all.

If you want to get down to what's real about this, you need to stop comparing yourself to others. This is hard. I'm certainly having trouble with it. But, it doesn't matter what kind of house your buddy, or your brother, or Jennifer Aniston, or Richard Branson live in. What matters is what kind of house makes you happy.

Here's another hint: I'm happiest in my 840 sqare foot cabin in the middle of the desert. I certainly didn't expect that, or realize it until I started staying here for extended periods of time.

I can save you a lot of time on this one. Your clothes, haircut, car, house, jewelry, and toys may temporarily amuse you. But, they won't make you happy. Especially if you go into debt to get them.

The point is for you to examine a variety of experiences and notice how you feel. Find the things that make you honestly happy. Those are the things you should do more of if you want to be happy. Identify the things that make you uncomfortable, angry, or disappointed. Stop doing them.

You're probably asking yourself, "Why is Pat talking about happiness? I thought he was going to write about how I can get rich. What's up?"

Well, yea. You're right. Thanks for pointing that out. Here's the deal-

To me, happy equals rich. One of the components of happiness is having enough money to do the things that honestly make me happy.

So, let's talk about money.

My big turn-around about money came when I realized that I was responsible for my own income.

I would have made a great trust fund baby, by the way. I would have enjoyed a lifestyle of decadence as I scooted between my homes in Paris, Berlin, Sao Paulo, and L.A. on my private jet, partying with the (other?) beautiful people, drinking champagne from crystal goblets, and checking out TMZ and Gawker to make sure my press agent was keeping me in the public eye.

Unfortunately, my parents weren't rich. No trust fund. Damn.

I dropped out of school when I was 17 to be a rock star. My assumption was that somebody in the music biz would see my obvious talent and rescue me from whatever bar I happened to be playing and catapult me to fame and fortune beyond the dreams of avarice (and avarice, in my youth, dreamt big).

30+ years later, I was still waiting.

Nobody was going to save me. I spent a few weeks curled up in bed with Napoleon Hill, Ayn Rand, Randy Gage—not literally. I can't believe you think like that. I mean, I got a pile of really good books about personal responsibility and read them. It changed my life.

Around this time I had an interesting conversation with Joe Vitale. You probably have heard this story—he asked me what I wanted out of life and I answered, "I just want to pay my frickin' rent."

There's more to the story. He asked me, "what are you doing to be successful in the music business? How many press releases do you send out a week? What sort of advertising do you do? Are you building a mailing list of people who came to your shows? Are you in contact with labels, publishers, music press and agents who could help you get to the next level?"

I wasn't doing any of that. I was waiting for the rockstar fairy to fly by and sprinkle me with pixie dust, I guess.

I was broke. That was old news. I was broke and *it was my own damn fault*. That was an epiphany. Whoa!

Then Joe snuck me into a seminar he put on in Austin. I discovered Internet Marketing just about the time I discovered that I was responsible for my own income. It took a few years, a lot of work, some dumb mistakes and a lot of help—but, one day I looked up and I was, by my standards, rich. Then came the seminars, book deals, coaching programs, etc.

But, it all started with me realizing that I was responsible for my own income. Not my parents. Not the government. Not my girlfriend. Not society. Me.

That simple realization was the turning point. Try it.

For me, the vehicle was Internet Marketing. It's not for everybody. For a long time I thought it was. It was so right for me I figured it would be right for everybody.

Wrong.

Here's some things about Internet Marketing you should know.

1. You work alone. Mostly. Especially at first. If you're not comfortable with your own company and need people around

to motivate you, go get a job.

2. You work with your face stuck in a computer screen. I have two computers here in my office, another in the living room so I can work while I talk with Betsy. An iPad, so I can work from anywhere—and I never leave home without it. An iPhone—Last Tuesday I pulled over to the side of the highway between Junction and Fredricksburg, logged onto PayPal from my iPhone, and paid one of my employees who was in a jam and needed an advance. Then, I checked that day's sales, scanned Facebook, read and responded to a few emails—then, got back on the road. Internet Marketing is like that. If you don't like computers, you won't like Internet Marketing.
3. The scenery changes fast. Tools that I rely on today didn't exist a couple of years ago. Sales pages that converted like gangbusters last year have stopped converting—and must be changed fast. Channels like Facebook, iTunes, YouTube, Amazon, etc. are where the action is. SEO rules change constantly—stuff that was OK yesterday gets you slapped hard today. If you like doing the same thing over and over in a safe environment that never changes, you're gonna hate Internet Marketing. The only thing that stays the same around here is the constantly increasing rate of change.
4. You don't get a paycheck. Even the best entrepreneurs have to deal with wild swings in income. I deal with this by keeping my burn rate relatively low, so that even in my slowest month I can break even. It takes discipline and the Internet Marketing highway is strewn with the smoldering wrecks of marketers who based their expenses on their income when times were good—and then crashed and burned when they had a bad month. It only takes one bad month to wipe you out. If that scares you, get a job.
5. The higher your profile, the more haters you get. If you can't take criticism, this ain't for you. A sub-set of this is that the more sales you make the more refunds you have to process.

The more customers you have, the more unhappy customers you have. Of course, you do everything you can to keep this to a minimum but, as John Carlton says, "If you don't have at least a 5% refund rate, you're not really trying." 5% of a thousand sales is 50 unsatisfied customers. Of course, if you never launch a product and never make any sales, you never have any unsatisfied customers. If you're totally unknown you'll never have any haters. *Thick skin + good karma = happy Internet Marketer.*

Finally, remember this: you can be as happy and as rich as you want to be IF you recognize that your happiness and wealth are your responsibility.

MAGIC

GOING FOR IT

The rehearsal hall was in a converted motel attached to the Austin Opry House. A few years earlier, Willie Nelson had bought the property and dropped some of that outlaw country money on making a place for music to happen.

My band (but not me) had been signed by the same management company that handled Z.Z. Top, which was a mixed blessing. But, they did provide a rehearsal room, a Dodge van, and some nice gigs. A tour with Cheap Trick was coming up and we needed to get our show together.

My friends were at the Armadillo World Headquarters drinking beer and watching great music shows. I was stuck in a room with three other sweaty musicians practicing for a future that might never arrive.

That kinda sucked.

Fast forward a couple of months: the tour happened and I found myself on huge stages playing to tens of thousands of people. Watching Cheap Trick from the side of the stage, partying backstage with the various rock stars who came by to visit, and building memories that still make me smile. That made the hours of rehearsal and the deferred partying worth it.

Rewind back to the rehearsals. The renovation of the rehearsal hall pretty much consisted of throwing away the furniture. Walking out of our rehearsal room and looking around, the walls and carpet still looked like a cheap hotel.

But, there was magic in the air.

Walking down the hall, I could hear Chris Geppert and his band, Christopher Cross, working on the tunes that would soon become their first album. Chris won five grammys for that one, beating out Pink Floyd's *The Wall* album.

In the next room, Eric Johnson was working on his album, *Seven Worlds*, and redefining guitar playing. He wouldn't win a grammy until 1991, but while he was waiting for his contract to expire, he played on several gold and platinum records, toured the world, and became every guitar player's favorite guitar player.

Up a few steps and to the left, Stevie Ray Vaughan and Double Trouble were perfecting their rocking blues. They went on to sell over eleven million records and win a grammy.

Something was going on. But, was it magic?

A year earlier, I'd been playing in a lame country cover band in Kerrville, Texas.

Christopher Cross was one of several more or less interchangeable "frat bands" that played cover tunes for drunk college kids. Eric Johnson played bars with the Electromagnets. We all knew he was good, but nobody predicted he'd be an international superstar.

Stevie Ray Vaughan had been playing with blues bands in Austin at Antones and other blues clubs. To be honest, there were probably half a dozen or more guitar players in Austin at that time who played rockin' blues like Stevie.

What changed?

How did I go from playing to twenty or thirty drunks in dumpy bars to playing to twenty thousand people a night?

How did Chris go from playing frat parties to having the number one album in the world?

How did Eric go from playing little bars in Austin to being the guitar world's hero?

And Stevie—especially Stevie—how did he differentiate himself from all the other Texas guitar slingers to become the best-known guitarist of his generation?

What changed?

I can only speak from my own experience, but from talking to the others and watching them I know we all went through the same process.

We went for it.

What does that mean?

We started taking ourselves seriously. Instead of doing the least amount of work to get through the gig, we started paying attention to details. Tone, time, gear, chops—it all adds up.

Remember, at this point in time none of us were making any money. Opening acts don't get paid in anything but "exposure," and exposure doesn't buy gas, food, guitar strings or hotel rooms. If you add rent, utilities and living expenses to the equation, it just doesn't make any sense.

That's why most musicians slog along at their day jobs and show up at the gig tired, unrehearsed, and sloppy.

But when you're going for it you're not looking at where you are, you're looking at where you're going.

It's a subtle thing. The look in the eyes is different. The attitude is different. You may be playing to twenty people that night, but you're playing as if twenty thousand were watching because that's where you're going

I've never known a musician who went for it who didn't eventually succeed.

Why am I talking about musicians? Because the same "going for it" philosophy applies to Internet Marketing.

I decided from my very first exposure to Internet Marketing that I was "going for it." At my first seminar I hung out with the speakers and realized that they were "just folk." They weren't supernatural. But, they were speaking from the stage at a seminar and I was in the audience.

I attended that first seminar with a friend who had been dabbling in Internet Marketing for a year or so. Neither of us could afford to stay at the hotel where the seminar was held. During the ride home I told him I was going to be on that stage next year. I could do this. I was going for it.

Later, at other seminars, I met the other members of my class. Today, a few of them are household names. Most of them are back at their day jobs or still working on their first product. You can tell who's going for it and who's just coasting.

Just like musicians, Internet Marketers who go for it pretty much always succeed.

There are constraints: personality, risk aversion, bandwidth, talent, work ethic—those differences separate six figures a year from seven and eight figures a year.

I've noticed it through the years at seminars. I'll see somebody at a few seminars and they'll be just like everybody else—just coasting—talking about what they're *going* to do. And then something changes. They decide to go for it. You can see it in their eyes.

At the next seminar, instead of talking about what they're *going* to do, they're talking about what they've *done* and what they're *doing*. Instead of joining another coaching program or buying another product, they're running their own coaching program and selling their *own* products.

Success is a combination of outer game and inner game. The outer game is easy. You already know what to do. My blog alone has enough Internet Marketing training on it to get you to your first hundred thousand dollar year.

Here's the Internet Marketing outer game in a nutshell: you need something to sell and people to sell to. Websites, autoresponders, shopping carts—the rest—is just details. Read the first part of this book for more information about that.

The outer game stuff is easy but actually doing it requires a strong inner game.

The big inner game change happens when you take responsibility for your own life and your own success. You don't need anyone's permission to be successful. You don't have to get in line and wait for your turn.

You decide where you're going and you go there. It's that simple.

You blog even though you think nobody's reading because where you're going thousands of people read your blog regularly.

When you get an idea for a product, you make and market it. You don't worry about the competition. You don't let the fact that some alleged guru already did one in that niche slow you down. You realize your customers are relying on you to provide solutions for them. Where you're going, you've got thousands of customers relying on you.

When you get a glimpse of where the business is going, you jump to the front of the line—even if you're standing there alone. The fact that everybody else is going left when you think the market is going right doesn't mean you're wrong. In fact, it may mean that you get there first.

You don't look over your shoulder. You don't wonder what some superstar marketer might say about your product or promotion or blog post. That person is *not* your customer.

Sometimes going for it sucks. The Superbowl is on and you have a sales letter to write. Which one is it going to be? Everybody's going to the Continental Club to see Red Volkhart and you have an autoresponder series to crank out for tomorrow's promotion. What are you going to do?

That's the difference between going for it and not. It's also the difference between success and failure.

Whether it's "all your friends are out partying and you're practicing with your band," or "the Superbowl is on and you're stuck in your office or a coffee shop writing a sales letter," you've got a choice to make. Are you going for it or not?

Fade into Antone's, a blues bar in Austin. It's a Thursday night in the early '80s, almost closing time. I'm playing with the W.C. Clark Blues Review. Chris Layton and Tommy Shannon, who play in Double Trouble, are sitting in because our regular drummer and bass player have other gigs and Chris and Tommy can use the twenty bucks.

In the dark club that can comfortably hold a few hundred, through the smoke I can see ten or twelve people scattered around. Drinking, talking, not really paying a lot of attention to the band.

Stevie Ray Vaughan slopes into the club. He pulled up in the equipment truck.

When Chris and Tommy get off stage they're driving to Dallas for their gig tomorrow night. This is long before Stevie Ray and Double Trouble became household names. They were just one more blues band from Austin.

W.C. asks Stevie Ray if he'd like to sit in. He goes out to the truck and brings in a battered Stratocaster and plugs into W.C.'s amplifier.

Stevie Ray turns to me. "*Things I Used To Do*, in A flat," he says.

Then he closes his eyes, juts out his chin, and Antone's fades away. He's playing to fifty thousand people in Alpine Valley. Every note comes from his heart. He sings as if he's pleading for his life and the firing squad is just ten paces away. The music swirls, crescendos, drops to a whisper, and then thunders like a Texas tornado.

It's infectious. I feel the stage lights. I hear the roar of the crowd.

Stevie Ray is almost levitating. He's lost in the music and we're lost with him.

He's not playing where he is. He's playing where he's *going*. And, that's the secret to the inner game of Internet Marketing. Actually, that's the secret. Full stop.

If you're going to do it, do it.

Write every blog post as if your life depended on it. Design every product as if you were going to die tonight and your chance of getting into heaven depends on that product. Write every email as if it was your last chance—ever—of getting your point across.

Because, where *you're* going, what you do and what you say is important.

Go for it.

I originally wrote this as a chapter in Connie Ragen Green and Geoff Hoff's book, *The Inner Game of Internet Marketing.*

HOW TO PROGRAM YOURSELF TO ATTRACT MORE MONEY

Dr. Joe Vitale

My father taught me that the best way to double my money was to fold it over and put it back in my pocket. He also taught me that the best friend I would ever have is that dollar bill in my pocket. Interestingly enough, I never made much money as long as I believed his limited thinking folk wisdom. I had to do a lot of deprogramming to become wealthy.

Let me explain.

Last year I interviewed Steve G. Jones, celebrity hypnotherapist and my partner on several projects, such as Wealth Trigger I and II, and the Law of Attraction Practitioner Certification course. I found him fascinating and insightful.

One key principle from our interview is worth sharing with you here. Steve pointed out that your subconscious mind looks for and offers you proof for your thoughts. That may or may not be news to you. But let's look at it in real life terms, and specifically in how it can help you attract more money, and see how it ties in to what you attract into your life.

When a person says, "It's not possible for me to attract love into my life because all the good ones are taken," their subconscious mind begins to look around for evidence to support that belief.

They may then find themselves attracted to a person, only to get more information and discover the person is not ideal for one reason or another. Then the person with the belief "all the good ones are taken" announces, "See! All the good ones are taken!"

Of course, that's not true. Not in objective reality terms. After all, there are seven billion people on the planet. Surely there's a match for the person seeking love.

But let's dial in on this and take a closer look.

When you say, "I can't attract more money" — or anything along the lines of "It won't happen for me" — then you are simply delivering a belief to your subconscious. Your inner mind will then do what it is designed to do: prove your belief is true.

Even if you say, "It's obvious the world is suffering financially," or "Making money today is harder as the competition is so thick" or "I must be destined to struggle," all you are really stating are your beliefs.

Are the beliefs really true?

Are they measurable as facts that we can all agree on?

NO!

Do you see how important this is?

It means what you are telling yourself and accepting as true will become true in your own life if you continue to believe it! It means you have to become very sensitive to how you think. When I — or anyone — suggests you can have, do, or be more, what is your first thought? If it's anything like, "Hogwash! You are just selling hope and it will never happen!," then you are of course commanding your own mind to prove your own limiting belief to you!

But it's not objective reality.

These days I sometimes do consulting with people. I constantly hear them voice beliefs they don't realize are beliefs. They think their statements are clear observations of reality. They think their observations of reality are reality. But that isn't always so.

This is why a coach is so crucial. It's why I started Miracles Coaching years ago. You need someone to hear your statements and point them out to you, help you question them, and then release them or replace them.

My interview with Steve really made me aware that none of us listen to our language closely enough. I sometimes catch myself complaining or stating a limiting belief. I have to pause and ask myself, "Is the belief true in objective reality?"

In other words, is it a fact we can all agree on and even measure?

More often than not, it isn't.

Years ago, when I trained with famed bodybuilder and Olympia winner Frank Zane, I was urged to watch my mouth. Frank would tell me, "I pay attention to how people speak. Your statements are usually empowering, but when you got under the squat rack, you started to say you couldn't do it."

He was right.

Frank wanted me to learn that my thoughts were leading me to create my own limitations. My statements about what was possible were in fact programming me to expect the very thing I declared. I was programming a robot: me.

I'm inviting you to monitor your thoughts and your language. What you say is programming you. As Steve pointed out in our in-depth interview, your words are speaking reality into being. But the reality you speak is one fabricated because of what you speak.

Here's what Steve suggests you do right now to remedy this:

Speak as if what you want is already true. "I am a multimillionaire." "I am in love with the perfect person for me." "I am healthy." You get to choose. Make it now, present tense, and positive.

Watch for clues. Your subconscious will hear your new language and begin to offer evidence for it. It will, in a sense, test you. Be sure to take action on the opportunities that arise, to prove you are becoming that which you speak you already are.

Be that person. In other words, feel as though you already are what you said. Your emotion will stir motion in and around you to bring the desired state into being.

As you review this post, what comes to mind?

What are your thoughts right now?

Do you believe you can reprogram your mind?

Do you believe you can have, do, or be virtually anything? Do you believe you can attract more money this year and in the future?

This is all part of the process of deprogramming the mental robot in you. It's about freeing yourself of limitations. How you answer reveals your beliefs, not objective reality. You can remain programmed by circumstances and upbringing and past beliefs; or you can begin the process to take control right now and reprogram yourself for what you want.

My father meant well, but his advice was actually nothing more than his expressed belief system. When I left those old beliefs behind, my wealth began to expand.

Remember, your subconscious mind will look for evidence to prove what you believe and expect.

So, what would be really good for you to believe about money right now?

Dr. Joe "Mr fire!" Vitale is the world famous author of numerours bestselling books, from *The Attractor Factor* to *Zero Limits*. He's also a movie star, being in several moves, including *The Secret*, and he's a musician, with five albums of original music available.

His main website is www.JoeVitale.com.

YOUR RELATIONSHIP WITH MONEY AND SUCCESS

Steve G. Jones

Hi, I'm Steve G. Jones, Clinical Hypnotherapist, and before I begin exploring more about your relationship with money and success, I want to tell you a little about myself. I've spent years in education, earning a Bachelor's degree in Psychology from the University of Florida, a Master's in Education from Armstrong Atlantic State University, and a Doctorate in Education from Georgia South University. I'm a certified clinical hypnotherapist, serve as President of the American Alliance of Hypnotists, and am a member of both the American Board of Hypnotherapy and the National Guild of Hypnotists.

With over two decades of experience in hypnotherapy, I've been fortunate enough to work with people across a broad spectrum, from celebrities to professional athletes and Fortune 500 executives, in order to help them increase their income, boost their confidence, unblock barriers and enrich their lives. From my office in Beverly Hills, I worked with people like Tom Mankiewicz, the writer of *Superman* and many James Bond films, as well as Jeraldine Saunders, the creator of *The Love Boat*. I have been interviewed on national news networks such as CNN and

Fox News, and frequently travel around the world to visit with clients and teach classes on hypnotherapy.

This is not meant to be boastful, but rather to impress upon you that I am not only fully certified and qualified, but also keenly experienced in the field of helping to guide others to their success. I'm happy to share with you my wealth of experience and knowledge to explore ways to help improve your life.

In the Wealth Trigger program I produced with Joe Vitale, we explored the relationship one has with wealth. I'd like to take a moment to underscore one of the key points from that program as it tends to lead much of one's thinking with regards to money and success. Your relationship with success and mindset about wealth will ultimately work to define the outcome of your endeavors.

The pursuit and gain of money and success is not a sin. Let me repeat that: having money and success is not a sin. Remember being told that, "Money is the root of all evil"? Where, and more importantly, why, did we learn that? Many of us are conditioned through either our upbringing, social strata or environment at large to believe that there are limitations to our success in life. That simply isn't the case, nor is achieving those goals and pushing ourselves for even greater gains. It is okay to be successful. It is okay to make, have and share wealth.

Achieving success will allow you to share that success with those around you. The pursuit of your own success can become a fortuitous virus in your life, spreading from your own experience into those around you. As you become successful, your immediate friends and family begin to feel the impact of that positive energy and wealth. Your success impacts those that you do business with as you create more opportunity and ideas. Your success leaves a mark on your community as you're able to contribute more time, energy and yes, money to the programs and people around you.

These are all good things. I would encourage you to meditate on your current relationship with success and try to discover if there is any inner monologue that might be blocking your road to improving your life. Is there some script inside of you that says, "I deserve to be happy and have a good life, but not too good"?

Do you find yourself getting complacent once you've reached a certain level of professional or financial comfort?

Challenge that thinking. Realize that the only limitation to your success in life is your own approach. Your relationship with success is defined by your own understanding of what it means to be successful within your own life.

If you find that your subconscious mind is steadfastly locked on limiting your success, or that you're regularly putting barriers in your own way to stifle your own growth and prosperity, consider exploring hypnosis as a tool to make a positive change in your life. In my online programs, available at stevegjones.com, I offer tools that will speak to that subconscious mind and help reprogram your mindset about success. Programs like Discover Abundance, Program Yourself for Wealth and Unlimited Wealth Hypnosis and Hypnotherapy help you take control of your life through hypnosis and power your mind through hypnosis to affect change in your life with positive messaging.

Have you visualized yourself being successful? Many of us may think, "Someday I'm going to be wealthy," but then don't invest much energy in imagining what that wealth would actually mean within our lives. By taking the time to actually envision that success, to picture what wealth and prosperity would bring into our lives, we're creating an image of a potential self within our minds that helps to inform our subconscious mind that yes, success is possible. Visualize what an outstanding life you would have if all of your dreams were realized, if every mark of success and wealth had been achieved. Would you be on a beach in the Caribbean right now, having whisked your family away for a surprise vacation? Or maybe driving down the Autobahn through Bavaria in that luxury sports car you've always wanted? Perhaps it's an even closer goal of living in a beautiful house where your children have acres of land to play in and you wake up to the most breathtaking view every morning.

The point is to give those goals and dreams a real place in your mind, to envision your desired life in a real way. By creating that image you're helping to desensitize yourself to the subconscious fears that may be blocking your path to success. You may not even realize that you've carried around a fear of failure, or a fear of having money or success. In telling yourself that it's okay to be successful, that it's going to feel wonderful to achieve those goals and live a life of wealth and success, you're training your mind to accept and pursue that prosperity. You are showing your subconscious self that money is going to allow you to live a bigger life, to have more opportunities, to be a bigger and better you that has the ability to express your success in so many new and amazing ways.

It's also important to understand that there are opportunities for success and wealth at every turn. Years ago, and specifically before the dawn of the computer age, money was made in fairly traditional platforms: you'd shuffle off to a brick-and-mortar establishment day in and day out to earn your living and provide for your family and yourself through biweekly paychecks. Many of us still do that of course, but our interconnected and globally-linked modern world has opened up a new playground for wealth opportunities.

The next time you're at the coffee shop, take a look around at all of the people sitting in front of a computer. They've probably just paid over $5 for a drink, may be wearing tennis shoes having just finished a morning jog, or might have on a beautiful sundress in preparation for a picnic in the park later. It's a Tuesday mid-morning, and a fair number of those people will be working. They're sitting there comfortably and not only enjoying their lives but also making money.

Your opportunity for wealth is not linked to any one geographical location. With our technology, you are now available and free to explore the world around you and still support your life financially. By being open to those opportunities around you that allow you to think and work creatively, you're also opening doors to experience life in a new way. Many global corporations are beginning to understand the importance of this flexibility as well. With companies now offering their employees the freedom to work remotely—sometimes simply from a home office when a child is sick, but also while travelling—executives have learned that their staff tends to be happier, and consequently more productive, when they're given the flexibility to push back from the cubicle and explore work within the comfort of their own life.

Similarly, you are free at every moment in your life to redefine and reinvigorate your approach to making money. If you're not happy or fulfilled getting up every day before dawn and driving for over an hour through congested traffic to sit behind a desk until the sun begins to set again, you have the freedom to challenge yourself to find or create a new opportunity to make money. This can be as simple as finding an established agency or person that has a need for what you can provide, or creating that opportunity for yourself and defining what it is that you want to do, then finding a way to market yourself and make money at it.

Julia Cameron, the author of *The Artist's Way*, wrote that, "When we do what we are meant to do, money comes to us, doors open for us, we feel useful, and the work we do feels like play to us." Think about that. Money isn't the goal, it is the means by which your life and happiness is bolstered. It allows you to be successful and share that success with the world around you. Money is a tool that is instrumental in impacting all facets of your life: your general wellbeing, your relationships, your career, your experiences and your opportunities.

You are responsible for your relationship with success. No -one or -thing is going to reposition your life for you. You have the power and the tools at your disposal to take charge of your own success, to chisel a life out for yourself that is fulfilling and meaningful. There are no apologies due when you take control of your own success and create opportunities within your own life to achieve your goals, live happily, and make a positive impact on the world around you. When you've positioned yourself for success and happiness, when you're making money in a way that is rewarding both financially and personally, you're creating a positive energy in your own life that is transferrable to everything around you.

The money you make is an energy that can flow from any source. It's not a static block of value. Money is inherently transferrable, and I don't mean simply the transaction of moving funds from accounts or tendering payment for a service or product. The great entrepreneur Harold Honickman, leader of one of the nation's largest privately owned bottling and distribution organizations, said that, "Wealth is a great thing to have and a great thing to share."

It's that understanding that wealth and money are transient values that helps drive true success. After the Great Depression, the United States saw a widespread mindset of fear around money, and to a degree, given the recent economic struggles both within the United States and on a more global level, we're seeing a level of that discomfort now.

Perhaps you saw your neighbor lose their house through foreclosure and it's created a fear within your own life that the same thing might happen to you. Or maybe your spouse was laid off from the job they've had for decades because of company downsizing and now everything feels like it's a race to gather the funds every month just to pay your bills. It's those fears that can become crippling to your success. You can become so afraid of running out of money that you don't enjoy the money that you have.

After a period of experiencing financial challenges, of feeling like there is not enough or struggling to pay for bills, it's easy to develop a fear of money. There is a fear of losing money, of not making enough money, of disbursing money in ways that will leave you without the resources that you need to survive. And it's that fear that creates a wall, either consciously or subconsciously, around that energy that would actually bring you more money.

If you exist on a mental plane where money becomes a survivalist weapon and the absence of money, to any degree, initiates a panicked response within your psyche, it's time to reposition your thoughts and to find a healthier way of understanding money and success. Money shouldn't use you; you should use money. Unblocking your fears around money will open new doors of success into your life, and you'll be grateful for the opportunities that money affords instead of fearing whatever losses you can imagine around it.

It's important to understand that money is an energy, and to be open to that influence within your life. If you are afraid to make money, you will be blocking yourself from those opportunities to make new gains in your life. And without allowing that energy into your life, you will then not have the means to share that energy with those around you.

Let's be clear: money will not buy you true happiness. Money can't buy you true love or peace of mind, it won't create a family or a lifetime of joy. Your relationship with money, however, can help you achieve the priceless riches available to you. If you enjoy a truly healthy relationship with money, receiving it with gratitude and giving it with pleasure, you'll have unlocked a key to allowing that energy to flow unimpeded through your life. As that energy flows, you will find an abundance of prosperity around you, which affords the opportunity to embrace your true happiness.

How you relate to money is just as important as how you relate to the people and things you care about. Creating a healthy relationship with money, taking the time to explore your understanding of the implications of money in your life and discovering how it fits into your experiences, will help create a healthy companion of money. Just as death and taxes are eternal mainstays in the human condition, money too becomes a lifelong partner, and having a symbiotic relationship with money will help ease any burden you feel with regards to your experience with success and wealth.

"Financial health is having a conscious and purposeful relationship with money that is satisfying and isn't overly stressful," said Brad Klontz, PsyD, a financial psychologist and director of research at H&R Block Dollars & Sense. Remember that money is the means, and that in making and saving it you are able to make yourself, and the people you love, calm and comfortable.

Dan Millman, author of *The Peaceful Warrior's Way*, also said, "Money is neither my god nor my devil. It is a form of energy that tends to make us more of who we really are, whether it's greedy or loving."

I encourage you to explore your relationship with money, unlock those opportunities for wealth around you, and explore your true potential for success. You are welcome to visit my website at http://stevegjones.com where you will find 22 books on hypnotherapy and over 3,000 hypnosis recordings available as downloadable mp3s or CDs. These recordings will program your mind to achieve your goals and empower your life. I also have audio books available where I am sharing with you, in a very dynamic way, techniques that you can use to improve your life and the way you do things.

HOW TAPPING CAN HELP YOU DEAL WITH YOUR ENTREPRENEURIAL FEARS

Nick Ortner

Are you finally ready to be free?

If, through reading this book, you have fully committed yourself to new levels of productivity and abundance on your own terms, then congratulations; you've just set off on quite possibly the most important adventure of your life. It's downright thrilling, and maybe even a little scary.

What if it's very scary?

I bring this up because I've seen so many people set off in the direction of their dreams only to return with a whimper soon afterwards. Sadly, it's not because they failed, but so often because they were scared of failure. That fear can trip you up as you're challenged along your path, and if you're not in the right frame of mind, it can seem like the end of the road. It doesn't have to be. Thankfully, there's a very simple way for you to deal with this. It's called Emotional Freedom Technique, or EFT for short. Commonly known as Tapping to those who use it all around the globe, EFT combines ancient principles of Traditional Chinese Medicine still used in acupuncture today with modern Western psychotherapy. Best of all, it's a modality you can practice on your own without a practitioner, extensive training or tools of any kind. It's easy. It's free. It is simply the most powerful personal development tool I know of.

Interestingly enough, it's through teaching, researching and spreading the word about EFT—in addition to using it on myself—that I've been able to unlock my own personal abundance. Allow me to break down just how that happened, and then we'll get into how it can turn your life around as it did mine.

In what I like to call a former life, I worked in the real estate industry, and any success I had was matched only by my deep dissatisfaction. Come 2007 on through 2008 however, the scales finally tipped in favor of this malaise when the economy went bust.

I already knew about Tapping at this point, and was even working with a few clients and helping them through their personal struggles with weight trouble, financial difficulties and even illness. Still, I hadn't fully unlocked its power in my life or fully committed to making a career with it. Now however, I was at the crossroads.

Through Tapping, I was able to repurpose my life, to come to the realization that I didn't want to be in real estate at all, and that I could never outrun the stress or dissatisfaction it brought me with any amount of "success" it produced in my life. I needed to come to that success on my own terms in a way that was fulfilling to me and helped others at the same time. By tapping on myself, I was able to acknowledge and ultimately dissolve the many fears that had tethered me to this unhappy profession. It seems so obvious now, but what I saw was that the answer was actually tapping itself!

That's when things really got fun, though no less challenging.

Along with my sister and my best friend, we embarked on a filmmaking adventure, setting out to produce a documentary about the wonders of tapping. We traveled across the country, documenting cases and speaking with experts. We exhausted ourselves and maxed out our credit cards in the process. In many ways, it was more taxing than my real estate work, but it was so much more fulfilling.

And it paid off. We christened the film *Try It On Everything!* and later renamed it *The Tapping Solution*. It was a great success, and launched the business I run today. I continue to work very hard, but my life has never been this utterly amazing.

Best of all, our company is run by wonderful employees who work remotely all around the country. Our business is part of the new paradigm being heralded by this very book, a new way of doing things that allows everyone financial success without requiring them to strap into a desk and chair at a depressing office somewhere for 40 hours a week.

So, how can Tapping help you overcome the fears you're facing in your journey to this new employment nirvana?

First, you'll want to learn the basics of Tapping. The easiest and fastest way to do so is to check out the video on our homepage (http://thetappingsolution.com/how-to-tap.php). In it, my sister Jessica walks you through the meridian points used in acupuncture and acupressure that we also use in Tapping.

Once you've done that, return to this article and follow the script below. It's a basic Tapping routine that addresses the common fears one faces when embarking on an entrepreneurial adventure. Best of all, once you've completed it, you'll have a very clear sense of how you can create Tapping scripts of your own in the future.

As always, we start by conjuring up the fears and worries that are plaguing us. We don't want to run from them. They're the raw materials that we're going to alchemize into motivational fuel. Simply think about and fully feel what's bothering you. Hold it in your focus, rate its intensity on a scale from 1 to 10, and begin tapping on your Karate-chop point as you repeat the set-up phrases below, even if they feel a bit funny to you.

"Even though I'm worried that I can't make it, I deeply love and accept myself."

"Even though I feel as if I could never be a success, I deeply love and accept myself."

"Even though I'm scared that I don't have what it takes to make my entrepreneurial dreams come true, I deeply love and accept myself."

Starting this way allows us to feel safe expressing our fears, even if only subconsciously. We often feel that it's weak to admit these things, but this denial always comes back to get us in the end. Here we acknowledge and accept our feelings of limitation.

Next, move through the Tapping points while following the script below:

Eyebrow: "I don't know how I'm going to get this done." Side of Eye: "It seems impossible."

Under Eye: "What made me think I could be successful?" Under Nose: "What made me think I could take this risk?" Chin Point: "I'm so delusional."

Collar Bone: "I'm going to fail miserably."

Under Arm: "I'm hopeless."

Top of Head: "Everyone who thought I was crazy was absolutely right."

Take a deep breath, now start again at the eyebrow: Eyebrow: "This is the hardest thing I've ever done."

Side of Eye: "I should have played it safe."

Under Eye: "What a waste of time."

Under Nose: "I'm washed up."

Chin Point: "I'm going to end up an utter failure."

Collar Bone: "I'm going to be the laughing stock of all my peers."

Under Arm: "I simply don't know what I'm doing."

Top of Head: "I'm a failure."

Take another deep breath. How are you feeling? Although it would have been difficult to verbally address those feelings, you might surprisingly be feeling a bit calmer, slightly more settled. This is because you weren't repressing those feelings; if they stay bottled up inside they can lead to anxiety, stress, trouble sleeping, even physical symptoms. You have to let them out.

Rate how you're feeling. Has it decreased any? If it hasn't, repeat this routine a few times until your clocking in at a 2 or lower. Also feel free to add any insights about your emotions or things that happened in your past that arose while you were tapping. These are likely deep-seated feelings that are influencing how you've been feeling recently.

Once you've made it down to a 2 or lower, get ready to tap again. Now we're going to focus on "installing" some positive feelings that will aid you on your mission.

Eyebrow: "I've been feeling scared, but I can do this." Side of Eye: "Who am I kidding? I can't get this done." Under Eye: "No, I can. I really can."

Under Nose: "Feeling scared is only natural."

Chin Point: "I know I can overcome these fears." Collar Bone: "I can get it all done."

Under Arm: "I may not have all the answers right now." Top of Head: "But I can figure them out."

Eyebrow: "I am smart and industrious enough to find my way." Side of Eye: "I have what it takes."

Under Eye: "I've always had it."

Chin Point: "I can live and work on my own terms."

Collar Bone: "I can bring success into my life without slaving my life away."

Under Arm: "This is do-able."

Top of Head: "I am getting it done. I'm going to win."

It's really that simple. Repeat this whole process whenever you see fit, be it once a week or twice a day. I promise you that it will make a radical difference in your life. It will transform you as it did me.

Along your journey, you'll hear so much about the power of positive thought, and while it's true, the part that's almost always left out is the essential need to fully address and manage the negative thoughts and feelings that plague and hinder you.

It's only if you can get a grip on them that you can make room for the positivity-powered motivation that will get you where you need to be.

You can do this. I know because I did it myself. With EFT in your toolkit, you can tap into the drive, vision and focus to make your dreams come true…literally.

HOW MUCH IS ENOUGH?

One day, if you stick with Internet Marketing, you'll have to make a choice. You'll see an opportunity that, if you took it, would allow you to make a lot more money. But it's not fun. In fact, it may be downright distasteful.

I've had a few of those. I'll see an opening, and see that it will lead to serious dinosaur bucks, and…

Every time I've fallen for that I've regretted it. I've learned to see those for what they are and just say no. That's why I don't do any media interviews anymore, for example.

There are so many ways to make money in the IM field that *are* fun and ethical that I recommend listening to your gut. Get in touch with your feelings. When an opportunity comes along, take a minute to think about it.

We started out talking about balance. There are, believe it or not, some things more interesting than money. If you're good at the game, you'll make plenty of money. Really winning is doing it without compromising yourself and keeping it light and fun.

However, let me tell you a story. One day I casually mentioned a tax issue I was having to a guitar player friend of mine. He said, "My gawd, how much did you make last year?"

Like an idiot, I told him.

He looked at me with quite a bit of judgment and asked, "how much is enough?"

His position was that every dollar I made was taking a dollar away from some poor soul who needed it. He thought it was criminal that I was making so much more than the average worker.

What I tried to explain to him was that 1) there is an infinite amount of wealth in the world and 2) it wasn't about the money. If you successfully find a way to make money doing what you love, you're going to keep doing it because you love it. I'm long past sitting in front of my computer watching the "you've got mail" emails. I have friends who make my annual income every two weeks or so and they're working just as hard as they ever did.

It ain't about the money. It's about the love of the game. And, in my opinion, that's the key to living a balanced life. As Internet Marketers we're in a privileged position. We can make money from anywhere doing what we love. It's not for everybody. If it's for you, you'll know it. If you find that you love the game, play it to win. When it starts feeling like a treadmill, jump off. Just to prove that you can.

THE POWER OF THE MASTERMIND

Chuck Pennington

How do you think the world's most powerful, influential, and wealthy people got that way? Do you sometimes sit back and wonder what the secret handshake is? Have you ever driven through the "rich part of town" and wonder what these people do differently?

I know I have...and I've spent a pretty good amount of time figuring out what those people do that sets them apart from the from crowd, which, trust me, is somewhere you want to be.

The folks that are in this book know one of the most powerful secrets to success that has been proven to work time and again in all its different forms. Pat knows it, Joe knows it, those folks in the rich part of town know it, all the authors in this book know it and have used it to create the success they've experienced in their lives...they all know the power of the mastermind.

Masterminds have existed in many forms throughout history. Rockefeller, Wrigley, Ford, Ben Franklin and the rest of the founding fathers of the United States, and the list goes on down through the ages and continues into the future.

Pat understands this power so well that he made masterminding part of the famous UnSeminars he created. He wanted to make sure that his students got an infusion of this creative process and to go home knowing they had an extremely powerful tool in their quest to create an online business and make money from anywhere.

I've had the pleasure of running the UnSeminar mastermind sessions for Pat over the past few years and I have to tell you that I've seen a lot of some really cool transformations happen and a ton of new relationships form. Some of the groups that have been formed at an UnSeminar last months and years afterward.

But I must say the absolute coolest thing that I see happen the creative environment that swirls into existence during the first mastermind session. People all the sudden just light up like the sun. The massively creative element that is part of every human being gets ignited and just glows brighter and brighter from Friday morning till on Sunday folks are just exhausted with the energy flowing through them.

It's truly inspiring to be part of it. I feel lucky to have been the leader of these mastermind sessions. Well, I say leader…it more like having the fun of lighting the fuse to all the fireworks on the 4th of July. Once you light fuse, its just fun to watch and its absolutely beautiful.

Most everyone considers creativity to be the realm of artists, poets, and musicians and they hold the self image of actually being that "creative being" at arms length from themselves their entire lives. It's incredibly awe inspiring to see people coming to the realization that they to are creative beings. Not that they are artists, musicians, or poets, necessarily, but that they, in their own unique way, are that creative being. When folks don't feel creative to solve to problems in their lives they lack the ability create solutions and thus they fall powerless in a great number of areas of their lives…that's very unfulfilling way to live.

When I've seen people light up with creativity, they begin to realize that they can create more personal freedom in their lives. During the mastermind sessions, you can see shackles falling from tensioned bodies, light bulbs going off, wings sprouting, ideas and businesses being formed…it's truly incredible to witness. As I look out across the groups of people during the mastermind sessions and when I talk to the folks during the weekend, the sheer joy on their faces comes from the realization that they are creative. In what ever flavor that is for them, they found it, they found their creativity, they found their freedom.

I've said in every testimonial I've given for Pat's UnSeminars, the coolest thing that happens is the creation of the "UnSeminar Environment". I know that the mastermind sessions are the catalyst for that powerfully creative environment.

So, why do masterminds work?

I was a systems engineer for over 20 years, and just sitting down and talking a problem out, getting a different perspective on solutions is very valuable and if it doesn't completely solve the problem, get you going ion the right direction. It's because everyone comes to the table with ideas from a different angle than you are coming from.

I'm also a musician and songwriter and I've had home studios most everywhere I've lived. With today's technology especially, you can record all of the tracks by yourself. You record the drums and play them back while you record the guitar, and then the bass, and so on. Sure you can get an idea for a song recorded and possibly even do a good job at it, but it's so much more fun and I usually come out with a better song and recording when I work with my band or other musicians. Just the different energy and outlook adds to the seed of the idea and invariably makes it better.

In a mastermind where a group of people are dedicated to improving each other, you get a different perspective on your problems, on your issues, what kind of things you've been working on. It's just so valuable, because you don't get that in your everyday life.

The UnSeminar environment I spoke about earlier is about being in tune. It's about being in harmony with nature. Harmony of energy is everywhere in our lives. It's there in color. It's there in music. It's there in our relationships. It's there in our thoughts and how our thoughts become things.

Masterminds help you maintain this tune. It's like being a guitar player. You can have one of the finest Martin guitars in the world, and it's one of the best blues musicians in the world. But if the thing's completely out of tune, it's not going to sound very good. Being a blues musician, Pat knows how to retune a guitar very quickly to get it back in tune where it's going to sound beautiful.

That's what a mastermind does for you. It helps you tune those parts of your life that get out of tune.

All of that creates this creative environment. Where in your life do you get this kind of thing? Where do you show up in your life and get a group of people that just want to make sure you succeed and want to see you succeed to your fullest potential?

We normally don't get that; from our friends, from our family, from the self-talk we have, from the media, from the workplace. If we still have our day jobs, all that stuff is impinging upon your new creative environment. This environment is so important that you need some tools to protect it.

A mastermind is an internal firewall that helps you protect from the information that's going to detract you from your goals, from what you want and from what you really desire. When you start a new business or take on a significant life change on purpose a lot of folks around you will think you're nuts. Your group can help you get through that by providing you with support and ideas without blowing smoke up your butt.

A mastermind gives you trusted sources. You can go to these people and they will help you like no other people will, because they don't have any of the baggage that comes in with a lot of your personal relationships. They want you to succeed just like you want everyone in your group to.

It's also intrusion detection. If you go off in the weeds and you get some weird idea, your mastermind group's going to go, 'No,

"Don't go down that rabbit hole." So, its rabbit hole protection to keep you from getting off in the weeds.

Image you're a computer system. You always need new

knowledge. Internet marketing, just like anything else in life, is a constant learning curve. So you've always got to patch your systems with new and good information, and the mastermind helps you do that. If your group can't specifically solve your problem they can usually get you pointed in the right direction.

You're a systems designer and the system that you're designing is yourself. A mastermind group helps you run through that design process and helps you basically write good code. It keeps you in check. It keeps you from running bad routines in your life. It helps get you out and keep you of the weeds.

Your mind-brain combo is highly plastic and programmable. A lot of people give credence to go into the gym, and they lift a weight and their muscles get bigger and stronger. But yet, when they look at their mind, they don't think to use their mind to actually make these changes. Much like a personal trainer at the gym, a mastermind group can help you get stronger and more fit, mentally.

And so, your mastermind group, through this new perspective that you're going to get, helps you get those skills that you're going to need and iterate over ideas quickly and effectively. Not only making sure you get the right answers, but that you are asking the right questions.

Why would you ask the mastermind?

Why don't you just stew on it by yourself in your corner and get mad at yourself and frustrated? Because I kind of do that a little bit. I have an analytical mind, so it just goes and goes and goes....

So I can get distracted with my own self. If I stay inside myself too much, I'm going to go off in my own little rabbit hole, and I look up a couple of weeks later and I'm going to be behind on stuff that I really needed to get done, because I was off on some tangent.

I've had mastermind groups snap me out of that because part of the mastermind is accountability. You've got a place where you set your Smart Goals. If you're not getting your Smart Goals done every week, well there's something going on. There may be something else you need to ask the mastermind.

Your mastermind is a receptive audience. Its fertile soil to grow your new ideas, your new life, and it's always recreating a life that's ever better. Your mastermind's a safe harbor to develop your resolve and confidence. It's a place for positive reinforcement you don't normally get from friends, family, coworkers, and definitely not the media.

It's your personal consulting group you've got access to on a weekly basis. It's very likely that the group of people you're going to end up with have a far different skill set than you do. You're going to be able to take very good advantage of that.

So look around your life. Who around you wants you to succeed, to be free, and to enjoy your life and all it can be. Where have you ever sat in a group people and had that experience? It's an awesome feeling, and that's the same thing in a mastermind. You get your group of six to eight people, and it's a group of people that are dedicated to making each other's lives better, to helping each other.

The mastermind is like your band. It helps you be a rock star. It helps you be a bad ass. When you're creating products, stage presence, all the world's a stage, including the Internet. The stage presence factor; It's walking up on a stage and saying, "Look at me." It's walking up on a stage and playing guitar and saying, "There it is. That's your product." What do you create and when do you call it a product…That's your product presence.

Is this a product? Hell yeah, it's a product. Why? Because you say it is. That's it. I've had this conversation with a lot of people. It may be a small product. It may be a big product. It may be an inexpensive product. It may be a very expensive product. A three-page PDF can be a product simply because you say it is.

I was talking to Pat the other day. I've always had this idea of selling one single sentence for 37 bucks. I guarantee you will find 37 bucks worth of value in that sentence. He said sell it for $97. One sentence, I guarantee you it will make 97 bucks worth of difference in your life. Married or trying to have a relationship of any sort is a hot topic. The only reason that's not a product right this second is because I haven't said it is. So stage presence equals your product presence.

It is now a product at www.bestcomplimentever.com…just because I said so.

Your ability to stand up and say, "That product exists because I say it does." Masterminds will help you get there.

What are the different types of Masterminds?

There are a bunch of different types and styles of mastermind groups and meetings. The structured masterminds are best to start off with. Once you've experienced the structured types and have worked with a group for a while you can expand into longer more free form versions that suite the style and needs of the group. Some very high dollar, strategic mastermind sessions last over weekends or several days depending on the scope and needs of the group.

Here are few of the basic models to get you started:

- Structured – open topic
- Structured – single topic
- Expert – student
- Hot Seat

In a structured, open topic mastermind, you agree with the group on a set duration and then divide the time equally among the members. In this type of mastermind the members can bring any topic to the table they want to discuss. You come to the table with whatever you want to work with, and the group works with you on that.

There are structured masterminds with a single topic or specific intent; we created the Good Energy Movement in a mastermind where that that's all we did. There were seven of us in there, and it was based on how do we create the good energy movement? What we need to do? We all had different aspects of the movement we were working on and we got input from the group on the different aspects of the project.

In the beginning, and as a general rule, a time structure mastermind meeting will work best. If you've ever been in a bad business meeting that's gone on forever, that can happen at a poorly structured mastermind. If you haven't been working with the people or if it's a new group, you can get off in the weeds if you don't put any time constraints or any other kind of constraints on it. So they're good for getting started.

The expert-student mastermind is great for adding to your business and a back end product offering. You can offer a small group of student individualized attention by being the expert and your student have a time slot where they can ask you what ever they need to. The other student will benefit from hearing the answers as well. It also work well to bring in other experts as an added benefit.

The Hot-Seat is not for the faint of heart. It's where a single person gets in front of a panel of experts and works on the issues and goals of their business. You are generally open to a no-holds-barred discussion when you agree to this…so be ready.

How do I Mastermind?

Meeting in person is very powerful. Looking people in the eye and discussing your issues and goals has a huge impact on what you ask and what you get in return. When discussing uncomfortable topics or something that is exciting, body language plays a key role in determining what the mastermind delivers. It's also just easier to stay engaged during a face to face meeting.

All that being said, sometimes it's just impractical or impossible to be in the same room. There are several free conference call services that you can use to run your group meetings (I'll list them at the end of the chapter). There are no setup fees or monthly charges. You simply sign up and the service will email you a call in number and PIN code to enter. You then email that info to everyone you want on the call…simple and free!

In this crazy old world, folks are generally busy and sometimes are rushed just to get to the meeting place or on the phone to get on the call and so I've found that people often need to spin down and relax before being it the best state of mind to give and receive help.

I found that if we open the mastermind with this introduction, it's slightly meditative, I've jumped on the call right in time, and this opening gives you a little bit of meditative sort of release. You can certainly modify this intro to anything that relaxes you and your group.

I release myself to the mastermind because I am strong when I have others to help me.

I believe the combined intelligence of the mastermind creates a wisdom far beyond my own.

I understand that I will more easily create positive results in my life when I am open to looking at myself, my problems and opportunities from another's point of view.

I decide to release my desire totally in trust to the mastermind and I am open to accepting new possibilities.

I forgive myself for mistakes I have made. I also forgive others who have hurt me in the past so I can move into the future with a clean slate.

I ask the mastermind to hear what I really want; my goals, my dreams, my desires, and I hear my mastermind supporting me in MY fulfillment.

I know, relax and accept, believing that the working power of the mastermind will respond to my every need. I am grateful knowing this is so.

After the intro, each person in the group in the order of showing up will do a round of gratitude. A very simple, very short, very sweet statement of what the person is grateful for. "I'm grateful for every single person in this meeting today and energy they've shared this morning. Thank you very much", something very simple. Gratitude is so important in our daily lives, and that gives us an opportunity to show that gratitude and to get into that vibration.

After you do your round of gratitude, everybody gets their time slot. And if you're doing a seven-person mastermind in an hour, generally that's about seven minutes. So until you've gotten familiar with your group, you want to introduce yourself, spelling your name is slightly hypnotic, but it's optional. Did you complete your Smart Goal for the week? State the category of your question, and then ask your specific question.

When you're running a structured mastermind, you've only got seven minutes, so you don't want to go into a long story about, "Well, if I could do this, it would really be awesome," and you lead into it for about two or three minutes. You want to have a specific question. "I want to learn about list building, specifically, how can that create a freebie opt-in page in a WordPress blog?" So it's a very specific question.

If you meander about stuff, you're going to get vague answers, and the people in the mastermind aren't going to be able to effectively help you. So it's very good to have a specific category and a specific question in mind. Then you just rinse and repeat that for the folks in the group.

In the same order, after everybody's finished their mastermind session, in the same order you state your Smart Goal. The Smart Goal, you have to be able to have the specific, measurable, attainable, relevant, and time bound goal. It can't be, "I'm going to write some articles this week." How do you know you did that? "I'm going to write four articles by next Wednesday on widgets." That's specific, measurable, and time bound. You want to be able to know when you're done, pretty much.

And then next week, when you go back and say, "Did you finish your Smart Goal?" It's a yes or no answer. There's no judgment, just accountability to yourself.

At the end, once everybody has stated their Smart Goal, we have a closing that we read. And that kind of ties up the energy; it seals it up. It's a nice little package around the mastermind.

I now have a covenant in which it is agreed that the mastermind shall supply me with an abundance of all things necessary to live a success-filled and happy life. I dedicate myself to be of maximum service to my fellow human beings, to live in a manner that will set the highest example for others to follow and remain an open channel. I go forth with a spirit of enthusiasm, excitement and expectancy.

That's the closing of mastermind. This can also be modified to fit your group or if you don't like it, you can simply close the meeting without the statement. It's certainly not required, but I find it a nice way to end the meeting. The most important thing in all of this is that you take action and do it!

So those are the basic steps to having a successful mastermind meeting. Here's a recap.

The Basic Outline of the Mastermind meeting

Step 1—Introduction – 7 Mastermind Principles

Step 2—Round of Gratitude

- State your name, spell your name (till you get to know each other). State what you are grateful for. Each person states one thing they are grateful for right then, short and sweet.

Step 3—Each person gets their 7 minute time

- My name is ________________. (Saying and spelling your own name is slightly hypnotic)
- Spell your name the first few weeks or until everyone knows each other.
- Did you complete your S.M.A.R.T. goal for the week? (Yes or No) no explanation or reasons…just yes or no. (1st wk no answer of course)
- State a category for your question (keep it short and to the point)
- Ask your specific question (Be as specific and brief as possible) Rinse and repeat for each person

Step 4—SMART Goals

- In the same order that you did the Round of Gratitude and the Questions, go around and set your S.M.A.R.T. Goal for the week. If a person seems to have a vague goal ask, "How do you know you'll be done?" How will you measure it?

S.M.A.R.T. GOALS

S—Specific – what is the exact goal? Clarify and make it specific

M—Measurable – Each goal must be measurable, which allows you to see "forward movement."

A—Achievable – If you cannot achieve the goal, what point does it have?

R—Realistic – It must be something while it stretches your abilities; it is something you feel you can do.

T—Time Bound – A reasonable time limit set for accomplishing your goal.

Remember Goals are much more meaningful and much more likely to work if they are written down.

Step 5—Closing

- Here are some helpful hints for running a successful mastermind meeting:
- When you state your Smart Goal, it's a simple yes or no answer.
- In your seven-minute sessions, when you get your time, state the category and the question and state a very clear question that people can help you with, not a lot of back story, not a lot of rambling.

Choose one person to be the timekeeper and one person to be the moderator. So, one person can come in and write down the order of the people and make sure that you don't go over time. Timekeeper should give a one minute or 30 second "heads-up" when a person time is about up. Look for a brief lull in the conversation to do this. Try not to step on the conversation. Just say "one minute" or "thirty seconds"

If you are the facilitator or leader, try to keep things moving if they get bogged down or off topic. If somebody starts rambling or going off, you can kind of check and say, "Let's get a specific category and a specific question so that you can get the most help you can."

Start on time and if you commit to a group, respect their time by showing up. If you can't make or the schedule isn't working for you, let the group know.

Send out reminder emails to the group. Everyone gets busy, so a quick reminder often helps.

Put the meeting time and dates in your scheduling software so you get a reminder.

As facilitator, if someone is having a problem with getting a specific question out, help them along and keeps things moving. If the person starts to ramble, get them back on course by suggesting a topic or subject matter and try to lead them into a specific question to ask the mastermind group.

If a person asks a question and you get crickets or a big gaping silence, ask for input from the group.

When folks are setting their S.M.A.R.T. goals, help them to make sure they are realistic and measurable and that success can be answered with a simple yes or no.

Mastermind for fun and profit

Here are some situations where masterminding has proven to be very effective in solving problems and creating and extra stream of income.

Backend product offers. Have people pay you to help them implement your specific product or affiliate offer.

Coaching. Offer a general coaching program for a monthly fee.

Facilitating. Provide a service where you offer to run mastermind meetings and keep them organized.

Bring in guests. Bring in expert guests to your meetings as a way to keep thing lively and fresh. This also works well for affiliate offers.

Fund raising efforts. Masterminds are a great way to make sure you maximize your fund raising efforts for your cause, team, or group you want to help.

Causes or Movements. Want to bring awareness to your cause or start your own movement?

Bands and artist groups. You may want to put on a festival or showing in your community as way to expose folks to your work. You can get multiple bands or groups to work together through your community and beyond.

Business groups or Chamber of Commerce. Trade groups can benefit from using masterminding to increase business and visibility in your area. For example, all of the hair stylists and beauty solons could get together and have a make-over day in the town center. Or all of the health food store, message therapists, and chiropractors could get together on a wellness day for the community.

So how do I get started?

Decide to do it (sounds too simple, but that's where most people stop)

Decide what you want to accomplish.

Find your group…at least start it. Social media is a great place to find folks. You can start with just one or two other people and build from there. Meetup groups are good if you want to meet in person.

Set a definite schedule.

Show up. Respect other people's time.

Set SMART Goals

Work on those goals

Attend your scheduled mastermind meetings

I've put together a free Mastermind "getting started" pack that includes everything you need to get started with your group. You've gotten a lot of it just by reading this far, but there some additional reports and a cool one-page printout that you can use to make running your meetings easy and stress free.

You can everything you need to get started masterminding right here: http://www.MastermindBasics.com

Those free resources are also available in my "Personal Empowerment Starter Kit" at http://www.HarmonicThought.com.

Here are some free conference-calling services you can use to hold your meeting on the phone.

- http://www.freeconferencecall.com
- http://www.freeconference.com
- http://www.freeconferencing.com
- http://www.freeconferencecalling.com.

CHOOSING YOUR OWN TARGET

I've noticed that people need someone to look up to and someone to look down on. That's unfortunate. But, how do you know how you're doing if you don't compare yourself to something or someone?

Recently, I got a lesson in letting go of these comparisons. It changed my life in a good way.

The upstairs porch at Brewsters Pizza is one of the most delightful places on the planet, with an elevated, shaded area with room for maybe fifty people to stand or twenty to sit comfortably. There are tables and big, comfy chairs .

The view is stunning. To the left is the road to Devil's Backbone, a spectacular drive popular with sports car and motorcycle enthusiasts. Straight ahead you're looking over the Wimberley valley. Hills, trees, and spectacular sunsets stretch as far as the eye can see. The hills slope down to the Blanco River, which isn't really visible from the porch, but you can tell where it is.

The noise can be distracting. In addition to the sounds one would expect in an upscale pizza restaurant your peaceful reverie can be broken by Harleys and sports cars blatting down the hill—all of which would benefit from mufflers, in my opinion.

Recently, Dr. Joe Vitale and I had a late lunch on that porch. I'd been out of town for a month, visiting my off-the-grid cabin in Terlingua. In addition to being buddies, Joe and I are business partners so we get together every now and then to catch up on what we've been doing and to plan future adventures. Joe's fascinated by my stories of Terlingua. He says, "it's not just another world, it's another planet."

I won't bore you with the personal stuff, although I will share just one…while I was in Terlingua, my birthday came and went. Joe surprised me with a present—an Erlewine travel guitar, and not just any Erlewine travel guitar. This one was one of the ones that Mark Erlewine made himself in collaboration with ZZ Top's Billy Gibbons. It's a little jewel, precision designed and crafted out of natural wood. It looks like a toy, but is in fact a serious rock and roll implement of pleasure. I was delighted, and it now is displayed prominently along with the rest of my guitar collection.

So, let me set the stage. I'm sitting at a table on the elevated porch looking out over the hill country. Joe is to my right. In front of us are a couple of Vitale steaks, with trimmings. (Brewster's is a pizza joint, and one of the best in the galaxy. There are some off-menu items that Bruce can be persuaded to fix if you give him some lead time. The Vitale steak is one of those. It ain't a cheap thing, but it is possibly the best steak money can buy. Anywhere.)

Very nice cigars and very old scotch round out the table settings.

To my left sits Bruce Collie.

In a nutshell, I am surrounded by two of the most effective over-achievers on the planet. Joe is the author of 50+ books, a movie star, and one of the best Internet Marketers alive. Bruce is a former NFL star with two Superbowl rings. He's run successful construction businesses, invests successfully in real estate, and his current restaurant/brew-pub is a smashing success. These guys know success. It's where they live.

In the middle, there's me.

Here's where the lesson happens. I'm a real good guitar player, but I'm not as good as Joe Bonamassa, Eric Clapton, or Eric Johnson. I used to make records, and they're also good, but not as good as The Beatles.

That's always bothered me. No matter how well I did, no

matter how cool my gigs were, there was always someone who was doing better. U2, for example, make more money in one night than I made in my entire music career. Thinking like that can make you wonder why you bother.

Now, I'm also an author. I've written five books, two of which were best-sellers. In most gatherings of authors, I'd feel pretty successful. However, I'm sitting with a guy who has written 50+ books, many of which were best-sellers.

I'm also a pretty good Internet Marketer, and I teach Internet Marketing. However, there are Internet Marketers who make more money than I do, and in Internet Marketing, that's one of the ways we keep score. As a matter of fact, there are Internet Marketers who make as much money in a week as I do in a year. Joe's one of those.

It's kind of like being a reasonably good entertainer, and your buddy is Elvis. In the Internet Marketing world, Joe is Elvis. He's also a real nice guy. He'll listen with interest while I talk about what I'm doing. Then, he'll share what he's been up to.

Amazing promotions, trips to Russia, Poland and Chile, best-selling Nightingale Conant programs and books, and private masterminds with the top minds on the planet. Compared to Joe, I might as well have stayed in bed.

And then there's Bruce. I've done some interesting things, but nothing I've done compares with winning the Superbowl. In American iconography, that's about the coolest thing you *can* do. And Bruce did it twice.

After the steak, we fired up some amazing cigars, topped off our cups, and had a mini-mastermind meeting. Maybe it was the scotch that led me to bring up the subject, maybe it was the cigars, but I brought up the subject of comparison.

I told Joe and Bruce that I constantly compared myself to them and other successful people. And, in those comparisons, I didn't always come off as the uber-successful person that I wanted to. My question was, "who do you compare yourselves to?"

The answer surprised me. They both said, "I don't."

I asked for clarification. Everybody compares themself to somebody, right?

Bruce said, "I'm only competing with me." He then went on to talk about injuries, car wrecks, pins through bones, playing football games with broken bones, and businesses that seemed to want to fail. He viewed the apparent adversity as a challenge, and used those challenges to get stronger. When a business wasn't working, he either closed it or changed it and worked even harder to make it a success. Bottom line, he may fail, but not for long. The game ain't over till it's over, and ultimately, he's going to win.

Joe had a different take: "I look for projects that would be fun," he said. "I look for something new and interesting that I want to do, and then I do it."

I got the feeling that although Joe is very aware of what others in his industry are doing, he doesn't really look to others for inspiration. They're old news.

I also know Joe constantly asks himself the question, "what would be better than that?"

So, I suspect, based on years of observation, that he comes up with an initial idea that he thinks would be fun and profitable, and then plays the "what would be better" game with that idea.

There are people who are more successful than Bruce and Joe. The lesson for me is that they spend absolutely no time thinking about that.

That conversation took place a couple of weeks ago, and the more I reflect on it and learn the lessons from it the better I feel. Of course, The Beatles made better records than I did. However, thousands of people enjoy my music. It's OK that I wasn't as successful as they were—by a long shot. I made the best Pat O'Bryan records that I could make, and they stand on their own.

The same deal with guitar playing. Yes, when Eric Clapton closes his eyes and starts channeling a long dead blues master his playing is transcendent. At my best, I'll never be that good. And yet, I can make a blues band chug like a locomotive. I've watched the dance floor fill to capacity when I start laying down the blues.

I could always be a second rate Eric Clapton, but it's more fun and healthier for me to be a first-rate Pat O'Bryan.

And then there's Internet Marketing. Music can be a matter of taste and opinion. In IM, we keep score with money.

At one point, I looked at Joe and said, "how will I ever catch _______?" (fill in the blank with the name of a very successful Internet Marketer who I have been trying to "catch" since I started.)

Joe said, "you don't have to."

And I exhaled.

Over the next few weeks, I got it.

I'm not a better Internet Marketer because I make more money than one person, and another person isn't better than me because they make more money than I do. We're all who we are, and we're all competing with ourselves.

All we have to do is be the best we can be and that can look a lot of different ways.

For example, I not only run one of the best Internet Marketing coaching programs in the world, I run (I think) the cheapest Internet Marketing coaching program in the world. I could, and possibly should, charge much more. But, there are other benefits to me besides money. I get to work with absolute beginners who are just starting out. Beginners usually don't have a big budget, but by working with them, I can keep them from getting hurt—among other things. I don't do upsells to my coaching clients. I transparently show them what I do that works, what I've tried that didn't work, and help them achieve realistic goals that, over time, has brought some of them to pretty substantial success. That's success to me.

One day I was talking to Ray Wylie Hubbard, who is a pretty famous songwriter/performer and a neighbor. We're neighbors and have played some gigs together. I don't get to hang out with Ray and his lovely wife Judy as often as I'd like, but I always enjoy it when I do.

We were talking about success. Ray's pretty successful, but he's not as successful as, for example, his friend Willie Nelson.

Anyway, the way Ray put is was, "everybody else is ganged up shooting at that target over there," he said, pointing to his left. "I'm shooting at this one over here," he continued, pointing to his right.

In other words, you define your success.

To Ray, it's not about having the hot hit single of the moment. It's about creating the next great song, and adding it to a life's work that contains a lot of great songs, a stream of interesting gigs stretching decades into the past and, hopefully, into the future.

Ray, like Joe and Bruce, is very successful. They're successful because they define what success means to them, and don't let others define them or their success.

To me, that's remarkably liberating.

So, it's ok for me to take the night off to watch the sun set and the stars come out? It's ok to take a day off and go for a ride through the hill country with Betsy? It's ok to write a book that I want to write, instead of one I know will sell?

The answer is a resounding "yes!"

It's not about maximizing income. It's about maximizing life.

Once I got that, I felt like a huge weight had lifted. I decide what target I shoot at. Nobody else gets a vote.

Try it. See how that feels.

Here's the punch line. Once I stopped comparing myself to others and just set my own course, I started making more money.

Pick your own target. Define success your way. And then shoot for the bulls-eye.

You can't miss.

LEAVING THE BOAT ON THE SHORE

There's a Buddhist story about four travelers who used a boat to cross a stream that is worth reflecting on.

Once on the other side of the stream, they decided that a boat was a pretty useful thing to have so they picked it up and continued on their journey.

It turned out that if you're not crossing a river, a boat can be a drag on your journey. They carried it on their heads, so they couldn't really see where they were going. It was heavy, and it slowed them down.

Finally, someone pointed out to them that the boat was useful for crossing a body of water, but once you're on the other shore it's best to leave the boat behind.

Of course, that's a parable.

The boat can be a belief, or a defense mechanism that has outlived its usefulness, or a habit. Sometimes, we can find ourselves reacting to something happening based on experiences we lived through years ago. Those are all boats best left on the shore.

My favorite example of a boat is the famed "protestant work ethic."

I've heard people say, "he's a hard worker," as if that was a compliment. I find that confusing. Does his work give him pleasure? Does it bring him money and resources to make his world a better place? Or is it just work for the sake of being able to say that he worked hard, and is therefore a good person?

To me, work is a boat. The more interesting thing to focus on is "where is that boat taking me and am I there yet?" If it's not taking me where I want to go, I'm changing boats. If I'm "there," I'm dropping the boat.

The target I'm trying to hit by working is to make money. I'm looking for the work that most efficiently transfers funds into my bank account. The work isn't the target or the goal. It's the boat. Sometimes I have to change boats to get where I'm going.

It's easy to fall into the habit of doing the same thing over and over again. It's easy to lose sight of why you're doing it.

I've met Internet marketers who found something that worked—maybe they put up a website, bought adwords, and managed to make more from sales than the advertising cost. Then something changed. And, if there's one thing you can count on it's change. Sales went down. Their keywords got more expensive. So they put up more sales pages and bought more keywords. They worked really, really hard. And the harder they worked the more money they lost, and they were confused.

The confusion comes from focusing on the boat instead of the destination.

Where, precisely, are you going?

I've found that a lot of Internet Marketers focus on the boat. And they teach boat, too. WordPress, SEO, PPC, etc.

Those are all very fine boats, and if they're taking you to your chosen destination you should certainly use them—until they don't.

But don't confuse learning that stuff with learning Internet Marketing.

What's Internet Marketing? Well, the way I practice it is something called the "Portable Empire System." Here's how it works: you find people who have a problem. Then, you solve that problem and sell them the solution. (Notice that "finding the people with the problem" comes before "providing the solution.") That's it. You make money by helping people.

People who want to be helped and will pay for solutions to their problems. When I started out, the most effective way to provide that solution was with eBooks. eBooks are PDF files, and they're tiny little things. They're easy to make and you can download them over a modem (remember those?). The focus should be on delivering *content*. Many Internet Marketers focused on the creation and delivery of *PDF files*. Those can be the same thing...but they don't have to be. Time passes. Things change.

Content can be delivered as an audio or video now and many Internet marketers are focusing on those boats. You can buy courses on how to make audio and video products. Go for it, but remember they're just boats. The *destination* is solving problems and getting paid for it.

Once you get that distinction, you'll find that as new boats come by you can easily adapt your business to them. If you're really smart, you'll hire people to do the "boat stuff" for you.

That brings us back to work. Here's a fun little fact for you: the less work I do the more money I make.

Truth.

For example, I used to make web pages. I spent hundreds of hours learning Front Page, which was an archaic method of making HTML pages. Then I learned Dreamweaver, which was a more elegant way of doing the same thing. Now, I either ask my "web-guy" to make the page for me or go to http://fiverr.com and hire somebody else to do it for five bucks.

It would take me hours, and my time is worth a lot more than $5/hour.

So is yours.

So I focus on the destination, which is making money and helping people with problems. I'm a detective. I'm on the lookout for interesting problems, and groups of people who have those problems and will pay for solutions.

Finding the problems is the tricky bit. The solutions are easy. If you already know the answers, you're there. If you don't, just find somebody who does. Interview them. Video-tape or audio record the interview. Package it. Sell it.

I've seen people work desperately hard. And they don't get the results they want. So, they work even harder. They've been trained that hard work will eventually lead to success. "Never give up," is the advice they've internalized and they heroically persist in working very hard and achieving diddly squat.

That is insane.

That is being way too attached to the boat and not focusing on the destination.

Years ago, I wrote "if something's working, do more of that. If something's not working, stop doing it."

I've found that you can quickly tell if something's working or not if you've got a good definition of "working."

"Working" is *not* "I have a beautiful WordPress blog" or, "I've done meticulous keyword research" or, "I have a domain with my keyword in it, my meta-tags have the keyword, and I've sprinkled my keyword so liberally through my content that it reads like gobbly-de-gook."

"Working" *is* "I'm achieving the results I want from my efforts."

That's an *important* distinction.

I'm reminded of an email I got this morning. It was from someone I coach, and they had a problem. They were intensely passionate about a particular subject. They felt like the world would be a better place if everybody had access to the information they wanted to sell, and once they heard about it everybody would buy their information.

They were wrong.

They were doing a pretty good job of telling people about their information, but people weren't interested.

Bottom line, my student wasn't making any money.

I pointed out that they were looking at one target and shooting at another.

If the target they wanted to hit was "getting their information in front of people," they were hitting a bullseye. However, if the target they wanted to hit was "making money," they were missing wildly.

The person who wrote me that email had a boat. It was his information.

The options I offered were to find a *different* problem to solve or find a way to *reframe* that information that would make it interesting to the people with problems.

Change your list or change your marketing.

He hoisted his boat up over his eyes and trudged on.

It all comes down to reality.

I don't endorse everything Byron Katie says, but one of her sayings is, "don't argue with reality. You'll lose. But, only every time." I strongly endorse that.

It's easy to try to live in the world the way we think it ought to be.

However, if the world "the way we think it ought to be" is different from the way the world really is, we'll be confused. We'll fail.

It's noble to work to make the real world the way we think it ought to be, and if we could all agree on how it "ought to be" things would get better quickly. We can't.

One person's perfect world is another person's nightmare.

But, especially when we're talking about something as quantifiable as making money, living in the world the way it *really is* will streamline our efforts and get us to our destination quickly.

If you're marketing essential information that everybody must know about underwater basket weaving, for example, you may want to explore the possibility that even though everybody should be interested in the topic you feel so passionate about, they're not. If you market the hell out it, drive lots of traffic, and your conversion rate is sleeping with the fishes—it's time to put that boat down and refocus on your destination.

By the way, there are other destinations besides money. As long as you're clear about your destination, and have a good definition of what "working" is, I heartily recommend pursuing other destinations. I've been doing a lot of music lately, and I haven't made a dime. I've succeeded wildly, because my definition of "working" is: 1) I enjoy it, 2) I make other people sound better, 3) it gives me an excuse to buy fun toys like guitars and recording gear, and 4) I enjoy it.

If I judge my music projects by the same criteria I use to judge my Internet Marketing projects, I'd fail. If I judge my Internet Marketing projects by the same criteria I use to judge my music projects, I'd fail at those, too.

Different destinations. Different boats.

"I CAN DO IT IF ________"

Try this.

When you're working on something and you reach that place where you say, "I can't do it because ____________," replace that sentence in your mind with "I can do it IF __________."

Here's an example.

I was recording a song in my studio. On my CDs I usually play all the instruments. I found myself saying, "I can't do this because I can't play guitar like Billy Gibbons."

And, I can't.

That stopped the project, and also stopped everything else. I was stumped.

However, after some thought I realized that I *could* do it if I could come up with a lead guitar part that filled the space in the same way that a Billy Gibbons lead guitar part could. Not everything The Reverend plays is technically difficult. Some of it is just a matter of tone, time and space.

I can do that.

Consequently, the song is finished and I can go on to the next project.

Let's look at an Internet Marketing example.

For the first few years that I was an Internet Marketer, I couldn't make a web page that looked good. And, I had friends and business associates who would explain this to me at great length.

I also couldn't afford to hire somebody to do it for me. This is back in the stone age, when web designers were expensive.

I couldn't put up a web page that looked good, but I *could* put up a web page. I figured the important thing was to get the information online so people could understand the benefits of my products and buy them.

I discovered then, and I still maintain, that the increased sales and profit good graphic design bring is important, but marginal. If I stopped working because I couldn't make a *great* website, I wouldn't make *any* website.

Consequently, websites were made and products were sold. Which is the point, right?

In my coaching program I run across this all the time. "I can't do it because ______________"

That "because" can be just about anything: I don't have the time, I don't have the money, I don't know how, I don't have the courage, I don't have the (fill in the blank).

What I try to do as a coach is help my students focus on what they *do* have and what they *can* do. Maybe the problem is traffic. They can't spend thousands of dollars a day on Google Adwords.

Fine.

They *can* write articles, put videos on YouTube, be active on Facebook and Twitter, work the forums, write blog posts, write guest blog posts—in fact, when you start looking at your business from a place of possibility, you'll find that you *can* do a *lot* of stuff.

Doing what you CAN do can also provide the funds and information you need to do the things you previously couldn't do.

Objects, businesses, and people in motion tend to stay in motion.

And, often, doing what you *can* do leads you to be able to do what you formerly *couldn't* do, which is a lot better outcome than stopping because you can't do something.

So, what's stopping you?

How would you finish this sentence? "I can't do it because ______________."

Now, flip it.

How can you finish this sentence? "I can do it if ________." Remember, the important thing is to do it.

THE SHORTEST PATH

On one of my weekly Portable Empire Coaching UnWebinars I was listening to some new marketers talk about their adventures in getting started in Internet Marketing and had a thought.

Then, a more experienced marketer brought up an issue that they were having with one of their coaching clients, and that added to that thought.

Here's the thought: you won't take the best path to where you're going if you haven't clearly defined *why* you're going.

For example—let's say there are two roads. Road 1, which is 5 miles long, curves through beautiful hills where animals gambol freely. There's a waterfall with a peaceful pool where you can sit and watch the clouds reflected in the water while graceful birds swoop and dive. Further up that road there is a quaint café that serves excellent coffee and home-brewed beer. Some days a local string quartet drops by to practice. You can sit and talk to your friends, drink the brew of your choice, and enjoy the music. It ends up at your destination.

Road 2 is 1/2 mile long and goes directly to your destination. There's not a lot to recommend road 2 except that it's short. No scenery to speak of.

Which road are you going to take?

It all depends on your "why," doesn't it?

If your house is burning down, you don't have a phone, and the fire department is at your destination, you'll probably take road 2.

What's this got to do with Internet Marketing?

I think it's important to make money quickly when you first start out. Internet Marketing is a *business*. A business that doesn't make money either fails or gets relegated to hobby status.

And, when you first start there's a suspension of disbelief that is essential. Internet Marketing, although it's a mature business now, is still new to a lot of people. It's hard to believe that you can make a good living sitting at home or in coffee shops pecking away at a computer.

If you don't get some positive reinforcement fairly quickly, it will be *very* hard to believe and you'll stop doing it.

You could choose road 1, leading to the great American eBook which will not only be the last, final word on your topic but will require years of research, professional design, editing and an expensive promotional campaign.

Further up road 1, you'll find technical challenges that take months to conquer, blog posts that never get posted because they're not perfect, and changes of direction that require you to start over several times.

There are lots of places to stop on road 1 and very few people who take it actually get where they're going.

By the way, it's possible to work very, very hard on road 1. It's not necessarily an easy road to travel. You could find yourself huffing and puffing up a steep hill congratulating yourself on your strenuous effort, and still never get where you want to go.

Or, you could take road 2.

Road 2 goes directly to making money. The road map is in my book, *Money From Anywhere*, but the basics are easy: you find a group of people with a problem, gather those people so you can talk to them, and then solve their problem and sell them the solution.

That brings us to the big question: "*Why* are you going?"

If you're in Internet Marketing because you like to design web pages, or you have a point of view that you think is important to tell people about, or you like to fantasize about getting rich—you will achieve your goal.

If it's designing web pages that turns you on, that's what you'll do.

If it's telling people your point of view or fantasizing about getting rich, that's what you'll do.

Congratulations.

But, if your criteria is designing web pages and you're successfully designing web pages but not making any money you can't honestly be disappointed or frustrated because you're not making any money, can you?

It's important to be honest with yourself.

There's nothing wrong with either road.

But, if you're not finding the financial success you want you may want to have a talk with yourself and discuss "why" you're traveling the Internet Marketing road.

Yes, there are definitely things in life that are more important than money.

But, don't judge them by money or the lack of it.

If your criteria for success is how much money you make, take road 2.

This works for any goal: happiness, artistic fulfillment, relationships. The trick is to be honest about what your goal actually is.

WHEN THE SPOTLIGHT HITS YOU, IT'S SHOW TIME

There's a difference between "rehearsal" and "performance." In a rehearsal hall, when you make a mistake—or stop and grab a cup of coffee—nobody cares or knows.

In a performance, when it's show time, it's "SHOW TIME!" Nothing matters but putting on the show. The spotlight pops on, and it's pointed right at you.

One of my mantras is "this is not the rehearsal."

What I mean by that is that this is your life. As far as I know, you only get one and you might as well live it to the max. That directly leads to my "on my deathbed" story—you can only do one thing at a time. When you're on your deathbed, reflecting back on your life, is what you're doing *right now* going to make you smile?

And don't tell me you're doing something you don't want to do because you "have to." Unless there is a gun at your head at this very moment, you are not a slave. You have choices.

Every moment is a choice.

You can choose to watch TV, or you can choose to set up an opt-in page. You can't do both at the same time. You can choose to do the same old stuff every day until the edges wear off your life and the days slide by like gray cards in a solitaire game—no hearts, diamonds, spades or clubs—just gray cards hitting a table one at a time until the deck is gone and the game is over.

Just imagine the choices you could make:

- Stay home or go traveling in Europe.
- Take a bus or charter a plane.
- Eat at a fast-food joint (which is guaranteed to kill you and suck your soul into the ancient grease vat) or have an organic feast on the boulevard in Paris.
- Stay with the guy you don't particularly like because he's a "good provider," or be with the man of your dreams.

It's "either/or" and you have to choose.

How do you make those choices?

Well, first you have to realize that you *can* make the choice.

There is not one aspect of your life you can't change—the fact that you're experiencing it means you've chosen it.

- The dead end job—or no job at all.
- The lousy relationship—or no relationship at all.
- The boring life—or no life at all.

Why wouldn't you choose a life of vivid color over a gray, dull life?

The excuse I hear most often is, "I can't afford it."

That's why I've been saying, and taking a lot of flack for it, that every spiritual quest requires a financial quest.

You can't self-actualize if you're hungry and homeless. I've tried and it can't be done.

You can't hike up the Himalayas, boat down the Nile, or even meditate successfully on an empty stomach. To live your best life you need a budget—like a film producer needs a budget—you need a location, wardrobe, script, catering, travel expenses—this is your movie and you're the star. You're also the writer and director.

So, step one is to realize that your world is a world of choices. Step two is to *consciously choose.*

Step three would be to put this plan in action, and for that you need an income.

Personally, I like being able to generate an income from just about anywhere.

Right now, I'm about to saddle up the 4Runner and head for Terlingua. If you follow my blog or get my emails you know about Terlingua.

The bumpersticker is: I bought a cabin in the Chihuahua desert off eBay a few years ago. It's off the grid: solar, well, and there's broadband Internet access, which is very strange.

My cabin, surrounded by mountains, sits about 20 miles from the Rio Grande and Big Bend National Park.

Some afternoons I choose to sit on my front porch and watch Nine Points Mesa reflect the sundown. It starts off green from the vegetation. But as the setting sun shines on the rocks it goes from orange to red. Then, as the sun finally sets, blue to purple. If there's a full moon, it will never quite fade to black. When there's no moon, it just sorta disappears, but you know where it is because there's a Nine Points Mesa sized hole in the stars.

And, the stars. It's 52 miles to the nearest city and there are a lot of mountains in the way so there's no light pollution. Usually, there's no air pollution, either. The stars are so close you can just about pet them and the milky way looks solid enough to drink.

Life in the desert is vivid. Some of the roads require your full attention—six inches to the right and you're going down 100 feet onto rock. Speaking of rocks, they tell you that they fall on the highway, but they don't tell you when. And there are snakes…

I always feel more alive in the desert. There's nothing like knowing that a careless move could be your last one to keep you in the moment and focused.

But, if I didn't have my Portable Empire, I couldn't hang out in the desert. I couldn't afford the 4Runner without which I couldn't even get there. Cabins, solar panels, water wells—these things cost money.

I spend a few minutes online while I drink my morning coffee and the rest of the day is mine to enjoy. And, I can teach you how to do it.

The beauty of it is that with a Portable Empire, you make your money by helping others.

Your dream life may not include a cabin in the desert.

But, whatever your dreams are, I want you to consider the possibility that today would be a good time to start living them.

Behind the curtain, back stage, what I really want to talk to you about it self-actualization. We really need to talk about extracting all the juice from a life, so that when we leave it behind we're just leaving the skin and seeds. We really need to talk about the stuff that's beyond money and things…the stuff that matters.

But, until you get past the money thing, it's hard to pay attention to the important stuff.

Because this isn't the rehearsal.

ANCIENT CHINESE WISDOM THAT WORKS

Once upon a time in a land far, far away a young girl was carrying a pail of milk down a dusty trail.

It was a cool and sunny day. Tall trees shaded the trail, so the sun was filtered and dappled washing the forest in sepia tones. The girl skipped along the path and the pail swung gently at her side.

It could have been an unseen rock. Maybe it was a silver fox that streaked across the path tripping her. Perhaps a forest sprite was just feeling frisky that day...

History does not relate the cause, but the girl tripped. She lost but quickly regained her footing. Wardrobe and knees were spared, but the pail of milk was a goner. On the dusty trail, the pail skidded to stop on its side and milk darkened the ground in a pool that spread quickly downhill.

At this point, the young girl had some options:

1. She could scream, cry, stomp her foot on the ground, and curse her luck.
2. She could grab a stout limb from one of the trees, rip her bodice to bare her back, and punish herself by whipping her soft, white skin until it bled from a thousand stripes.
3. She could fall to her knees and pray to the divinity of her choosing to intercede and present her with a filled pail of milk.

4. She could sit down on a grassy patch with her back to a tree and visualize a full pail of milk. She could imagine what it would feel like to have a full pail of milk. She could recite affirmations like: "I have a full pail of milk" a thousand times while visualizing.
5. In the end she could either 1) go forward without milk or 2) go back and get more milk.

Once the milk leaves the pail and hits the dirt, it's over. What would you do?

For the last…wait a sec, let me check…*year*, I've been working on a new book. It's called *Everyday Tao te Ching*, which is probably not the sexiest title I could come up with. I'll deal with the title problem after I finish the book.

When I was a 19 year old college student, signing up for college classes was done by crowding into a gym with all the other students and filing past tables where the professors had their paper class rosters. Some tables had lines—those were either really popular courses or required for all students. The professors at those tables were usually pretty aloof. They were going to sell out their courses so they didn't need to do any selling.

Other tables were empty except for a desperately gregarious professor with a hopeful smile—and a sparse class roster. Their class may not "make" unless they can convince students looking for elective classes to sign up. If the class didn't "make," the professor didn't get paid. They had lots of time for talking to confused students.

After I had signed up for all the classes I had to have for my degree plan that semester, I had room for a couple of electives. That's how I found myself signed up for Oriental Philosophy. It was an advanced class and I had none of the prerequisites, but the professor at that table wasn't real particular. He needed butts in seats and names on his roster. We made a verbal agreement that guaranteed a minimum passing grade in return for my signature on his roster.

I didn't have high hopes for the class. I liked taking oddball classes like holography and this sounded pretty dry to me. What could a bunch of dead Oriental guys have to say that would have any relevance to me?

Imagine my surprise as, over the course of the semester, I was introduced to Lao Tsu, Chuang Tsu, Shunryu Suzuki, D. T. Suzuki and their Western counterparts: Gary Snyder, Alan Watts, Baba Ram Dass (Dr. Richard Alpert), and realized that there was some deep, powerful stuff going on that I didn't even know existed.

During that semester I was exposed to a lot of books. The one that stuck and made the biggest impression was the *Tao te Ching*. I don't remember which translation we used for the class. Today, I have about 30 different versions in hard copy or digital format.

After studying the Tao for almost 40 years, I decided that the existing versions were missing a very important point. Very few modern readers are actually rulers of kingdoms and the reports of perfect, almost prehistoric Chinese ancestors were kinda irrelevant.

There's a *lot* in the *Tao te Ching* that can be extracted and used in twenty-first century capitalistic countries to have a better life. I decided that a book that extracted those things and presented them from a point of view that had some relevance to readers in New York, San Francisco, Miami, London, and Berlin would be a good idea.

So, I did it.

Let's talk about the girl who, until recently, had a pail of milk. The Tao teaches that feelings come from thoughts. By studying the Tao and implementing its teachings you can, over time, learn to control your thoughts. The Tao doesn't concern itself with good or bad. However, it's real concerned with efficiency. It's smart.

Yesterday, I was talking to someone about this and they responded, "yes, but…what if I authentically feel sad and angry about the spilled milk?"

I pointed out that those feelings, regardless of how "authentic" they appear, are the results of thoughts. What were the thoughts behind those feelings?

In every case, the thoughts involved the phrase "I wish" or a related phrase.

And, in every case, the wish was for the past to be changed—which ain't gonna happen.

Regardless of your thoughts about the milk, the milk will remain on the ground until it evaporates. It's not going back in the bucket.

So, wasting time wishing the past was different is, at best, inefficient. At worst, it brings suffering and pain.

We then had an interesting side conversation about punishment. "I screwed up. I spilt the milk. I'll feel bad unless I'm punished. I need to at least look like I'm sorry."

The Tao has no room for the concept of sin and punishment.

And, after you've ripped your blouse and whipped yourself into a bloody frenzy, where is the milk?

What have you actually accomplished?

In the time it takes to wish, whip, visualize, etc. you could have gone back to the dairy, refilled the bucket, walked home, and played video games or surfed the web or some other profitable exercise.

Pain, suffering, guilt, and punishment are, in the kindest light, highly inefficient.

The sooner you can get to "what is, is" and stop arguing with reality, the sooner you can get on with your life.

And, once you learn and metabolize this simple strategy, you can spare yourself a great deal of needless pain, suffering and guilt. The *Tao te Ching* was written in China about 2,500 years ago…roughly around the time that Buddha was teaching in India. And, it's 81 chapters are just full of fascinating, useful strategies for living the best possible life. My job was to make it readable and relevant.

You can see the results at EverydayTaoTeChing.com

CAN YOU REALLY CONTROL YOUR REALITY?

Those of us who have been using "new age" technologies like affirmations and clearing audios have known all along that we can. Now, the scientific community is catching up.

Let's look at a few concrete ways that we can control the world we live in, and make our experience in it better for ourselves and others.

Scientists have been researching reality and perception recently and coming up with some fascinating results. It turns out that our expectations are major determining factors of our experience. For instance, brain scans reveal that expectations about a wine's quality (based on price or a critic's review) actually change the level of activity in the brain's reward centers when a person takes a sip.

I'm working from "How the Power of Expectations Can Allow You to 'Bend Reality'' from October 2012 issue of *Scientific American*. I made up the following scenarios, but they're based on solid scientific research.

The Wine Experts

A group of wine experts sat around a nice oak table in comfortable chairs preparing to perform a scientific experiment. There were candles on the table, appropriate stemmed glassware, and a group of unmarked wine decanters. Each participant was an expert in the analysis of wine.

Each decanter held a bottle of wine. Some of them were silly expensive. Some of them came from boxes.

The experts tasted each bottle. They swirled the wine in the glasses to see if it had "legs." They inhaled the bouquet and let the wine settle on the palates. Then, they assigned each bottle a grade.

Conclusion: wine experts don't know anything about wine. At least, that's one conclusion you could draw. There was no correlation between the price of the different wines and the grades the experts gave to the wines. In fact, some of the cheapest wines got the highest grades.

When the experiment was repeated, but with the wine in its original bottles, the experts gave the highest grades to the most expensive, highest-rated wines.

Heavy Lifters

Carl was competing in a power-lifting competition. He was good, but the competitors were the best in the region. Carl's coach knew that on his very best day, at the height of his abilities, he could probably win.

Before the competition started, Carl's coach took Carl to a private office. He said, "take these. They're powerful performance enhancing drugs. They won't show up in a drug test. They'll make you unbeatable."

Carl was surprised, but he trusted his coach. He took the pills, and very quickly he could feel an awesome power coursing through his body.

Carl not only won the competition, he beat his own personal best by a wide margin.

The pills? Placebos. Sugar pills.

The Wall Flower

Skip was a loser when it came to women.

He spent his time in his parent's basement playing video games.

He wasn't bad looking. His breath didn't stink. He took regular baths. He just felt awkward around people in general and girls in specific.

One day, he got a new adventure game. Before he could play, he had to choose an avatar. An avatar is your graphic representation in the game. More interestingly, it's who you are in that game. Skip picked a tall, handsome Avatar and loaded it with the very qualities that he lacked. The avatar was brave, handsome, and the females in the game all wanted to be with him.

In his imaginary(?) world, he easily kicked nine shades of poop out of his opponents, had plenty of friends, and all the girlfriends he could want.

Here's the odd part. The more he played the game, the more he took on those qualities in real life. After a few months of being tall, brave and desirable in the virtual world he discovered that he had friends in the "real" world, too. He also had a new, hot girlfriend.

The Negotiator

And, here's one from my own personal experience. I was talking to my meditation teacher, who occasionally has to negotiate with government officials and business associates. She's wildly successful.

I asked her how she, a middle-aged "hippie chick" from Austin, could stand her ground and consistently accomplish her goals in these negotiations with high-powered adversaries.

She told me that there was a Buddhist goddess who was a warrior queen. Before she went into these negotiations, she meditated on this goddess and "assumed her affect." She, internally, became that warrior queen. Although the government officials would make quick work of a middle-aged hippie chick, they stood no chance at all against the warrior queen.

So, what's real?

Good question.

Those of us who study the Law of Attraction and other "new age" techniques have known about this all along. When we're using Clearing Audios, affirmations, hypnosis, and other alternative means of enhancing our lives, we know the results we get. That's why we use them.

What's fun for me is that the rest of the world is catching up.

WHY YOU'RE NOT RICH—PART 1

I discovered Internet Marketing in 2003, launched my business in 2004, and my life changed. Forever.

James Taylor, talking about his first record deal, said something like "it was like a door opened, and the rest of my life was on the other side." Finding Internet Marketing was like that for me.

And that's the happy ending, although the story never ends and it's not always been happy.

Before the happy ending there were years—decades—of struggle and pain. And good times, of course.

Some of the best fun I've ever had happened in clearings and back yards and didn't cost a thing. Well, almost nothing. We'd pool our change for beer and wine because a guy with a guitar who can sing the blues isn't going to go thirsty at a house party. Or get lonely.

A group of talented (but broke) musicians sitting around a fire sharing songs, whether it's in a forest in the Texas Hill Country, the pickin' circle at Luckenbach, or around a campfire at Cowboy Chris' ranch in Terlingua, is entertainment you can't beat and can't buy.

So, we've established that it didn't suck all the time.

But mostly, being broke did suck. Bad.

My son and I lived in a single-wide trailer in a trailer park outside Wimberley, Texas. Honestly, I liked that trailer. The park was a nice one, an easy walk from Jacob's Well, and surrounded by forest. The trailer eventually got repossessed because I couldn't make the payments, but I kept it long enough for my son to have a very Tom Sawyer like childhood. He didn't know we were broke.

My lot rent was always late. I kept making deals with the utility company. Some months my overdraft fees exceeded my deposits. Tortillas, beans, and cheap beer in the fridge.

Somehow I managed to keep us sheltered and fed with the money I made playing bars ($30-$50 a night) and doing odd jobs. I taught high school, gave guitar lessons, and ran a little music store—though none of these things really worked or provided much money. I have no idea how we survived.

Occasionally I would write a hot check for groceries. It wasn't theft, as such. I was playing the float, hoping to cover the check with future income before it got to the bank. Sometimes I managed to beat the check to the bank. More than once I didn't.

I got a notice from the grocery store that my check had bounced. I went to the grocery store, paid the check plus penalties, and promptly forgot about it. It had happened before. It would probably happen again. It happens to people in America every day.

Three years later, driving home from taking Betsy's son to a seminar at Rice University in Houston, I was almost home when a I was pulled over on Ranch Road 12 for going 42 in a 35. Lovely. As we were sitting in my truck waiting for the cop to finish writing the ticket I looked back and noticed that another cop car had arrived—he'd called for backup.

"Mr. O'Bryan," he said, "I have bad news and worse news. I'm writing you a speeding ticket and taking you to jail on hot check charges."

Right. I got out of the truck, gave Betsy my ATM card and told her to withdraw enough cash to cover the check and fines, and, surrounded by nervous cops, allowed myself to be handcuffed and deposited in the back of the cop car.

I went to jail. The grocery store had failed to notify the DA that I'd paid that check and the fines. I could have gotten a lawyer and made some noise, but I was a still a broke guitar player then and couldn't afford a lawyer. It was cheaper to pay the fines.

A few uncomfortable hours later I was a free man. I tell that story so I can tell this one.

One of the terms of my freedom was that I was required to attend a Hot Check Class. Insult added to injury. I have a degree in accounting. I can balance my check book. I just didn't have any income. Hot Check Class wasn't gonna help that—in fact, I had to pay a few hundred dollars for the privilege of going to the class.

I'll skip the class itself. The teacher and the students all knew we were just killing time so a friend of some politician could make money owning a Hot Check School. But, at the end of the class the teacher asked an interesting question.

"Now that you've seen how the system works, do you think you'll ever write a hot check again?"

She went down the rows, asking each student. "No." "No." "No."

"Probably."

That was me.

The teacher stopped. Nobody had ever said anything but "no" to that question. Who was this guy? What sort of hardened criminal was in her class?

"If my son was hungry and I didn't have any other way to get food I would *definitely* write a hot check to get food," I answered. And I not only meant it, but, at the time, I assumed I would do it.

Fast forward a decade and imagine me writing about that. I've been running a successful business for years. Within some pretty broad limits, if I want something I can buy it without causing myself or anybody else any pain.

But, I can vividly remember being broke. It was the first thing I thought when I woke each morning, the thought bounced around in my head as I tried to go to sleep at night, and the filter through which I looked at the world each day—all day long.

Sometimes when I wake up *now* it takes me a few minutes to remember that I'm relatively rich now.

And it's not just my life that's providing that inertia. Poverty and "just getting by" go back generations in my family. Rich folk were kinda looked down on. "We ain't rich, but at least we're honest," was a phrase I heard a lot—although, objectively, we weren't all that upright or honest. But, the meme I absorbed was that we could be rich if we'd do the low-down, lying, cheating stuff that rich folk do to get rich. We're better than that.

We could win by losing. The mere fact that we had no money made us self-righteous. We could look down our noses at those rich folk in their fancy cars and fancy houses.

We had a lot invested in losing. It was the only way we could win.

With that kind of programming in my head, it's no wonder it took me 50 years to break free of it.

I invite you to examine what comes up for you when you think about rich people. What happens in your stomach when you imagine yourself as rich.

What does "rich" mean, anyway?

To me, it's the freedom to do what I want, where I want, when I want. Your answer may be different. You may even have achieved it. Either way it's an interesting exercise.

Because, if you're not living your definition of rich, you need to examine why. There is a *definite* reason.

It's not because you don't know how to make money. Between my free books and what I write on my blog, you can learn enough to make a fine living without spending a dime.

That's the easy part.

If you're not living your dream life right now it's because a counter-intention, program, filter, meme—something your mom or dad told you, or a teacher told you, or you saw on TV—some glitch got installed in your mind when you weren't paying attention or were too young to protect yourself.

What to do?

Well, the first step is identifying the problem.

Try this: visualize yourself happy.

Now, look around. Where are you? What are you doing? Who's with you? What are your surroundings like?

Start there…

WHY YOU'RE NOT RICH—PART 2

The facts are mostly irrelevant. What matters, when we're trying to understand the world we live in, are the stories we tell ourselves—the narrative.

What you put in your mind, and what was put in there for you, dictates how you interpret the world.

For example, here's a story I carry around in my head:

During the Great Depression of the 1930s my father was a school kid. He was born in '21. So, by the time the depression was really kicking in he was about 14.

His father, my grandfather Thomas, had a good job as a bookkeeper for the railroad. I've still got his pocket watch, which was as important to him as your computer or iPad is to you—only more so. A good pocket watch will last generations. Your grandkids probably won't hold onto your iPad.

The depression hit and the job with the railroad disappeared. Thomas took to the road to try to find some kind of employment. Eventually, he hooked up with the Works Progress Administration (WPA)—a government job corps and grandma Bessie joined him at the WPA camp leaving my dad and his much older sister at home.

Dad's sister, Rosalie, was ten years older than dad and without a doubt the best unknown barrel-house piano player I've ever heard. She did odd jobs, taught piano lessons, and did what she could to make a home for dad—but she was in her early 20s, for gosh sake. Thomas and Bessie sent home what they could but…

One day, Dad and Rosalie heard a knock on the door. It was the gas man, and his instructions were to get the back gas payments or turn off the gas. Rosalie didn't have the money—so, Dad made one last pot of rich Louisiana coffee and he, Rosalie and the gas man each had a cup. Then, the gas man turned off the gas.

Dad never related what time of year it was, but for him—even at that age—going without coffee was worse than freezing.

What's the lesson? "You're going to lose anyway, but lose with grace and class. And pride."

Here's another story that's stuck in my head—at that time, every pair of pants my dad owned had holes in them. Today, that can be a mark of high fashion but in the '30s it was a sign of poverty. The other kids made fun of him, so he quit school. Out of embarrassment and pride, I guess.

That story had a silver lining of sorts—one of the jobs he was able to get was writing stories for the local paper. It didn't pay much, but he learned he could write. After World War 2, he used the GI bill to attend LSU and study journalism. Later, he became an award-winning journalist with his own column and radio show in Houston. But, that was much later.

The stories in your mind are what you use to make sense out of what happens to you and what you observe.

That's why it's so important that you fill your mind with positive stories—when you're choosing what books to read, what movies to watch and…well, we could talk about TV, but my advice is to unplug the damn thing unless you're using it to watch movies or Anthony Bourdain.

And also when you're choosing who you hang out with. That's *really* important.

Dad never outgrew his poverty mindset. He never owned a new car, for example, even later in life when he could afford one.

That poverty mindset was handed down to me.

The only tools I had to make sense of my environment were poverty tools.

People have asked what steps I took to get out of poverty thinking.

Well, in 2003, I met Joe Vitale.

We'll eventually talk about Internet Marketing, and how I managed to create a thriving business—and, that's interesting, I guess.

But, the more important stuff is even more interesting. Listen up.

At first, I was Joe's guitar teacher. Later, we became business partners. We were in a mastermind group together. For the first few years that Joe and I hung out together, every time I'd see Joe he'd tell me about a book he was reading. A lot of times, if he liked a book he'd buy several copies and give them to his friends.

Not all his friends would take the time to read the books, but I did. Some, like *Think and Grow Rich*, I read several times. Joe was also very interested in new, positive ways of looking at the world. Just sitting at the table with Joe over cigars and coffee was inspirational.

I was lucky.

When I met Joe I was broke. My trailer had just been repossessed. My music career was going nowhere. I came to the realization that everything I was doing was wrong and everything I thought was true wasn't.

That's a real good thing.

If I had been partially successful, or had a job that I hated but paid the bills—I might not have been so open to new ways of thinking about the world.

It turns out that when what you're doing isn't working—and you *know* it isn't working—that just leaves everything else.

I knew what was in my head wasn't serving me, so I was open to deleting what wasn't working and replacing it with something else. Something that worked.

If you get the opportunity to hang out with Joe, I recommend you do so. However, he would tell you—and, I'm telling you now—you don't need anybody else to make the changes in your life that you want and need to make. It's not your fault, but it is your responsibility. It's your head. You control what goes in it, which will dictate what tools you bring to the world. With better tools, you'll have a better life.

When the thoughts and beliefs you have in your head aren't bringing you the life you want, be brave. Be honest. Get rid of those thoughts and beliefs and replace them with better ones.

That's the single most important advice I can give you.

We can talk about Internet Marketing, and we will, I promise. We can talk about web pages, blogs, traffic. Apparently, I'm an expert in that stuff now, and I watch proudly as my students achieve greater and greater success using my strategies.

But, that ain't the important stuff.

For example, Joe can't make a web page.

I can, but these days I don't.

The mechanics of running an online business are fairly simple.

Go read my free best-seller, *Money From Anywhere*, and you'll have 90% of what you need to do that. (It was a best-selling book on Amazon.com. Now, I give it away. Or, you can go to Amazon and buy it if you want.)

Listen closely—none of that will help you if you don't have your inner game straight. If you're still looking at the world through limiting beliefs, if you've still got the poverty mind-set, if you're still hanging around with negative people and reading negative things, you're going to continue to have a life filled with poverty and negativity.

That's a fact.

What to do?

First, honestly look at the stories you tell yourself.

Identify the beliefs that aren't serving you and replace them with better beliefs.

Observe what you read, what you watch, and what the people around you say.

Are they bringing you stories that make your life better?

MAKE MONEY FROM ANYWHERE?

Why not?

This is actually a chapter about Internet Marketing. But, it's also an exploration into "what does it mean to be rich?" Hang with me here while I set it up. If you're just interested in the "make money" part, skip on down.

Last weekend I played several gigs with some local musicians. Since my cabin is up to 40 miles away from some of the gigs, I decided to live in my RV for the weekend.

It gets about the same gas mileage as my 4Runner and has a comfy bed, bathroom, kitchen, and a kick-ass music system.

As far as I was concerned, I was living like a King. I was rich. And, other than gas, I didn't need to spend any money.

I *did* spend some money—a local writer had a book-signing in Lajitas, and I bought one of his books. And, I used enough gas to drive about 100 miles, in total. That's about 5 gallons. Down here, that's a little over twenty bucks.

And, I bought breakfast. A big bowl of fresh fruit, a tasty breakfast burrito, and a pot of French Roast coffee, which I ate in the courtyard at La Posada Milagro in the Terlingua (TX) ghost town while I was working Saturday morning. A bit of a splurge, at about $15, but delish.

Friday night, we played the High Sierra in Terlingua. The gig was fun and—although I was just sitting in, the club gave me food and drinks. I had a few beers over conversation with the other musicians, Laird and Charlotte. They've lived down here over twenty years, and have great stories to tell of life in the desert.

Then, I went out to my RV, read a few chapters in Chris Moore's new book on my iPad, and got a great night's sleep under an almost full moon. Then down to La Posada Milagro for an excellent breakfast.

The next night, we played at the Lajitas Resort. That gig was better. The crowd was pleasant and pleased with the music. A local singer (Betheny) showed up and sat in. Tim, the harmonica demon of Lajitas, played some blues with me.

After that show, I drove the RV to the Lajitas RV park, which is luxurious, and enjoyed half a bottle of organic Shiraz, read some more Chris Moore, and then slept for about nine hours. The next morning I got up and checked out the pool—but didn't feel brave enough to go swimming. The quick evaporation rate out here keeps the water cold, and also freezes you when you get out. Too vivid for me. I did take a shower and enjoy the air conditioned sitting area.

Then, back at the RV, I made some tabouli for breakfast, along with a couple of tangerines and an apple and a pot of locally roasted Italian Roast coffee in my French press. The RV has a propane-powered kitchen. Boiling water for coffee was a breeze.

Later that evening, I drove to the local Pizza parlor where the pizza is good, the beer cold, and the music was even better! In addition to the singer who sat in Saturday night, Ted Arbogast, who owns the local recording studio, showed up with a bass. It was Easter Sunday, and the crowd was slow—but the people who showed up got a hell of a show. Laird was on, Charlotte sawed away on her viola like the award winning orchestral player she is, and with Ted on bass and me laying down the leads—well, you won't find a better show in South Brewster County on a Sunday, that's for sure.

After the pizza parlor show, I drove the RV back to the cabin, unloaded my gear and stuff, and—other than a missing toothbrush—did I leave it at Lajitas?—I was back home.

Here's the Make Money From Anywhere part.

Everywhere I stayed I had great Internet access. The High Sierra, Posada Milagro, Lajitas RV park—all I had to do was settle into one of the Captain's chairs, open up my MacBook, and I was in business.

To me, this is just stunning. It's odd enough to have fiber optic broadband at my cabin. But, to sit on the patio in the Terlingua ghost-town, the parking lot behind the El Dorado, and an isolated RV park in the mountains in Lajitas and have good, fast Internet access—it's a whole new world. You really can make money from anywhere.

Dr. Joe Vitale and I promoted a "flash sale" of one of our Clearing Audios (Clearing For Money) over the weekend. If you're on my list and took advantage of that sale, you got a screaming deal on a very powerful tool for clearing your blocks around wealth and money.

If you're not on my list—why not? There's a box in the upper right hand corner of my blog at http://patobryan.com/blog. Go put in your email address so you don't miss any more sales.

So, all weekend, while I was bopping around the mountains on the Texas/Mexico border, I was also running a pretty impressive Internet Marketing launch. I was in constant contact with my tech staff. I had up to the minute analytics. I knew how many people were coming to the site, how many bought the product, and we were able to make changes and adjustments as needed in real time—when they were needed.

By logging into my autoresponder, I was able to keep in touch with my list and let them know how much longer the sale was going on.

There were a few customer service emails that needed my attention. No problem. I just leaned back in my chair and took care of 'em while watching the sun play on the mountains.

My customers are happy—they got a screaming deal. My tech guy is happy—he had the support from me he needed. Joe and I are happy—it was a very profitable weekend. And, it's important to remember that if your business doesn't make a profit, what you have is a hobby.

I also had a few conversations with Betsy, a fascinating email conversation with my son, and kept up with my Facebook correspondence—and finished Chris Moore's new book, *Sacre Bleu*, which I enjoyed.

So—let's recap the weekend. I played 3 gigs. Counting gas, I spent about $35. If I had driven back to the cabin each night, I would have spent 3 times that much. I had a great time—I got to play good music with some very talented musicians for some very appreciative listeners. I got to work on my chops, which is why I do this. "Use it or lose it" very much applies to playing guitar. And, I had a sort of mini-vacation in my RV.

And, I made a metric poop-ton of money. And that brings us to the point.

Maybe you're already rich?

Am I rich?

I'm writing this from the second floor office/recording studio in my off-the-grid cabin in the desert near the Big Bend of the Rio Grande in South Texas. Out one window, I'm watching the sun reflect off of Nine Points Mesa—lots of orange, pink, and red going on there. Out the other window, the sun is moving toward the west. The ocotillo are in bloom—the desert is spotted with red dots from the flowers.

One of the things you need to consider, when you're deciding if you're rich or not, is your burn rate. What does it cost you to stay alive per month? In my case, the cost of owning this cabin on ten acres and the RV is about half what it cost for the house in Wimberley. I don't spend any money out here. There's nothing to spend it on. And yet, I don't miss a thing. I have plenty of groceries, wine, water, excellent music (Miles Davis' Sketches of Spain) on the studio monitors, company and conversation just down the road, a hell of a view out my windows, guitars, keyboards, recording gear, video and still cameras, hundreds of books on my iPad, the Internet, and...well, just about everything I need.

I have friends out here on the border living on a few hundred dollars a month. They think they're rich, and I agree. They've defined happiness on their own terms and work just enough to fund the lifestyle of their dreams. They live in RVs, campers or domes. They've got impressive yards and a sky that goes on forever.

I've also got friends back in the city who are making a lot of money and don't think they're rich. They're too busy to enjoy their lives and, by the time they pay their bills, they don't have the money (or the time) to have fun.

It's entirely possible to have a beautiful house, fancy cars, and all the trappings of wealth—and be broke. In fact, there were times in my life when, if I could have just gotten back to zero, I'd have been way ahead. If you're upside down on a car or house you know what I mean. You ain't rich if you're broke, no matter what material possessions you've got. You're also not happy.

I made enough money over the weekend to live for months out here—and there are more promotions coming.

The bottom line is that "rich" is a very personal thing. Not everybody wants to live in the desert, for example. I'm happiest here. The lack of Starbucks, restaurants, night life, crowds, entertainment, and traffic (especially traffic)—for me, that's a positive thing. Some people need crowds and amenities. There is absolutely nothing wrong with having a big house and impressive cars, as long as they make you happy and you can easily afford it.

There is no right or wrong to this.

What's important is that you have a long, honest talk with yourself and decide what happiness means to you.

Close your eyes and feel what happiness feels like. Imagine being happy. Then, in your mind's eye, look around. Where are you? Who are you with? What are you doing?

As you go through your life, keep an inventory of the things that make you smile. Do more of those. Also notice what makes you unhappy. Those are the things you need to stop doing.

Here's the tough part. Notice the people who make you feel good. Spend more time with those people. Then, notice who brings you down. Avoid those people.

There's a tough love aspect to this.

It's your life, and, as far as I know, you only get one.

It's a beautiful gift, and it's a mistake to waste it.

And yet, most people stumble through their lives with their eyes shut. They accept what they're given and react to what happens to them. Why?

It's just as easy to live a conscious life. Demand happiness. Don't settle for less. And don't let anybody else define happiness for you.

I have friends who drive expensive cars and live in big houses. I could, too, if I wanted. I was actually tempted—how would people know I was a successful Internet Marketer if I didn't have all the trappings of one?

The cars and houses make my friends happy. My cabin in the desert makes me happy. And, business is fine. It turns out that there are a lot of people who "get" what I'm doing. I'm living a no-compromise life. I'm demanding happiness on my terms.

You can, too, if you only will.

I pay for my lifestyle by doing Internet Marketing. It's easy and doesn't take much time. If you're still learning the "how" of how to do that, you'll want to check out my coaching program—several of my students are making a good living online, which makes me proud and happy. You can, too.

The "how to" is easy.

What's harder is the inner game stuff.

There are a lot of tools available to help you with those. We work on inner game stuff in my coaching program, for example.

Clearing audios can speed things up. There are a lot of free eBooks on the web—*Think and Grow Rich*, *Acres of Diamonds*, *As a Man Thinketh*, that are just a Google search away. You should check those out.

But, the most important inner game decision you'll ever make is to *demand* happiness, and define it for yourself. That's the only way you'll know for sure whether you're rich or not.

MAGIC! 7 STEPS FOR CREATING MASSIVE SUCCESS IN THE NEW ECONOMY; ANY CAREER, JOB, BUSINESS...AND IN LIFE!

Deberah Bringelson

Do you live your life like magic?

I love magic! I love the magic of becoming aware of something I want to manifest and having it show up in my life, sometimes in days or even hours!

Do you have the magic touch? You do! I promise!

Do you know how to use it? If not, read on.

Of course, the word "magic" is just a fun way to describe the ancient laws of manifestation upon which our entire world rests. These laws have been hidden and until recently known only to a select few. But over the past few decades, they are coming into view for the masses.

Anyone can create. Even you!

Whether you realize it or not, the world is changing. What used to be successful businesses are now failing. Jobs are disappearing and new ones are being created. In the 1980 and 1990s many people still plotted out a career and stuck with a company until retirement. Most companies provided retirement, 401Ks, and health insurance. Not anymore. Health care, 401Ks are being dramatically reduced an in a lot of cases, eliminated completely.

Many people are seriously discussing whether a college education "buys" you a great career and future. Honestly, when I think about my college education, I seriously question whether I have ever used anything that I learned. Sure, those required geology and astronomy class were interesting, but I've not used one thing I learned in them to earn a living, put food on the table, or provide for my family.

The economy has changed and it is changing more and more every day. Everything is happening faster and faster. And, I'm not just talking about technology. Have you noticed that the time between expressing thoughts and manifesting the outcome of those thoughts is happening at lightning speed?

Where the "manifestation gap" used to take weeks or even years to complete, often the distance between thought and creation is now a mere 24 hours or less.

While all of this change may seem scary, I view it as incredibly exciting. Your opportunities are exploding. The upside of is that you can now have what you want faster than ever before. But, you better be focused on what you want; really zero in on what you do want and allow the experience of it into your life.

Equally important; let go of everything that you do not want. Let go of negative thoughts, negative people, and destructive emotions. They are all toxic to your life, your body and your abundance.

Life can be an incredible, exciting journey. You are moments away from beginning to take your first steps on your amazing new path. Enjoy!

What Is Success?

For many people, success is defined primarily by financial and/or career goals. If you are successful in your work, making a lot of money, then you are a success. While monetary success is certainly a part of overall success, that definition is really quite limiting.

If someone has $30 million in the bank, but no love in their life; are they a success? If the millionaire has poor health or is spiritually unfulfilled, can she be defined as successful?

So, really, what is success?

Webster's Dictionary defines success as:

> *a: degree or measure of succeeding b: favorable or desired outcome;* also*: the attainment of wealth, favor, or eminence c: one that succeeds*

That definition, I believe it too limiting. It is too limiting for my life. Isn't it for yours?

I define success as:

> *complete and total prosperity in all areas of life; financial, spiritual, emotional, and physical abundance.*

For me to be successful, I want to have the money and resources to travel, meditate, read, play, think and grow every single day, as my heart desires. I want people in my life who love me and whom I love. I want spirit flowing through my body and inspiring me every day. I want a body and mind that are healthy and active. I want a life filled with joy. I know I deserve it. And, I know that you deserve it too.

So. What do you think? Which definition of success works for you? Mine or Webster's. I'm taking mine! Come along with me and I'll show you the way.

What Is Your Definition of Success?

Obviously, you have to decide what success really means to you. It's different for everyone. But because everyone in our society needs money to live and enjoy life, professional and financial success naturally flows into life success. With that in mind, we are going to make some assumptions. First, we're going to assume that making money, a good income is a key component for a successful life.

For most people, the reason we work is at least in part to earn a great income. With that income, we provide for our family, we buy food, pay the mortgage or rent, travel, and have fun!

Whether you are someone who wants to donate millions to save the rain forest, build schools in third world countries, and feed underprivileged children; or someone who dreams of a house in the country with a pool and a convertible in the garage, a great income makes life more pleasant.

Second assumption! Money is energy. Period.

I know it. *Quantum physics tells us it's true.* And on some level you know it. Money is energy. Like the light switch in your house, you just need to know where the switch is and how to turn it on to get the electricity, energy (or in this case…money) flowing.

Are you the master of your money? Or are you controlled by it…or the lack of it.

If you are not currently the master of your career, money, or life… that changes, starting today.

The Laws of Money

Smart Tools + Smart Business Practices
+ Laws of Manifestation = Quantum Success

There are man-made laws of money and success. These are the "Smart Success Tools" and "Smart Business Practices" which can be used by themselves to create success and money.

Then there are the energetic laws of money, "Ancient Laws of Manifestation" that also can be used to create success.

What if you had all 3? What if you walked into every situation, fully loaded with smart success tools, smart, practical professional skills AND all of the ancient laws of manifestation on your side?

What kind of massive success could you create then? Would you be the master of your money and your success or would they still be mastering and controlling you?

Manifesting Magic In Action

A few years ago, when the Mayor of San Francisco asked me to negotiate a deal between Sir Richard Branson of the Virgin Group and the State of California and the City of San Francisco, what I did not know at the time is that Branson and Virgin had already made the decision that California was not a state they wanted to do business in. Before my very first conversation with them, I already had three strikes and I was out. Period.

I pulled out all of the stops. I dug deep in my toolbox of Smart Business Practices, Smart

Success Tools, plus the Ancient Laws of Manifestation that I had been using for almost thirty years.

Nine months later as I traveled through Italy on a month-long and much needed vacation, in between beautiful monuments, great art, and scoops of gelato, I burned up the transatlantic phone lines, closing the biggest deal of my career, with estimated annual returns of $300 million. And, I later received a specially created award "Steal of the Year" for the deal that was never meant to be.

When you take the 7 Step to Manifesting Success, you walk into every situation, knowing exactly what actions to take to create the outcome you want. You have the power to create that outcome and you do it joyfully.

Work becomes play! How fun is that?

You CAN Do It ~ How I Know!

Several years ago, I was speaking at a graduation ceremony for a criminal justice, drug and alcohol treatment program that I had designed and funded. The program was for nonviolent women who were mothers. Instead of being sentenced to jail and being away from their children, mothers were sentenced to intensive and comprehensive treatment. Everything from drug and alcohol treatment to learning to balance a checkbook to how to cook nutritious meals for their children, and discipline and appropriate bedtimes.

After giving my speech to these amazing women and listening to the heartfelt and tearful comments of their grateful children, one of whom said "I am so grateful; for the first time, my mom takes care of me. She's not always passed out on the sofa," I was shocked by the perception that many of the people had about me.

While my immediate circumstances may have been very different from theirs; even though I was the speaker, rather than a graduate, I really wasn't all that different. But many of the attendees assumed that our lives were miles apart and that I had started life with a 'silver spoon in my mouth' and was destined for success.

They had no idea that while the scripts of our individual lives may have been a little different, the overall plot of our life dramas was very similar.

Like many of them, I too grew up in an extremely violent, alcoholic and abusive household. Like many of them, I knew the terror of being shot at by a "loving" family member, barely able to stand because my entire body was shaking so badly, it was like my own personal earthquake.

Emotional and sexual abuse was a part of my life from my earliest memory until I moved across the country hoping to survive. Like them and possibly like you, I've had challenges in my life. I've known fear. I've known desperation. But more than anything, I know that if I can make these tools work for me, you can make them work for you! I promise!

Creating Abundance in All Areas of Life

> *"Whatever may be said in praise of poverty, the facts remain that it is not possible to live in a really complete fulfilling or successful life unless you are rich. You cannot rise to your greatest possible height in talent or soul development unless you have plenty of money. For to unfold the soul and to develop*

talent, you must have things to use, and you cannot have these things unless you have the money with which to buy them."

Wallace Wattles, *The Science of Getting Rich*

So, I just said in a previous section that financial success is not a complete definition of success. Now I am telling you that I want you to be rich. Mixed message? No, it's not.

In our society, in order to travel the world, own the home, vehicle, toys of our dreams, and to have time to play, meditate and grow, we have to have currency to exchange. Without it, we are constrained. Our dreams are limited.

So, while I do not believe that money is the only key to success, it is the first one. When you have money, you have a great deal more access to everything else that makes a successful, abundant life.

Are you with me? Let's go!

Success—Why You Deserve It

Your body, mind, and spirit were designed for wholeness and wellbeing. As a result of cultural influences, misguided thinking or simply not knowing what to do, many people have gotten off the path of wellness. Are you living the life you want? Are your days filled with joy, peace and prosperity? Are your body, mind, spirit, and finances where you want them to be?

Whether you are a scientist and call it Energy or a practitioner of a religious philosophy and call it God, Allah, Jehovah,

Yahweh, Great Spirit, the Great I Am; or whether you are someone who practices your own form of spirituality and calls it Source, the Universe, or something else; I believe that there is a loving, energetic presence that flows through each and every person on the planet. Regardless of the name we use, this Source Energy treats everyone equally. What is available to me is available to you. What is available to Donald Trump, is available to you.

There is not one person who is more worthy of success than another. What would be the point of that? There's no logic to it. You deserve to have an amazing, successful, abundant life. I truly believe that.

Why Don't You Have It?

"Imagination is more important than knowledge."
Albert Einstein

Do you believe you deserve total wellbeing? I mean really believe it. Close your eyes right now. Go on, close them and see in your mind's eye your life of complete and total well being. How much money do you have? What is your home like, your car? How about your body? See yourself spending time every day thinking, reading, meditating or just relaxing. Imagine whatever is right and joyful for you.

Now, here's the key. How does that feel? How does it feel in the pit of your stomach? Does it feel fabulous? Are you thrilled? Excited? Energized? Ready to reach out and touch this life?

Or, do you have a little uncomfortable feeling? You want it. You long for it. But, come on, really. You can't have that life. You're not smart enough, pretty/handsome enough, talented enough.

Oh and then there's "Yeah but?" Yeah, but I can't because I don't make enough money. Yeah, but I don't feel well. Yeah, but my spouse left me. Yeah, but I had a crappy childhood.....

You know what? The "yeah, buts" can go on forever. They are excuses. And, what is most important....they are keeping you from having the life you deserve. *This is a fact.*

I have yeah buts too. We all do. There's not one person on the planet, (even those who are wildly successful) who has not had some challenge to overcome.

And, really think about it. Don't you know people who are less talented than you, who do have success or at least some measure of success? Don't you know some who aren't as pretty or handsome as you, but have an amazing love life or relationships? Don't you know at least one person that you are as smart as…or even smarter, but they've achieved greater financial success? I bet you do. I know I do.

The *only* thing that is standing in your way is you.

The really cool thing about that statement is this: YOU have all the power. YOU have all the power to change it. Are you ready?

Note: I have been using these Steps To Manifestation Magic in my life for almost 30 years. If I use them consistently, they work for me every time. I have manifested houses, cars, trips, money, and amazing opportunities! The most important advice I can give you—use them!

Step #1 What's YOUR Brass Ring?

Define YOUR Goals and Intentions

What do you really want out of life? No. I didn't ask what you don't want. I asked what you do want.

Exercise: Put this page down and get a clean piece of paper and a pen. Now, for the next 5 minutes, do not let your pen leave the paper. Continuously write what you want for your life. What does your home look like; your car? What do you do during the day? Do you travel? Where do you go? Who is in your life? What are your relationships like and with whom? Write them all down. Keep writing for a minimum of 5 minutes. Go on do it! Now! If you don't the next 5 steps will get you nowhere.

Did you do it? Ok. Now, go back and do this one more time, but bump it up. Make it better, brighter, more exciting. You deserve an amazing life. But….the only way you will get it is if you know what you want and grab it.

Step #2 Believe In YOUR Life

Align What You Want with Your Beliefs About What

You Can Actually Have

So, you now know what you really want. Do you believe you can have it? Do you really? I bet you don't …but you will!

We have already established that money is not everything, nor are the things that money can buy. However, they do make good examples. Here's one:

Say you really, really want a brand new, shiny, bright red Mercedes convertible, with soft leather seats. But, you're currently driving a beat up powder blue Ford hatchback. Do you know why you're driving the Ford and not the Mercedes? Because, you believe the Ford is what you can have. Your desire for the Mercedes doesn't align with your belief that you are a beatup-Ford-driving kind of person.

Trust me. It's true. You may not like it. You may not want it to be true, but it is. So, what do you do?

Try this. Put on some nice Mercedes convertible driving clothes. Don't forget the sunscreen! (and as a committed convertible lover, I also recommend a visor or hat!) Now, head down to the Mercedes dealership. Yes, you can. You deserve it don't you? Look at the convertibles. Touch them. Sit in them. Take one for a test drive…..with the top down! I mean it. If you really want to be a Mercedes convertible-driving kind of person, get in and drive one.

Feel it. Enjoy it. If you see someone you know, don't forget to wave!

Now, every morning when you wake up, very first thing, thank God, the Universe, the Creator, (whatever you believe in) for your beautiful new, shiny red Mercedes convertible with the leather seats. Do it again as you're drifting off to sleep. And, every time you get in the Ford, thank it for getting you where you need to be…..then feel that Mercedes and the wind caressing your face as you drive down the road.

You are now officially a Mercedes convertible-driving kind of person!

Note: When you're "future shopping" remember that the sales people are making a living too. Be respectful of their time. You would want the same respect.

Step #3 Fear

Don't Let It Eat Your Life Release The Blocks To YOUR Success

"Do or do not—there is no try."

Yoda

So, let's continue with the Mercedes example. You have gone for the test drive. Your desire for the Mercedes is stronger than ever. You love it. You want it. You now believe you can have it.

Oh but wait, here comes the fear. What will your family think? Your great aunt needs kidney surgery. Why didn't you send her a little of your Mercedes money? What will the neighbors think? Are you being snooty?

And, then how about the cost of insurance? What if it gets wrecked or stolen? Hmmmm. You really like that Mercedes….. and well….you do want it and deserve it, but well, now you're not so sure.

Fear is eating your life. Do not, I repeat, Do NOT let it.

Hold something non-breakable in your hand. Now—hold it. Now—drop it. Now—try to drop it. (don't hold it, don't drop it—TRY to drop it) Can you try to drop it? Nope. Fear is the same way.

Close your eyes. What is the fear you are feeling? Identify it. Don't wallow in it. Just acknowledge it. Now, let it go. See it dissolve. Feel the tension leave your body. I like to deeply exhale as I do this. Now go back and feel in your body. Is the fear still there? Maybe, but not quite as strong? Do it again. Just drop it. Let it go.

As you do this releasing technique, be gentle with yourself. When you are gentle and loving, you take the power away from whatever is limiting you. When you fight it or suppress it, you give it more power to control your life.

I have been using this process for a number of years. I still occasionally have fears that come up, but I allow them to come in and then just release them.

I'm a single mom, living in one of the most expensive areas of the country. Yes, I do sometimes have fear. I now let them go. I'm living my LIFE, not my fears. You can too!

Step #4 To Change Your Life—Change You!

Invest In YOU....Spiritually, Emotionally, Physically

> *It is possible to live in tiny, diminutive boxes of the soul and never venture out to live expansively; but this is not how we were meant to live. We must learn to live outside the box, outside our limitations—whether of our own making or the product of our past—because life is lived not so much on the outside of ourselves, but in the far-reaching boundaries of our own consciousness. To limit your grasp is to limit your purpose, your gift, your soul. Live beyond and you will encompass others in ways you might never have expected were you to continue in your small corner, curled up alone, afraid, and paralyzed.*
>
> Teresa Z. Crane

The number one tool that you can use to make your life what you want it to be is ....You.

Think of who you were at 15. Think of what you knew (what you really knew, not what you thought you knew!) Think of the person you were then. Now, think of who you are now, what you know, what you've learned as a part of experiencing the moments of your life between now and then.

You're different, right? You know more? At least I hope so. If re-lived the days and experiences you've had since you were 15, knowing what you know now, would you make different choices. The truth is, most people, with expanded experience and knowledge would.

Now, imagine if you had really invested in yourself during those years. Just as one example, imagine the impact that 1 nonfiction book a month would have made on your life. Think of all the things you would know. Knowledge is power, real power.

When you are investing in yourself....reading, learning, thinking, exploring, growing....you are investing in your amazing life.

Here's another example of knowledge as power. Take two children. One grows up living in a grass hut, with minimal food, no running water, and minimal or no education. The second grows up, experiencing the best education that life has to offer, travel, intellectual and spiritual discussions....the Internet.

Child one may have a happy life. I certainly hope she does. But child two will have a bigger life, hopefully just as happy, but with a much larger menu from which to choose. Her choices will not be limited to a view from a grass hut and minimal food. Her view will be of the entire world and what it has to offer.

Your life is exactly like that. Choose to expand your mind, your spirit and your life. Only by doing so will you have the big, amazing, abundant life you deserve.

Note: I will say it again. Money and homes, etc do not make anyone happy. Both children may be equally happy. I certainly hope they are. However, child 2 has so many more choices. The point of this, is to invest in yourself so that you too will have a huge menu from which to choose. The only way you can choose a Jaguar convertible over a Mercedes convertible is if you know the Jaguar exists!

Step #5 Passion Rules

Do What You Love And Feel Passionate About—Create Excitement To Move Forward

The best way to explain this is to tell you a personal story. A few years ago, I was working a decent job, making a decent income as the CEO of a business development company. In the beginning it was fun, creative and I enjoyed it. But over time, the long hours working on someone else's dreams, being paid what they thought I should be paid, began to wear. I started looking for a new job.

But, I had already used steps 1-4 to begin unlocking the doors to my abundant life. What I wanted out of life far exceeded anything that any "J.O.B." was going to get me. I wanted time with my daughter. I wanted to travel and show her the world. I wanted to be completely debt free. And, while I was making a decent income, it was not going to provide me with what my soul truly wanted and what I had become in alignment with.

So, I kept being passed up for jobs for which I was beyond qualified. I'm a turn around expert. I go in and fix companies that are failing….getting them back in the black and moving forward. One company that was in serious financial trouble actually told me when they chose someone else to be their new CEO that they were concerned that I would grow the company too fast!

See, my intentions for my life and my actions to get a new job were not in synch. A job would not get me the life I wanted.

The point is that I was not passionate about doing any J.O.B. I was passionate about creating a life. The Universe was not going to deliver to me something for which I had no passion. It kept saying "NO" move on.

What did I ultimately do? I quit looking for a job, started my consulting business we and am living the life I truly want. I take my daughter to school every day. I work from home…..a few hours a day….not 80 hours a week! And, when she's a little older, we will begin traveling together and seeing the world.

I now make what I deserve. Not what someone else has decided they want to pay me.

I am now living my passion!

Step #6 If You Love It—Let It Go

Define What You Want—Set Your Intention—Release It To The Universe

So, how do you release your desires to the Universe and why should you do it?

WHY: Because unless you are a teenager, you do not know everything. Sorry, you really don't. Say you want that new Mercedes we talked about back in Step 2. Do you know how you're going to get it? You could win it. You could buy it. The new love of your life (that you're going to meet next month) could give it to you as a gift. Or something else miraculous could happen.

You don't know. You have your tiny little, limited perspective. You cannot see or know all of the wondrous ways the Universe has to deliver your dreams to you. You simply cannot. So, don't fuss about it. Let it go and let God give it to you.

HOW: Here's another example. Say you go into a restaurant and order a nice meal. You expect that the waiter will deliver the request to the kitchen and it will be prepared and delivered back to you, right? Do you signal the waiter every time he passes to make sure he's delivered the request? I hope not. Do you go back to the kitchen to make sure the chef has received your order? Probably not. Do you run back to the kitchen periodically to be sure that the food is being washed, chopped, simmered and sautéed? No? Well, the same is true with fulfilling your desires.

Ask for what you want and then let it go having the complete expectation that your desires will be fulfilled, just as you have an expectation that your order for food will be fulfilled.

Note: Please note that just as a seed has to germinate, grow and blossom before it can produce beautiful, sweet smelling flowers; the seeds of your desires also have to germinate and grow, with loving care. You would never pull a growing plant out of the ground because it did not produce flowers or fruit within a day or two. Please don't do it with your dreams. Give the universe a little time to nurture and deliver your desires.

Unlocking YOUR Success
Building Your Wealth to Create Your Amazing Life

> *"Feel the fear and do it anyway."*
>
> Susan Jeffers

For several years prior to starting my own company, people have been telling me that I should start my own business. Repeatedly, I was told by almost everyone who knew me that I would be a great business consultant or life coach. You see, helping people solve problems and create massive success was something that I did and still do regularly with my friends and colleagues. And during the time that I was wanting to leave corporate America, it was suggested by a wide range of people that I should open my own consulting business. But there was just something so comforting about that biweekly paycheck. No, I wasn't really happy working for that paycheck. It limited me in a lot of ways. But it was comforting.

I was stuck!

But then, I got a kick in the pants from the Universe and discovered that if I really wanted a life of abundance as we discussed at the beginning, I had to give up the idea of earning what someone else wanted to pay me and learn to fly on my own. I felt the fear and did it anyway!

It was scary. I am a single mom. The cost of living where I live….and love…..is one of the highest in the United States. If I were to make it here, I would have to make it big.

So, what did I do? I used the 7 Steps to Manifesting Success. And, I manifested an amazing opportunity. It was an opportunity that just seemed to fall into my lap. But that is how it happens when you are using all of the steps, especially those related to the laws of manifestation.

Joe Vitale says "the Universe likes speed" and "and money likes speed." Those words were in my mind as I made the decision to start my own wealth education and wealth management business.

It's one of the best decisions I have ever made.

What Is Your Hearts Desire? What is Stopping You?

Are you willing to feel the fear and do it anyway? Will you let me help you?

You have to ask yourself, are you happy with things are right now? Or do you deserve something better.

I know the answer to that, do you? Re-read this chapter if you need to. Start right now, today and begin really living the 7 Steps to Manifesting Success.

They will make a difference in your life if you allow them to.

Step #7 The Icing On The Cake!

One of my very favorite expressions and reminders about how to create success is "praying rain". It's from a story about a Native American who lives in the dessert region of North America. It was a particularly dry "rainy" season. Even what was typically sparse rain did not come after months of waiting. For months and months there had been no moisture at all.

Going out into the dessert alone, the Native leader created a large rock formation by placing rocks in the shape of a circle along the ground. When the rocks were all laid out nice and neat, he proceeded to walk around the circle. He just kept walking. Walking and walking. While he walked, he said nothing. He just continued to walk for hours.

Finally he was finished and began to walk back across the dessert to his home. When asked what he was doing, he replied that he was "praying rain". "You mean, you were praying for rain?" he was asked.

"No. I was praying rain. I was thanking the Great Spirit for the rain."

"But it hasn't rained. Why are you giving thanks for something that is not?"

He replied, "I know that the rain is there, waiting. I give thanks for it. I know that it will come."

Everyone thought this man was crazy. It hadn't rained for months and months. It was not likely to rain anytime soon.

But by the time evening was falling....so was the rain.

This story is an excellent example of how to create true abundance in your life. Whatever it is that you desire, it is there as a response to your desire. If you have not yet received it, either time is not yet right or the doorway that it needs to pass through is not open.

Expressing gratitude is the absolute best way to open that door. By doing this, you "assume the win". And by assuming "the win" you help to ensure that the door between you and your desire is wide open.

How It Works

The Universe speaks in images and emotions (which are vibrations). Every moment of every day of your life you are sending messages or some call them prayers to the Universe telling it what you want.

When you think of something that creates a feeling in your body and images in your mind, those are sent out, like little messengers to the Divine, "Send me this!"

One of the very best ways to create what you want in your life is to allow gratitude and appreciation for what you want to wash over your body, like loving rays of light or mystical mists of joy.

Every morning when I wake up, before getting out of bed, I lie there and think about all of the things that I'm grateful for. Sometimes they are things that are already physically manifested in my life. This part of the exercise gets me going and sets the tone *and vibration*. I express thanks and gratitude for all of the blessings, friends, joy, experiences and "things" that make my time here on the planet a richer and more joyful experience.

These images and the expression of gratitude create images of all that I have. Those images create feelings of appreciation. I smile. I *feel* the feelings of joy and gratitude.

Then I move onto things that will soon be physically manifested in my life. I've manifested jobs, cars, opportunities, homes, and many other things by being grateful for them before they ever showed up on my door!

In my mind, I imagine the joy of staring up at the Eiffel Tower with my daughter. I imagine myself surrounded by Parisian cafes and beautiful monuments. I feel a thrill of excitement as I look in my daughter's face and see her excitement at taking the trip we have been dreaming about.

While this trip hasn't actually occurred (yet), I see myself in the scene and most importantly I *feel* the joy. That feeling sends a vibration to the Universe: "1 Paris trip for two is on order" and the Universe begins conspiring to make it so.

I then move onto things that I already enjoy, but want to re-enforce my appreciation and desire to have them continue: such as great health and a strong body. I feel the joy of having a vibrant, healthy body that supports me in having a great life. I immerse myself in thanksgiving both visually and physically for my beautiful home that shelters my family, nurtures my spirit and welcomes friends.

I do this every single morning before rising and every single night before going to sleep. It sets the tone for my day and gives gentle instruction for my subconscious and my higher self to go to work for me while I sleep.

When It Doesn't

Important Fact: There are NO negative images.

What I mean by that is: A picture is a picture. If you are picturing an image of a car wreck or hurricane, your perception of those images may be negative. You may be saying with your mental or verbal words "oh, please no! I don't want that. But the message (conveyed through the picture in your mind) is the car wreck or hurricane. How the Universe interprets this is "Oh, she wants a car wreck." Or, "here you go, hurricane You, headed your way!"

Recently there was an extremely high fire danger in our area. People were praying that the fires wouldn't reach them and that their homes would be saved.

I tried to explain to them that that's not how it works. The Universe does *not* hear or understand "no".

It's not possible to have a picture in your mind of something you don't want and have an X through it!

If you say, "please no fire"...what image are you seeing in your mind? It probably looks something like this one.

What feeling are you feeling? Peace or fear? Fear, of course. That fear, combined with the image of the fire (even a fire you do not want) tells the Universe, "1 fire please! Come burn down my home."

The vibration that is created by emotion is fuel for your desires. Fear is toxic poisonous fuel.

Make It Work For You!

The joyful expression of gratitude is the absolute best way to create what you desire. But, how do you make it work for you?

First thing I highly recommend is that you do as I do. Every morning before getting out of bed and every night before going to sleep, spend 10 minutes joyfully feeling and seeing all you have to be grateful for.

The better the pictures in your mind, the stronger the feelings, the faster your dreams will come true.

Once a few years ago, there was something that I wanted so very, very much. It was something that was not readily attainable for me. But I wanted it more than anything I've ever wanted in my life. I would go for walks around my neighborhood and daydream about all of the divine, perfect details of what I wanted. I would get so wrapped up in the joy of having it, that I literally would cry with joy. Within three months, voila, the Universe said to me "ask and it is given; here you go, it's yours!" and sure enough, it was!

And, at the point that I first began asking, there was very little hope or opportunity for me to have this particular gift. But the power of joyful gratitude is stronger than any earthy circumstance.

One other key to making this work for you is that you absolutely must be clear in your desire and your joy.

If in the midst of fire season you are joyfully grateful for your beautiful home that is so strong and sturdy and safe, you're sending the right messages. But if at the same time, those messages are tinged with fear, the Universe receives mixed signals. "Hmmm… is he saying keep providing his beautiful home? Or is he saying, burn it down or perhaps he's saying, provide it, but singe it a little?"

This is where so many people get hung up in manifesting their dreams. They say to me, "but I said I wanted a new car! Why did my old car fall apart?"

Here's what happened: They worried (fear) about their old car falling apart, while at the same time asking for a new car. Voila! Their old car fell apart and they had no choice but to replace it.

Not really what they wanted. But the combination of desire for the new car and fear about the old car created that exact scenario.

How could they have made it work for them? Appreciate all of the wonderful things the old car does for them: safely getting them to work or to their child's soccer game for example. And, at the same time, visually and emotionally enjoy the delightful new car that is waiting to be a part of their experience.

Periodically re-read the steps. Use them! Every single one of them, every single day. I know for a fact that they work. They have helped me create hundreds of millions of dollars for my clients. The will work for you.

But, only if you use them!

Wishing you the most magical life possible!

Deberah Bringelson is a nationally recognized Business Development Expert, Certified Advanced Law of Attraction Practitioner, and Certified Wealth Consultant. She is best known for negotiating the deal between Sir Richard Branson and Arnold Schwarzenegger, with annual returns of $300 million, for which she received the specially created "Steal of the Year" Award.

Deberah is the founder of "Make Your Passion Happen" and the "Quantum Success Academy", two life-changing programs that teach people to create their own professional lives of success and personal and financial freedom and joy.

EMPTY BOATS, EX-WIVES, MASS MURDERERS, AND OTHER IRRITATIONS

I was introduced to the Buddhist concept of "empty boats" by Stephen Mitchell in his excellent book, *The Second Book of the Tao.* Mitchell, who is Byron Katie's husband, and the author of many books—mostly translations or interpretations of Oriental philosophy books. His interpretation of the *Tao Te Ching* is one of the best I'm aware of, and I've read dozens. I own a lot of his books, and enjoy them all.

The Second Book of the Tao, however, is my favorite. It lives on the table by my bed, and I've read and reread it countless times . From Amazon.com:

> *Drawn from the work of Lao-tzu's disciple Chuang-tzu and Confucius's grandson Tzussu, The Second Book of the Tao offers Western readers a path into reality that has nothing to do with Taoism or Buddhism or old or new alone, but everything to do with truth. Mitchell has selected the freshest, clearest teachings from these two great students of the Tao and adapted them into versions that reveal the poetry, depth, and humor of the original texts with a thrilling new power. Alongside each adaptation, Mitchell includes his own commentary, at once explicating and complementing the text.*

> *This book is a twenty-first-century form of ancient wisdom, bringing a new, homemade sequel to the Tao Te Ching into the modern world. Mitchell's renditions are radiantly lucid; they dig out the vision that's hiding beneath the words; they grab the text by the scruff of the neck—by its heart, really—and let its essential meanings fall out. The book introduces us to a cast of vivid characters, most of them humble artisans or servants, who show us what it means to be in harmony with the way things are. Its wisdom provides a psychological and moral acuity as deep as the Tao Te Ching itself...*

The story of "empty boats" goes like this. Imagine that you're lazily floating along a river in your boat. It's a peaceful day and you're leaning back watching the clouds dance in a blue sky. You're lulled into a meditative state by the easy flow of the boat on the water and songs of the birds in the trees on the shore. Then, abruptly, another boat bangs into yours, jarring you from your reverie. Your immediate assumption is that the person guiding the other boat has intentionally hit yours, you descend into anger and turn to defend yourself and possibly retaliate.

Turning, you see that it's an empty boat that has come unmoored and, quite by accident, run into yours.

The teaching behind this story is that empty boats are everywhere. The lying, cheating business associate that screwed you in a deal, the ex-wife with the bull-dog attorney, the driver who cuts you off in traffic—they're all empty boats. With the proper, Buddhist, state of mind, you should be able to view all these distractions with a detached sense of equanimity and be able to choose to respond from an empathetic, aware place—instead of an immediate angry response.

Easier said than done, I know. But, on those occasions when I can pull it off I find it's useful. Acting from an aware, empathetic place gives you space to choose your response. This is much more effective than just reacting. The phrase, "he made me mad," for example becomes a complete non-starter. Nobody can *make* you anything. You choose your response, and it helps to put a little space between the thing you're responding *to* and *your response*.

Like meditation, responding with an "empty boat" mindset takes practice. I'm working on it. Try it, and see how it works for you. It's an interesting concept, and useful as a model for living a peaceful life. What's surprising is that there's some hard science behind it.

Last night I was reading a collection of Malcolm Gladwell's articles in his new book, *What The Dog Saw*. (Yea, I consume books like a stoner goes through Cheetos. It's a benign addiction.) Malcolm Gladwell, in an article called "Something Borrowed," tells the story of a psychiatrist named Dorothy Lewis and her work. Actually, the article is about how a playwright plagiarized an article he wrote about Dorothy Lewis, and is a fascinating look at intellectual property rights, but the part that got me thinking about "empty boats" has to do with Ms. Lewis' work with serial killers.

She maintains that serial killers are not responsible for, or guilty of, their crimes because of "neurological dysfunction and childhood physical abuse." The difference between a crime of evil and a crime of illness is the difference between a sin and a symptom."

I've read several books about the effects of early-life trauma on brain chemistry and how these traumas can cause physiological damage and massive—detrimental rewiring of the neurological system—and this trauma doesn't necessarily have to be physical trauma. Surprisingly, severe psychological trauma can cause physiological changes in the brain chemistry and affect the function of the neurological biology. I don't understand this, but scientists assure us it's true.

You've heard the phrase, "they're just wired that way," right? Well, trauma messes with the wiring.

But, this is the first instance I'm aware of where a scientist actually went into the field and got to know actual criminals.

She interviewed them, learned their stories, and studied how they became "animals" that could kill innocent people in cold blood.

In every case, the criminals were suffering "disruptive neurological effects of prolonged periods of high stress." In some cases, they had been heinously abused, both sexually and physically.

In other words, their actions were the result of damage to their cerebral cortex due to early-life trauma.

Each of us is the cumulative result of our life experiences, which is why most therapists I know can afford to drive Mercedes Benzes. Most of us either deal with it or get help to deal with it, and, luckily, few of us actually act on our impulses to plant a meat cleaver firmly through the skull of those who, in our opinion, would benefit from such treatment.

Quoting Gladwell, "It is the function of the cortex—and in particular, those parts of the cortex beneath the forehead, known as the frontal lobes—to modify the impulses that surge up from within the brain, to provide judgment, to organize behavior and decision making, to learn and adhere to rules of everyday life."

If the cortex has been damaged through either physical or psychological trauma, it can't do its job. The science is clear on this. Irrational, even criminal, responses that lead to, in the case of the victims, possibly death and in the case of the perpetrators, long prison sentences, and possibly death, are caused by neurological damage.

So it turns out that jerks, vicious ex-wives, and yes, even mass murderers, really are just empty boats.

PRAYER PRESCRIPTION MEDITATIONS

Kate Loving Shenk

Larry Dossey, MD, took a leap of faith twenty years ago when he wrote the book *Healing Words*, about the power of prayer to heal.

The only study to prove the power of prayer to heal at that time was done by a cardiologist named Randolf Byrd. He prayed for half of his patients and left the other half prayer-less.

The control group didn't fare as well as the group Byrd prayed for.

This was the study that inspired Larry Dossey to begin praying for his patients.

Dossey describes his upbringing as Fundamentalist Christian in a Texan community, which he later rejected. By the time he was a doctor, he rebelled against any form of prayer or anything at all having to do with religion.

But the Byrd data provoked an inner change of direction for Dossey.

He decided to incorporate prayer into his daily morning ritual.

He said he locked himself in his office, brought out the incense and shamanistic rattles, as he calls it, and started actively saying unconditional prayers for the well being of his patients.

After these rituals, he felt well. He began to know that the world of medicine was much more than drugs and strict medical interventions.

As a Nurse RN/CRNP for 29 years, I know that "Nurses are healers but are called nurses instead." I found this out by praying when extreme circumstances in the life and death of my patients warranted intervention from the unseen helpers, whether these helpers were angels, gnomes, elves, gods or ghosts: the most important thing was to have faith in the healing effect of prayer.

The prayer for me is nondenominational and unconditional. Prayer evolved into what I now call "Prayer Prescriptions," meaning that it may be the only prescription you can give yourself without side effects.

What is Prayer? Praying is an act of Love. Prayer brings out all of the qualities of light and love and filters these through your loving heart. Pray now and Pray often for these wonderful heart filled moments to grow. Pray with your animals beside you.

Prayer is a meditation! When I write my daily prayers, I feel a deep sense of quiet and need for solitude. I cannot write prayers with music in the background, nor can I write them in front of a Television program. Quiet. Stillness. Meditation. Dogs. Cats.

Prayer Is A Song-Yes, it is true. Pray is an inner song of the heart. Are you singing to yourself? Are you singing to your dog and cat? Is anyone listening? Or are the unseen helpers not only listening, but preparing to usher in a lesson you need to learn related to the prayer you are singing? Look to your animals for guidance.

Internet Marketers can use Prayer Prescriptions to manifest goals in a timely manner, to work through troublesome challenges and relationships, to facilitate the flow of money. In fact, the uses for Prayer Prescriptions in the world of Internet Marketing is virtually endless.

Prayer Prescriptions can be added to what Pat O'Bryan refers to as "The Inner Game Of Internet Marketing."

As I worked (and played) with my own Prayer Prescriptions, suddenly the door opened, and I left the dysfunctional world of Corporate Medicine for good. For ever. Nothing else worked. Prayer Prescriptions pushed through the resistance I had to making such a monumental change.

No one knows how prayer works. It matters not if ten or more people pray for you or if one person prays for you, as long as the prayers are authentically done with a compassionate heart. The energy elevates the vibrational field to bring healing and love to all involved.

Prayer without the need to control outcome, with an attitude of surrender, of Thy Will Be Done, are the prayers having the most import. Prayer done fearfully with a desperate, bargaining with God mentality do not have any effect. These prayers are called Fox Hole prayers, the "get me out alive and I'll go to church every Sunday for the rest of my life" kind of prayer.

Why would you want to start writing prayers, to create your own Prayer Prescriptions? Write your prayers for all the free thinkers of the world, who listen to the tune of their inner symphony. Write your prayers for the animals in your life, for they are equal in the eyes of Goddess.

Write your prayers to:

- Heal yourself
- Heal other people
- As a meditation
- As a way to concentrate
- As a way to create something meaningful
- As a way to create something meaningful everyday
- As a way to slow down and tune into the animals in your life

When you walk every day with your dog and cat, your rhythmic step is a Prayer Prescription Meditation. All of life is about awakening and staying awake. Meaningful coincidences lead the way to experience life with a sense of purpose and meaning. As a result, you feel the life energy and dynamic excitement that flows from living a life with this sense of purpose, which gives vision to your destiny in this lifetime.

Walking with your dog and cat will do this for you. Simple. Waking up.

Fear and desperation are low vibrational energies that are best left in the trash heap of the psyche.

Prayer done with a vibration of love and compassionate has a high fast moving vibrational frequency that transforms rather than distorts, heals rather than harms.

Larry Dossey said that studying the effects of prayer in health led him away from the world view taught in Science that says when the body dies, we are gone forever.

The study and practice of prayer put him in touch with the infinite or "non local" part of ourselves that will never die.

Prayers of gratitude and Thanksgiving get us in touch with our own innate sense of optimism, goodwill and the peaceful silence that underlies all peaceful forces.

Albert Einstein said that we live in a friendly universe. By distrusting people and the goodness of life, we halt the body's great ability to heal.

Dossey's latest book, *The Extraordinary Healing Power Of Ordinary Things*, explores different healing modalities that have been known to cause spontaneous healing of incurable conditions.

He cites the use of maggots and leaches in modern surgery to debride diseased staph resistant ulcerations in Diabetic patients. People choose this therapy after trying everything else when modern medicine has failed them at every juncture.

Maggot and leach therapy may seem like a good alternative when all else has failed.

Or take the case of people in comas. When Christmas Carols are played, some of these comatose people rise up, take out their tubes and walk out the door. Carols create tremendous emotional memories that resonate deeply with some people. Maybe all of us raised with this music would have a similar emotional reaction.

Spontaneous healing, miraculous cure, prayer from great distances: these are all possibilities in a world full of loving potential. We can learn and immediately practice what Dossey teaches.

Touch your clients with unconditional loving intention. Pray for and with your business associates.

Direct healing rays to everyone you meet today.

You may suddenly realized that you are healed, as well.

Kate Loving Shenk is a writer, healer, musician and published author of the *Prayer Prescription Series*. She has been a nurse for 29 years. She believes all people are healers, but few are willing to own their power. She also believes healing takes place all the time, whether we are conscious of it, or not.

In her report, "22 Keys To Self Healing," she helps you access your own self-healing potential.

You can get it free at http://katelovingshenk.com

A QUESTION OF BALANCE

If you're an online entrepreneur, you probably already run into the problem of balancing work and life. If you're thinking about becoming an online entrepreneur, you should follow along, because finding that golden balance between work and play may keep you from burning out, getting divorced, or worse. It happens all too often. And can happen way too fast.

Before we get started, I need to stress that this is something I'm working on, not something I've mastered. It's a journey. The parameters change. However, I've been doing this nine years now and made some mistakes. Maybe you can learn from my mistakes. Maybe you will find new and interesting mistakes of your own to make. Hope this helps.

This is the first problem most IMers (Internet Marketers) run into. Has it happened to you? It sure happened to me. To most "normal" people, what we do is weird. For example, I don't keep regular hours, I work in gym shorts and t-shirt, and sometimes my most productive work is done under extremely unusual conditions. Right now, I'm sitting back in a comfy chair, smoking a Kristof maduro cigar and sipping some pretty nice Merlot. At least I have the laptop on my lap. Earlier, I was leaned back with my eyes closed—working. I've written blog posts from the dungeon of a castle in Germany, created products in motel rooms in California, and tend to work in hippie coffee shops in Austin regularly. My friends think that's cool now, but initially they were kinda judgmental.

By now, LaRoja (my wife-like girlfriend) is used to my work habits.

But it's hard when you're first starting out. Explaining what we do to "civilians" (non IMers) is tough. And, when you're first starting out you don't have a track record. You're taking a leap of faith. You can *talk* to others who have done it. You *know* it can be done and you're pretty sure *you* can do it, but how do you *explain* it? Most people are still trapped in industrial revolution thinking of "you need a job to make money," and they don't realize the industrial revolution is over and jobs are the *least efficient* way to make money. When you tell them that you intend to make money by sitting in coffee shops or hanging out in your PJs solving problems for other people and selling the solutions, chances are that they won't be real supportive.

And, when you're starting out is when you need their support the most. So, you've got the online world on one side telling you that you can do it and the "real" world telling you to get a job. How do you balance these opposing forces?

Recommendation: surround yourself with people who understand what you're doing. The Unseminar People page on Facebook is the best place to meet and hang out with other Internet Marketers (and great people) of all levels. You'll find newbies and pros there who will talk online with you about everything from family to autoresponders. When you're ready to kick it into overdrive, join the Portable Empire Coaching program. Ultimately, your best defense against the nay-sayers is to be successful.

Addicted to "you've got mail" emails.

The next balancing act happens once you start achieving a little success. You start making a little money. Now, I don't know about you, but when I started my IM career, I'd never made any real money. The money I had made was the result of unloading trucks in the hot Texas sun, or waiting tables, or playing guitar in bars. When I discovered that I could create a product—I mean, just make stuff up—put it online, sell it and make real money, I was hooked.

I know this is universal because I've heard so many of my coaching students talk about it, and I remember it *vividly*. During my first promotions I'd sit in front of my computer and have my email account open in one window, my shopping cart account open in another, and I'd just click back and forth between the two as the "you've got money" emails came rolling in. I'd stay up late at night and get up early in the morning, just to watch.

All good things come to an end. Eventually, the promotion was over. Sales would slow down to a trickle and I needed a fix. So I made up something else. That's my job description, you know—I make stuff up. I try to visualize what's not "out there" that should be, and I go make it. Luckily, significant numbers of people agree with me and buy the stuff I make up. The trick is to make up stuff that people actually need.

So, I'd get a big toke of "you've got money" emails and then they'd stop. The high would wear off and I'd immediately and feverishly go to work writing, working towards that next rush. This is back before I was making audio and video products. I wrote eBooks. One day I wrote an eBook between supper and bedtime. Most took longer—I'd camp out in a coffee shop with my headphones on and my iPod rocking, resource books spread out on the table in front of me, laptop on my lap, and I'd make up another eBook. Then, I'd put it online and sell it and get another fix.

All good things come to an end. That rush would end,too, so I'd do it again. After a while, LaRoja would stop me on my way up to my office and ask, "have we met?"

I was so tickled that I had an online business that I kinda neglected the fact that I had a family. It didn't help that I keep musician's hours. I tend to get cranked up about ten o'clock each night and work until I'm through. I've watched the sun come up over the hill country on my way to bed way too many times to count. Back then, the kids were in school and LaRoja had a career—I was there, but I wasn't *really* there. I was upstairs in my office with my nose in a computer.

Now, this is a good problem to have. At first. The ability to print money at will is a very cool thing. That rush, and the memory and anticipation of it, is what will keep you sitting at the computer long after you're ready to go do something else. Passive income, especially when you're starting out, is the result of massive action—and most of that action happens when you're alone with your computer. The work must be done, but you need to find balance between that and the "real" world.

Recommendation: Initially, don't worry about it. Get your business online and start making money. It's amazing how understanding your family will be once the cash starts rolling in. After you've established yourself, start thinking about taking the occasional day off. If you can work when the rest of the family is busy and take time off in the evenings when they're hanging out, that's good. If not, take a break after supper—then go to work when they go to bed. That's what I do. Now, unless I'm making a product or managing a product launch, I can keep my business going by working less than an hour a day.

It's better to burn out than it is to rust.

I disagree with Neil Young on that one. It's better to age gracefully than it is to burn out. Neil Young may have written that song, but Kurt Cobain lived it. So did Sid Vicious. So have several Internet Marketers. I'd rather be Neil, sitting on my huge ranch strumming my Martin D-45, personally. Or Paul McCartney, who, in my opinion, is aging just fine. I'd rather be Willie Nelson, going down the road in a cloud of smoke, than Hank Williams.

I don't personally know any IMers who have died from burn out, yet. I have seen some suspicious runny noses at seminars lately, so it's probably just a matter of time. However, I know several who have burned out. Now, they're starving consultants or "between jobs." When I point out that they could rebuild their online businesses easily—they've already done it once—they look at me like I'm the one who's crazy. They're as likely to get back into Internet Marketing as I am to go on another tour with my band. It ain't gonna happen. The thought of setting up an autoresponder fills them with dread like the thought of loading an equipment truck at 3AM scares me.

It can happen. It's almost happened to me.

It's easy to get on the treadmill, and like a mouse in a scientific experiment, as long as the positive reinforcement keeps coming, we keep scampering on that treadmill. Make a product, build the sales page, launch it, get a little chunk of cheese, make a product, build a sales page, launch it, get some more cheese. After a while, you need to change the scenery or the diet.

Recommendation: Get a hobby.

Recommendation 2: Monetize the hobby.

The absolute best deal you can create for yourself is to find something you love to do and then figure out a way to get paid to do it.

I started making videos for fun. My first one was of me playing my guitar and singing a song. I just wanted to see if I could do it. I set up a cheap video cam on a tripod, sat down on my desk, and played—I think—*Key to the Highway*. It's out there on the 'net somewhere.

I had a cheap video editing program, and I eventually figured out how to get the video off the camera and onto the computer and from there to the 'net.

It was kinda fun. It became my hobby. I started carrying that little camera with me when I went places, and including video on my blog. Then I videotaped my first UnSeminar, and that's when I really started learning how to edit video. It was hard, but it was new and different. Then, we sold the videos and made some money. Same cheese, different treadmill. I changed the scenery.

You'll find that if you carry a little flip-cam with you when you travel, and even when you're hanging out with friends, you'll find lots of opportunities to take interesting video. Put it on your blog.

Take your camera to seminars and meet-ups. Interview interesting people. You can make a lot of money selling interview videos.

Now, I have hundreds (and more coming) videos on my Youtube channel that have been viewed 1.5 million times, dozens of video products, and I'm known as a videographer. I have some very nice high-def video cameras and a professional video editing suite in my office. I'm working on a web TV program, and I'm doing a video project for a major magazine's website. You can see my videos at http://youtube.com/practicalmetaphysics.

The point is that video is something I do for fun, and I figured out a way to get paid for it. What's fun for you? You should do more of that. You should also figure out a way to monetize it. I do a lot of Internet Marketing video, but I also do a lot of music, travel and interview video. I monetize everything.

My other hobby is traveling. I love to go. I enjoy wide open spaces, vast vistas, and seeing things I've never seen before. Here's a little trick I've learned: As president of my corporation I assign myself writing and video assignments in interesting places. To make a video about Terlingua for example, I have to go to Terlingua. To write about Jack Kerouac, and his influence on writers and how that translates into the digital age, I had to go to San Francisco and Big Sur.

Oh darn. A tax-deductible trip to Big Sur.

And, if you're using your toys to make income that you pay taxes on, you can either expense or depreciate your toys. That's a tax deduction, too.

> ***Talk with your CPA, financial advisor, and attorney. I'm not a CPA or an attorney and nothing I say should be misconstrued as financial or legal advice. Your situation is probably different than mine.***
>
> My lawyers insist I include that caveat. Read and heed it.

Again, the trick is to find what you love and then find a way to get paid for doing it. I reserve the right to try any off-the-wall thing that catches my fancy. I'm delighted with my IM business, and intend to continue that as long as it's fun—but, to keep it fun, I need distractions and inspiration. You will, too. When you find the treadmill tedious, just get off. Take a walk. Read a book.

Let your mind wander.

AFTERWORD
HUMAN EXCEPTIONALISM

As Internet Marketers we communicate with people all over the planet. Unlike traditional manufacturers our reach is not bound by shipping lines and distribution channels. My hope is that our compassion can be similarly unbounded.

In the summer of 2003, a family—mom, dad, and their 6-year old son—went out to eat. There weren't many restaurants open, so the one they picked was crowded. Waving to some friends, they sat down, ordered dinner, and enjoyed a family night out.

Then, the bombs hit. Metal tore through metal and metal tore through skin. The noise was deafening and anyone who survived the blasts would have been traumatized. For the six year old boy, that's not an issue…for his parents, if they're still alive, it is.

What happened? It was Baghdad. There was a (false) rumor that Saddam was going to eat at that restaurant. Orders were given and obeyed.

What's your response to that story?

A. I have children. I can imagine the pain of losing my child and knowing that those people lost theirs causes me pain.
B. It has nothing to do with me. They're not members of my family, city or country.
C. Serves 'em right for being ragheads.

This chapter asks the question: "how big is your love?"

This has been coming up for me a lot lately, so I thought I'd just put it out there and see what you think.

Here's another story. This one happened to me.

"Would you be willing to pull the trigger yourself?" I asked. I was in West Texas at a social gathering and involved in a conversation about politics. I try to avoid them. But, sometimes…

"I ain't paying for lazy people's health care. If they want health care let them get a job with benefits like I did."

I had to respond to that. "Well, we could require that everyone who can afford it must purchase health insurance and let the government provide health insurance to those who can't afford it. That would be much cheaper than the system we've got now."

"That's socialism!" they responded.

We quickly determined my debate partner didn't know what socialism was, but was *sure* it was bad. We also determined that rather than have their tax money go to save the life of another person they'd be happy to watch them die.

"Well, then, a lot of poor and middle class people are going to die and suffer," I pointed out.

"Serves them right. They made bad choices."

"Like choosing their parents, where they were born, and their genetic makeup?"

I tried. I pointed out that, unlike them, I had been to England and Germany, specifically, and seen social medicine in action. It just works. I pointed out that uninsured health care was inefficient, cruel, and more expensive than paying for the insurance. I got nowhere.

So, I tried one more thing: "If your child was uninsured and needed medical care to save their life, would you pay for the medical care?"

"Of course," they said.

"What about if it was your brother's child?"

"Yes."

"How about your neighbor's child?"

"No."

"So, you're ok with your neighbor's child dying?"

"I guess so. Yes."

"Would you pull the trigger yourself? Would you watch as that child dies?"

And that's pretty much where the conversation ended…they hadn't thought about it that way and didn't want to.

That's how big their love is.

As it should be.

One last example. I was pointing out to a person that in my (childhood) home town, people with black skin *still* lived on the west side of the railroad tracks and people with white skin lived on the east side of the railroad tracks. I commented that the division seemed odd—in 2012—so long after the civil rights acts were passed.

His comment? "As it should be."

His tribe has white skin. If you don't have white skin you can't be in his tribe. He doesn't want you in his neighborhood.

A field of compassion that small leads to a primitive, tribal bonding that results in…

Well, let's look at it like this:

Some people's compassion extends to themselves and their immediate family. Actually, I've seen smaller groupings than that. When my son was in high school our home was a halfway house for several teenage boys who were kicked out by their parents. The parents' compassion didn't extend to their own children.

Other people have a geographic tribe: their neighborhood, town, state, country or state of mind. An example of this are the "secede" bumperstickers I see on trucks in Texas. A somewhat larger geographic tribe displays their allegiance by displaying Confederate flags. During the alleged oil crisis of the '70s there were bumperstickers in the South that read, "Freeze a Yankee."

Tribalism. Very small tribes.

Other tribes are financial-based. You won't find many equity bankers or their Maybachs at the Devil's Backbone Tavern or many cedar-choppers or their battered pickup trucks at the River Oaks Country Club.

And then there's the concept of "exceptionalism." It implies that the people referred to are, in some way, chosen people and anything they do, no matter how cruel or ill-informed is ok, because they're chosen.

The loudest example of this is "American Exceptionalism." The US can kill innocent children, civilians by the hundreds of thousands, assassinate total strangers for politically expedient reasons, depose democratically elected presidents, starve entire nations—and it's ok because we're *exceptional*?

And if a citizen or, gawd forbid, a politician should attempt to apologize for this outrageous behavior, pundits and press pile on. "Apologizing for America" is, apparently, a sin—regardless of how egregious the sin we're apologizing for.

Human Exceptionalism?

What would it be like if we adopted a program of *Human* Exceptionalism?

Remember the song we learned when we were young: "Jesus loves the little children. All the children of the world."?

Sounds like a good plan to me.

It doesn't say "all the *white* children of the world," or "all the children in *my* family, neighborhood, town, state or country."

It doesn't say, "all the children whose parents believe what I believe or vote like I vote."

It doesn't say, "all the children in democratic, capitalistic countries."

What if your love was that big? What if your tribe was that big?

What if, when you read in the news that a bomb launched by a US drone accidentally hit a wedding party in Afghanistan killing the bride, groom and attendees you could actually feel that as if it happened in *your* neighborhood?

What if, when you hear of children starving in Africa you go to maps.google.com and actually *find* that country on the map? Then, go to Wikipedia (or the source of your choosing) and see *why* the children are starving there. Then, visualize *your* child in that country living under those circumstances.

What if the whole world was your tribe?

And, from a Law of Attraction point of view, what are you attracting if you don't?

5236921R00172

Made in the USA
San Bernardino, CA
29 October 2013